IN TIME OF BATTLE

Graham John Parry

IN TIME OF BATTLE text © GRAHAM PARRY

COVER ARTWORK © G. J. PARRY

All Rights Reserved

**For my Wife, Children and Grand Children
With love.**

Novels by Graham John Parry

* * *

The Waves of War

In Time of Battle

Man of War

When D-Day Dawns

Fighting Command

* * *

TABLE OF CONTENTS

GRAHAM PARRY

CHAPTER ONE .. RISK AND REWARD

It was twelve noon on the shores of South America's great River de la Plata, and the sun burned hot from an enduringly bright sky. Those same gleaming waters of the 'silver river' lapped gently round the vast, sprawling port city of Buenos Aires. Sweltering in the hot, humid air, the docks and quaysides reeked of rotting seaweed and glutinous mud flats, of dead and dying fish and the ever present stench of discarded vegetables. The pungent odour of that busy waterfront permeated throughout the encroaching city banks and offices, and weekday or weekend, it made little difference to the port of Buenos Aries; it was business as usual.

At a stone quayside on the harbour's inner basin, the crew of a battered old three-thousand ton freighter were busy stowing the last unmarked crates of an important cargo. Officially registered as the S.S. *Castillo de Maria*, the ship was no stranger to the packed waterfront and across the years she'd become a familiar visitor as she plied her trade up and down the coast of the Americas. Worn by long years of service, streaked with rust and with her once pristine red paint now flaked and peeling, she represented all that could be expected of a hard working, old tramp steamer.

And on this Saturday, the 30th of November 1940, her early morning arrival had been more than welcomed by a member of the Port Authority's Official Federal. He was known simply to one and all as Guillermo Castano, the Harbour Master. An advance booking, made three months prior, had been liberally sprinkled with a large payment of extra cash, and the Harbour Master was only too pleased to quietly direct the *Maria* to a secluded berth reserved for those wishing to remain as unobtrusive as possible. Having escorted the ship to her mooring, Guillermo Castano waved a fat hand to the freighter's bridge and departed in his gleaming launch. The Argentinean flag flying on the highly varnished bow made a mockery of the country's legislative jurisdiction over the criminal underworld. Many knew it, most ignored it, and the Policia Federal conveniently turned a blind eye.

For those paid to look the other way it was no surprise therefore when shortly after the old freighter's arrival a large convoy of drab looking canvas covered trucks drove onto the quayside and parked next to the waiting S.S. *Castillo de Maria*. More than a hundred wooden crates of varying size and weight were smartly unloaded to the quayside, checked and signed for. Before the trucks had driven clear of the docks the crew had set about loading the precious cargo.

One man on board stood in the open sun with one foot balanced on the gunwale carefully watching all that went on below. Emil

Lorenz, born and raised in the port city of Hamburg was a trusted employee of the German Embassy. His right hand gripped the barrel of an American made Thompson sub-machinegun, surreptitiously held low out of sight. A friend of a friend from the Brazilian port of Rio de Janeiro had smuggled it aboard in the dead of night. An extra four magazines of bullets were also delivered. Money swapped hands, no questions asked.

It took until the high heat of mid afternoon before the bare-chested, sweating deck hands eventually secured the last of her hatch covers and paused to seek rest in the shade. Only then did the man with the gun turn away, raise a nonchalant hand to the bridge, and disappear below.

Standing up there on that bridge overlooking the forward hold, the ship's Capitán nodded his satisfaction and rubbed a large handkerchief across his swarthy features. His white uniform shirt showed dark patches of perspiration and the fine starched cotton clung to his back.

But nonetheless, Capitán Carlos Romero Menéndez was a happy man. This latest shipment had special significance and he'd lost many nights of sleep waiting for this moment. He smoothed his flamboyant moustache and patted the heavy paunch, his twinkling brown eyes narrowed with pleasure. And he had good reason to be happy. Not only was he the skipper of the *Castillo de Maria*, but he was also owner and operator having purchased the vessel from her previous owners at an auction in 1922. It had been an inspired acquisition.

Utilising a single, triple expansion steam engine the ship generated enough horse power to give her a sustained capability of ten knots. The boiler and engine quickly proved to be the most economically reliable he'd come across, and his Chief Engineer continually expressed his satisfaction in running such well made machinery. From the personal perspective of Capitán Carlos Menéndez, the *Maria's* bridge superstructure sat high and wide amidships, giving him good all round visibility, a necessity when navigating some of the world's most unforgiving harbours. With her strikingly tall, slim funnel positioned immediately abaft the main housing, seldom if ever were the fumes from the boilers directed down towards the bridge.

Menéndez pulled a cigar from his breast pocket, an aromatic, long, slim panatela. He clipped it, lit it and inhaled, and then allowed the blue smoke to dribble from lips and nostrils. He nodded his appreciation and then thought of the coming voyage. Before the war now raging between Germany and Britain the *Castillo de Maria* would occasionally take passage as far as Gibraltar, her holds chock full of precious grain. More often she would sail for Spain or Morocco to trade in luxurious hand-woven fabrics and exquisitely crafted jewellery before returning with highly prized European agricultural machinery, much sought after by Argentine farmers. Always profitable.

Then, a while ago, on his previous stopover in Buenos Aries, his brother in-law had invited him to dine at the upmarket "El Torredo" restaurant, an invitation he was hardly likely to refuse. It took special privilege to be considered for a table at one of the most fashionable eating establishments in the city. But of course, for Major Hans Günther Zeigler of the German Embassy, such special treatment had long been accepted as routine.

What transpired over the course of the evening was a proposal which Capitán Carlos Romero Menéndez found irresistible. His agreement to undertake such a risky adventure had made him impossibly rich, his crew well rewarded, and now with the hatch covers secured, put them all in the greatest of danger.

This time he and the crew would make their longest ever voyage in the old steamer. Firstly to Salvador in Brazil to replenish the coal bunkers, and then the long passage across the Atlantic to Cadiz to take on more coal, before sailing through the Bay of Biscay and on to the German occupied French port of Cherbourg.

Menéndez looked at his watch. He would sail

after dark. Prying eyes were best avoided.

More than a month later, in the January of 1941, an icy wind brought the first winter snow to England's southern shores. Overnight flurries fell on the rugged battlements of Dover Castle and heavy drifts blocked ancient streets in nearby Ramsgate and Folkestone. In the narrow seas of the English Channel turbulent waves lashed the snow covered Kent foreshore and gale force winds churned the sea into flying spume.

That same icy wind also brought snow to Chatham's Royal Navy Dockyard and as temperatures dropped below zero, lengthening icicles hung dagger like from the ornate ledges of Regency windows.

Behind the heavily curtained sash window of a room on the second floor of Admiralty House, a fifty-two year old bearded officer in a Post Captain's uniform, stood with his back to the fireplace and let the welcome heat of dancing flames warm his hands. Captain James A. Pendleton, R.N., D.S.O., was a leather-faced stocky individual whose magnificent beard was worn in the full tradition of the Royal Navy. His rich, deep bass voice could be utilised to convey a remarkable level of authority and woe betide those who fell short of expectations. Regrettably, from Pendleton's personal perspective, the reduction of the fleet in the years following the last war had eventually resulted in his reassignment to a shore based establishment, albeit with a promotion to "Captain of Destroyers". And as with all Royal Navy bases, tradition saw to it that only the honorific title of "Captain (D)" was displayed on the name plaque affixed to his door.

A loud knock interrupted his thoughts. It was the duty Petty Officer.

'Tea, sir?'

Pendleton blinked and tugged his beard before nodding. 'Please,' he said. 'Two lumps?'

Petty Officer Whitehead grinned. 'Right, sir, on its way,' he said and backed out.

Pendleton saw the grin and accepted the unspoken criticism. If you were a civilian two lumps of sugar amounted to a major portion of one person's ration. He shook his head. Right now he needed it.

He turned to face the roaring fire, extending both hands to the heat. His thoughts drifted to encompass all the destroyers in the Royal Navy, not just those under his own command. They were the backbone of Britain's war at sea and there'd been no let up in the varied urgent requests for their deployment. A seagoing Jack-of-all-Trades some said, a description not far off the mark. And because of their commitment to duty, their willingness to protect those in their care against overwhelming odds, many of the destroyer fleet had already been lost.

Few if any of those outside the Navy fully

understood the extent to which they confronted the enemy, but those engaged in the English Channel knew all about the furious non stop effort involved. In daylight, escorting vulnerable merchantmen left them open to dive-bomber, U-boat and E-boat attack, or long range shore based artillery fire. On night patrol they fought running battles with German minelayers, surprise encounters, close fought, broadside to broadside over open sights, the modern equivalent of a bygone era. From Scapa Flow to Southampton, battleships and cruisers required destroyer screens. At Dunkirk, Royal Navy gunners had duelled with German tanks, and many destroyers had been tasked with covert missions to raid enemy held positions on foreign soil. As each day passed, and with varying degrees of success or failure, the endless need to deploy and fight at the drop of a hat further reduced the Admiralty's ever shrinking number of destroyers.

Pendleton rubbed his hands and turned away from the fire. A large wall chart of the English Channel hung opposite his desk and for the umpteenth time in the last few hours, his gaze was once again drawn to the enemy occupied coast of France. A single blue marker-pin denoted the theoretical position of a small 'Hunt' class destroyer acting on his orders. The ship was H.M.S. *Brackendale,* but her exact placement was vague and determined by last known course and speed rather than up-to-date co-ordinates.

Stepping away from the warmth of the fire, Pendleton crossed to the chart and paused to stroke his full, grey-speckled beard. A frown knitted the dark eyebrows and his sharp gaze fastened on the second marker that he'd recently moved closer to *Brackendale's* pin. It was red and represented a small German convoy moving south down the coast of Belgium. It was closing in on the French port of Dunkirk. But even that placement was now subject to 'best guess'.

With an irritable shake of the head, he turned on his heel, strode to the desk and eased himself down into the chair.

'Tea up, sir!' Whitehead announced, and a large steaming mug landed on his desk.

'Thank you,' Pendleton muttered, reached for a cigarette and found himself wondering whether this latest deployment had not been somewhat rushed. Destroyers on offensive sweeps of enemy waters were not in themselves unusual operations. Night forays to disrupt German coastal shipping had been ongoing for the last eight weeks, particularly in the Le Havre to Brest area, with some success. But occasionally the Admiralty reacted without seemingly giving the decision proper thought and Pendleton felt this mission was a classic example. Unlike the Le Havre-Brest operations, this was a lone destroyer deployed at short notice against an unknown number of enemy vessels, and in filthy weather.

Pendleton stirred the hot tea, sipped it, and replaced the mug on the tray. He leaned back in the chair and tugged thoughtfully at his flowing beard. The fact that it had been his own choice on who to send across the Channel had initially seemed of great benefit. By chance, a young officer by the name of Richard Thorburn, for whom Pendleton had a great regard, was recently returned from convoy escort duties and it made *Brackendale* one of only two warships available. Knowing the young Thorburn from as far back as Hong Kong's China Station, and having been instrumental in his promotion to Lieutenant-Commander, it was natural enough for Pendleton to have chosen the man he believed would accomplish the task, particularly as he already had experience of offensive patrols across the Channel. He freely acknowledged young Richard could be somewhat headstrong, but his natural seamanship, tactical ability and sheer professional acumen made him the outstanding candidate. His recently awarded Distinguished Service Order spoke volumes for the man's courage under fire.

Unfortunately, it was not until Thorburn had departed for the French coast that Pendleton had felt the first misgivings over a hurried briefing and deployment. It was the Admiralty who'd recommended a single destroyer but in retrospect he thought that both destroyers at his disposal would have made for a better outcome, and the fact he was still awake in the early hours spoke volumes for his lack of certainty.

He was worried and he didn't mind who knew. He stubbed out the cigarette, rose from his desk and began pacing the room.

CHAPTER TWO .. THE HUNTER

Far out in the wind swept waters of the English Channel, a small Royal Navy destroyer thumped heavily into the oncoming seas. For the last forty minutes she'd been pushing relentlessly up the Nazi occupied French coast, and at this particular moment H.M.S. *Brackendale* was in the process of navigating the enemy held waters off Dunkirk.

Standing tall on the windswept, open bridge, Lieutenant-Commander Richard Thorburn narrowed his eyes against the biting gusts of wind. He swayed as the ship twisted through a tumbling crest and then slid awkwardly into a deep trough. Spray whipped from the bows and he blinked, tasting salt. The ship trembled in the effort to shake herself free, then clawed her way up from the depths and pushed headlong into the next wave. At a steady twelve knots and holding to a heading of east by north-east, *Brackendale* ploughed remorselessly on.

'Port five, steer oh-three-five degrees.'

Faintly heard from the wheelhouse compartment below the bridge an acknowledgement came up the pipe.

'Port five, steer oh-three-five degrees. Aye aye, sir.'

It was a minor alteration of course and

Brackendale settled quickly, continuing her uninterrupted passage along the hostile shore.

Thorburn grimaced, wiped his chin and jammed his cap tighter over the dark hair. The lines at the corners of his eyes creased as he squinted into the wind and he hunched a little deeper inside the almost black fisherman's roll-neck jumper. He wore the jumper half concealed beneath his shabby double-breasted jacket, and his trousers, once sharply pressed, now hung wet, wrinkled and stuffed unceremoniously into a stout pair of sea boots. In all respects Richard Thorburn gave the appearance of a time-served Cornish trawlerman, but regardless of his image, those under his command respected both the seamanship and fighting abilities of the man on the bridge.

He'd thought about sending for his duffle coat but had been distracted and it slipped his mind. He was beginning to regret the error.

He shifted position to the bridge-screen, head down behind what little extra protection it gave from the wind. He peered through the dripping screen and looked down on the forward gun turret, the pair of 4-inch gun barrels levelled out towards the bows. Half of the gun crew were stood to at the breeches, and Thorburn grinned. In all probability the Gun-Captain wasn't flavour of the month right now. Squinting to look beyond the barrels he managed to pick out the solitary 2-pounder situated in the bows, the modern equivalent of the so called 'Bowchaser'. It was unmanned at the moment, its primary purpose to fire down over the bows, a blind spot for the 4-inch main armament.

Glancing to his right across the starboard side Thorburn wondered if the German shore guns would show their hand. His lookouts were struggling with the poor visibility and it was as much as they could do to stay alert let alone manage a sighting in such poor conditions. Not that any watchkeeper lacked motivation; that enemy held coast lay only five nautical miles off their starboard beam. An icy gust blew in over the screen and he grimaced. This year's winter storms were proving to be a bitter reminder of what the weather could really serve up when so inclined. He turned up his collar and looked round to call for the bridge messenger.

'Sir?'

'My duffle coat, please. It's in my cabin.'

'Right away, sir,' the messenger said and hurried to the ladder.

Thorburn frowned as a thought struck him. The orders for his patrol had been clear and straightforward. The Kriegsmarine were sailing convoys down the French coast, and the Admiralty had received information that another small one would be heading down to Dunkirk this very night. To that end *Brackendale* had been despatched to find it, and Thorburn was to inflict whatever damage he could without placing his ship in serious jeopardy. For a brief moment a smile flickered across his weathered face. He had seldom if ever received an order that was uncomplicated, but he thought that just for once 'simple' was exactly what had happened. The mission briefing had taken no more than thirty minutes, and with orders confirmed he'd returned aboard and prepared the ship for action. The frown that now furrowed his brow reflected his concern over exactly what strength of escort he might encounter. He shrugged and dismissed the thought. Worrying over 'ifs' 'whys' and 'wherefores' only served to create a worthless distraction he didn't need.

He returned his gaze to the ship's bow and cursed the weather. Searching an enemy held coastline in a blizzard was not his favourite pastime. He clung on to the hope that the forecast proved correct and that the skies would shortly clear.

'Captain, sir?' The voice was raised, fighting to be heard above the wind.

He lowered the glasses and turned to find a Telegraphist at his elbow. 'What is it?'

'Signal from Captain (D), sir.'

'Tell me,' he said above the gusting wind.

'Convoy reported to have passed Ostend at 02.30 hours. Course two-five-oh, estimated speed nine knots. Believed to have two escorts.'

'That's it? Believed? Nothing more on the escorts?' A blast of wind stung exposed skin, nose and cheeks baring the brunt.

'No, sir. That's all.'

'Very well, acknowledge.' At least it was confirmation that they weren't on a wild goose chase. The messenger came back with his coat and Thorburn shrugged into the warmth. 'Thank you,' he said, glanced left at the port bridge-wing and picked out the tall, wiry figure of Robert Armstrong, his First Lieutenant.

'Number One!' he called above the wind, and saw him turn to move closer.

'Sir?'

'We might have company ahead.'

Armstrong's teeth glistened in the darkness. 'So I heard. Hope we see them first.'

'True,' Thorburn said with a slight nod, and ducked from the stinging spray. 'I thought to close the coast.'

Armstrong wiped his face and frowned. 'In this weather, sir?'

'All the more reason to give it a try.'

'If you say so, sir, but it gets very shallow and there's a lot of wrecks. Not much room to manoeuvre.'

Thorburn fixed him with a sharp glance. 'You seem remarkably well versed on this stretch of coast.'

Armstrong didn't meet his eyes. 'June last year, the evacuation from the beaches, before I joined *Brackendale*. We made two trips in all.'

'Of course, Dunkirk. Sorry, slipped my mind,'

Thorburn said apologetically. 'How many did you save?'

'Seven-hundred, give or take. Bombed twice. I was navigator.'

The destroyer's bows shipped water and threw spray at the screen. They both crouched but still came up dripping.

Thorburn persisted. 'Nonetheless, if I can get us inshore it'd give us the element of surprise.'

'Yes, sir,' Armstrong said slowly. 'Provided we make use of it.'

Thorburn smiled in the darkness. 'Oh, I think we will, Number One,' and he chuckled. 'I intend to leave a strong calling card.'

It was Armstrong's turn to grin. 'That, sir,' he said, eyes glinting, 'I never doubted.'

'Exactly,' Thorburn said, rubbing his hands and glancing round the bridge. 'So I think now would be a good time to bring the ship to Action Stations. Might help warm us up.'

Armstrong nodded. 'Very well, sir,' he said, and reached for the button press. The urgent clamour of the alarm shrilled through the decks, immediately followed by the clatter of boots on ladders, the slamming of water tight doors. Through bulkhead telephones and voice-pipes the familiar reports flooded in; officers, petty officers and leading hands verifying they were stood to at their stations. The First Lieutenant acknowledged each one until he finally turned to the Captain.

'The ship is closed up at Action Stations, sir.'

Thorburn nodded. 'Very well,' he said, and looked round to the compass binnacle. 'Pilot, I intend to take us inshore. I trust we have the right charts?'

Sub-Lieutenant Martin, the ship's navigator, nodded in return. 'Yes, sir, we do.'

'Good. And you will endeavour to keep us in deep water?'

A faint smile appeared on Martin's face. 'Indeed I will, sir,' he said, mimicking the Captain's formality. He ducked his head against the spray, crossed over to the bulkhead chart table, flicked a switch, and let the quiet glow of its dim light reveal the current chart and his pencilled calculations.

Thorburn moved to the raised compass housing and leaned to a brass voicepipe.

'Starboard ten.' He ordered.

From the wheelhouse beneath his feet, he heard an acknowledgement echo up the pipe.

'Starboard ten. Aye aye, sir.'

Thorburn smiled. The voice was that of Chief Petty Officer Barry Falconer. The Chief was a veteran, years of service; big ships, little ships, and everything in between, and known respectfully throughout *Brackendale* as the 'Cox'n'. He was a barrel-chested, stocky Geordie who'd grown up on the banks of the River Tyne, and Thorburn couldn't believe his luck in having been presented with such a stalwart in charge of the lower deck.

A more pronounced gust of wind struck *Brackendale's* port bow and she heeled awkwardly. He braced, watching the compass rotate.

'Steady, Cox'n . . . , steer seven-oh-five.'

'Wheel's amidships, steering seven-oh-five degrees, sir.'

Thorburn looked up at the snow speckled darkness. What he was about to do wasn't strictly by the book but he justified the move as being the better of two evils. He either kept to the original course and blundered headlong into the convoy, or took the risk of closing the shore. Others might judge it as reckless, but he felt that given the circumstances, it was the correct choice. A faint smile returned to his lips. No-one in his right mind would expect to find an enemy warship close inshore in this weather. The ship heeled and a sheet of spray whipped in from the bows. He wiped his dripping face.

'What do we know, Pilot?'

'A moment, sir,' Martin snapped, his words almost lost in the gale.

Thorburn heard the impatience and hid a grin. He was right of course. And young as he was a lot rested on Martin's shoulders, a fact which Thorburn well understood. He also appreciated that Sub-Lieutenant Martin was a fine navigator and being badgered while working out solutions for negotiating a hostile shore was not to be recommended. Thorburn bit his lip and waited.

The biting wind slackened, the snow gradually turned to sleet, thinned and finally cleared.

Martin straightened from the chart. 'We can take her in to eight-hundred yards, sir. We can hold that for three miles along the coast. After that there are shifting sands, unpredictable. I would prefer it if you allowed me to hold her at a thousand yards.'

Thorburn nodded. Armstrong's memory had proved to be correct. A thousand-yards was not as close to the shore as he wished but it would have to do. 'Very well, Mr Martin, I'm in your hands.'

'In that case, sir, ten knots if you please.'

Bending to the pipe, Thorburn said, 'Revolutions for ten knots.'

'Speed ten knots. Aye aye, sir.'

Brackendale thumped a wave, while Martin scribbled calculations, dividers stepping out across the chart.

'Port five, sir.'

'Port five.'

And from the wheelhouse, 'Port five . . . . Port five of the wheel on, sir.'

'Steer oh-seven-one,' Martin said.

Thorburn again bent to the pipe. 'Midships . . . , steady . . . , steer oh-seven-one degrees.'

The Cox'n's voice came faintly to the bridge. 'Oh-seven-one degrees, aye aye, sir.'

The heavy cloud that had brought such poor conditions cleared away on the wind, and a glimmer of starlight lifted the gloom. Thorburn took a breath of cold air and glanced at the lookouts. They were attentive, binoculars probing their sectors. He rubbed his hands to generate some warmth. Patience, he thought, was everything. *Brackendale* pushed on, rising and falling to the rolling sea.

CHAPTER THREE .. SKIRMISH

Less than twenty miles further up the coast towards Ostend, ten German freighters of the Deutsche Mercantile Marine, accompanied by their two escorting warships, were proceeding west-southwest at nine knots. The small convoy was on course and on time to make Dunkirk within the next two hours and the escort commander, Korvettenkapitän Wolfgang Herzog, was satisfied that despite the weather he would soon be reporting their safe arrival.

With a commendable early career in the officer corps of the Kriegsmarine he now held command of a thousand-ton Type 24 "Carnivore" class destroyer. Each of the "Carnivore" class had been allocated a name commensurate with such predators and the ship he captained had been granted the title of *Puma*. Others of the type such as the *Wolf,* (Flotilla Leader), *Polecat* and *Jaguar*, along with *Leopard, Lynx* and *Tiger* made up the rest of the class. In size all ships compared favourably with the Royal Navy's new 'Hunt' class destroyers, but had better top speed and held a significant advantage with the addition of two banks of triple torpedoes. This was Herzog's third convoy since assuming command, all of which, thus far, had gone surprisingly well. Thankfully the snow had stopped, although the state of the sea remained lively. As if to confirm his thoughts, the ship thumped headlong into another roller, the stern lifting to a following sea. A thin smile flicked across his angular features. In this weather he could see no reason why there should be any interference from the Royal Navy; absolutely no reason at all. He made himself a little more comfortable in the bridge chair and looked at the time. Not long now . . . , they would be well inside Dunkirk's harbour defences before daylight.

H.M.S. *Brackendale*, two miles north of Dunkirk, pushed steadily on up the coast towards Ostend. The weather had again deteriorated and Thorburn grimaced, the sleet and hail lashing in sideways.

Lieutenant Martin called from the chart table. 'Port five!'

Thorburn, braced securely against the compass binnacle, repeated it to the wheelhouse. 'Port five.'

Brackendale eased left away from the coast and Martin gave the new course. 'Steer oh-six-seven degrees.'

'Midships,' Thorburn said, and watched the compass steady. 'Steer oh-six-seven degrees.'

The acknowledgement came and he raised his old Barr and Stroud binoculars to scan the sea fine off the port bow. He held the search for a minute, but only the wall of foul weather filled his lens. Lowering the glasses he raised his voice above the wind.

'Eyes peeled, gentlemen. Any time now.'

In his mind's eye he could picture *Brackendale* heading east-northeast and moving steadily up a shoreline that lay hidden to their right off the starboard beam. In the darkness somewhere ahead, and on an almost reciprocal course was the German convoy. It seemed only a matter of time before they made contact.

Brackendale dipped and leaned, ploughing on through the heavy seas, and Thorburn let himself be swayed by the winding twist.

'Ship!' There was an unmistakeable urgency to the call. 'Bearing Red three-oh! Range two-thousand!' It was Leading-Seaman Allun Jones in the port bridge-wing.

Thorburn pressed the glasses to his eyes and instantly found a target. It looked to be a merchantman, maybe five-thousand tons.

'I have it.'

But was it the convoy? He panned right and picked up a shadow following on, another merchant vessel, a squat funnel abaft the bridge. But where were the escorts? He swept the binoculars to his left until he was at almost ninety degrees with the port wing. Another shadow in the swirling snow, smaller, more distant. It had the lines of a warship, sleek, a mismatched pair of raked funnels. He studied it for a few more seconds . . . , possibly a small destroyer. In all probability the leading escort. More decisions. Should he hold course along the coast and allow all guns to bear over the port side? Or wait for the middle of the convoy and turn between ships? The longer he waited the more chance of being observed. He was inclined to let a couple more freighters come past, turn for open water, and rake them as he went.

He bent to a voicepipe. 'Guns?'

Abaft the bridge, up in the Range Finder Control Tower, Lieutenant 'Guns' Carling answered. 'Sir?'

'You have them?'

'Four in sight.'

'That last signal said only two escorts,' Thorburn said. 'Not sure I believe it but I'll wait and then turn out for the Channel. We'll engage on the turn.'

'Aye aye, sir.'

Thorburn pursed his lips. Now it all hinged on his original supposition that their lookouts wouldn't be too interested on checking inshore. He raised the binoculars and found the next freighter coming into view. Just a few more minutes and *Brackendale* would make her presence felt.

Down in the sick bay, Surgeon-Lieutenant P. Waverly R.N., had prepared the 'tools of his trade' in expectation of casualties. Satisfying himself that there was nothing more he could do, he left the two sick berth attendants twiddling their thumbs and took the opportunity to nip up to the wireless room. With the Captain's nod, Waverly's secondary, but at times vital work of decoding incoming signals, had become a duty which made an intriguing change to his usual profession.

Easing the door open he squeezed in to the already overcrowded compartment, nodded to those who saw him enter, and tucked himself in the back corner out of harm's way. The 'on watch' Telegraphist was diligently tapping the Morse key and Waverly looked on in anticipation. A Doctor he might well be, but he was also a Royal Navy officer with more than one string to his bow.

The tapping continued and he waited. The wireless room would make good use of him as soon as the occasion arose.

More than a thousand miles south of Dunkirk in the ancient Spanish port of Cadiz, a three-thousand ton freighter was preparing to cast off from the old docks and set sail for the Cotentin Peninsula and the German held French port of Cherbourg. She was the battered, rust streaked S.S. *Castillo de Maria,* and had already completed a six-thousand mile crossing of the Atlantic Ocean.

Laden with contraband, her original departure from Argentina's capital of Buenos

Aries back in December went better than hoped for. From loading to sailing not one member of the crew returned ashore and the German Embassy were quick to note the British Embassy's failure to acquire any information regarding the ship's manifesto. Of course, the ship's captain and crew all had affiliations with Germany and although Argentina and Spain were accepted as being "neutral" by Great Britain, it was well understood in Allied circles that there were many sympathisers in both Spanish speaking countries.

The *Maria* had entered harbour in the early afternoon and Carlos Menéndez needed all his years of seamanship to navigate the congested harbour. A pair of small passenger ships carrying high paying guests were moored mid harbour and re-supplying for the next leg of their journeys. An oil tanker was off-loading at the refinery, the pungent smell lingering over the docks. Astern of the *Maria* a pair of tugs nudged and bullied a five-thousand ton merchantman into her berth, and a floating crane manoeuvred itself between a barge laden with iron ore and a coastal freighter preparing to make a trip to the nearby steel works. A three-masted sailing schooner lay moored to a buoy undergoing repairs to her bow, and a trawler returned to port trailing seagulls, fish in abundance. Rowing boats, dinghies, small fishing boats and pleasure craft of every size and shape weaved their way in and out of harbour.

Spanish Cadiz, at peace with the world, had continued with her lazy afternoon.

The stop off at Cadiz achieved two aims. One had been the necessity to refuel with coal, and secondly Capitán Carlos Menéndez wanted reassurance that his journey was not in vain and that the port of Cherbourg had remained under German occupation. After all, in adherence with his pre-sailing instructions, for the best part of a month he had been incommunicado. Much could happen in such a period of time and this last leg of his journey would be fraught with danger. If he was caught as a 'blockade runner' then the best he and the crew could hope for would be internment for the remainder of the war. The worst outcome was that the Royal Navy might shoot first and ask questions later, the crew of the *Castillo de Maria* dying as a result.

But after an exchange of signals between the German Embassy in Cadiz and the Kriegsmarine at Cherbourg, Carlos Menéndez had received the comforting news that Cherbourg was indeed still in the hands of German forces and that in fact the Kriegsmarine would come to meet him one-hundred kilometres south-west of his final destination and escort him into port. Heartened by the arrangements he had accepted the invitation to enjoy a good meal and much wine. Evening had fallen when Menéndez finally returned to the ship and prepared to leave harbour.

With a dark, cloudy night firmly established over the sprawling city of Cadiz, the rust streaked merchantman, coal bunkers full, cleared the port's outer breakwaters and turned west to skirt the Portuguese coast. And back in the familiar surroundings of his bridge, Menéndez ran a pair of dividers across the plot and nodded his satisfaction. If all went according to plan, in four days the *Castillo de Maria* would enter the German occupied port of Cherbourg.

CHAPTER FOUR .. DANGER

In the waters off England's south coast, two convoys, both escorted by the Royal Navy, were on passage to deliver their desperately needed cargoes. One of the convoys was designated 'CE' (Channel Convoy heading east) with its destination being the London Docks, the other prefixed with 'CW' (Channel Convoy heading west) was on route to Southampton.

While Richard Thorburn waited to commence his attack on the far side of the Channel, Convoy 'CE' comprising fifteen merchantmen and three Royal Navy escorts, was on passage from Portsmouth to the Thames Estuary. Currently they were in the process of making their way past the historic coastal town of Hastings.

It was a filthy night. Gusting winds made for difficult navigation, and intermittent sleet and snow showers continually blinded the watchkeepers. The merchant ships consisted of colliers, grain carriers, general cargo and a solitary oil tanker. Their final destination of London Docks impatiently awaited their arrival. The eight colliers were of critical importance to London's Battersea power station, carrying vital tons of coal to replenish rapidly diminishing stocks. With the bombing of Britain's railways leading to a lack of reliable transportation, freighting by sea was the obvious next best solution. And to secure their safe passage through English waters, the escort consisted of one new destroyer, plus a Flower class corvette, and an auxiliary minesweeper.

Lieutenant-Commander Charles Rutherford R.N., was Senior Officer in the new Hunt class destroyer H.M.S. *Cheriton*. Lieutenant-Commander Keith Sanford R.N., captained the Flower class corvette H.M.S. *Cornflower*, and the auxiliary minesweeper of Lieutenant-Commander J. I. Fielding R.N.R., swept the waters ahead.

Unbeknown to those in the convoy, and in the darkness of a night lit only by a few faint stars amongst the cloud and snow, a German flotilla of five E-boats spotted the minesweeper moving left to right across their bows. The Leader throttled back and waited. He had enough experience to know a minesweeper indicated a convoy; he would wait and see what transpired.

Eighty miles east of the unsuspecting convoy, Richard Thorburn stood impatiently on *Brackendale's* compass platform and watched the fifth freighter crawl past. Finally he leaned to the pipe.

'Port twenty! Full ahead together!

He straightened away as Falconer's acknowledgement came, heard the faint ring of the telegraph. *Brackendale* heeled sharply, swinging out from the coast. He felt the vibrations through her deck plates, speed increasing, bow-wave rising.

'Midships!' he called. The wind increased, cutting.

Falconer centred the wheel and the small destroyer lurched upright, knifing the sea. Ahead of the bridge the forward gun-turret traversed left, and astern, on the quarterdeck, the other twin mounting followed suit. As the barrels steadied "Guns" Carling gave the order.

'Shoot!'

Simultaneously, the four-inch guns hammered out a broadside. Four high explosive shells whipped across the void. Thorburn caught the flash of detonations as they struck home. Amidships, Sub-Lieutenant George Labatt's quadruple Pompoms joined the fray, their staccato barks thumping 2-pound shells at the freighter's superstructure. The main armament crashed off another salvo and the freighter's stern erupted in boiling flame. Then as fire engulfed the bridge, the ship veered off course shorewards. Thorburn saw *Brackendale's* guns then train right, over the starboard beam, and stop in line with the next vessel. He lifted the binoculars and found the target, an old tramp steamer, probably four-thousand tons. He guessed the range as eight-hundred yards. In that moment the guns thundered, and at that distance they couldn't miss. Two shells found the starboard hull alongside the forward derrick, detonated on impact and set fire to the cargo hold. The second pair of shells struck the bow plates, tearing a wide gash. Seawater poured through, flooding the bow compartments. The ship staggered, slewing away as the weight of water took effect, down by the head.

Then night turned into day as an enemy starshell burst high,

Thorburn cursed at being discovered, but determined to inflict yet more damage on the convoy. He lunged for a voice-pipe.

'Hard-a-starboard!'

Falconer spun the wheel, held it over, and *Brackendale* heeled to port. Below the starboard bridge-wing the 20-mm Oerlikon blazed into life, tracer raking the crippled freighter.

'Midships!' Thorburn yelled above the din. *Brackendale* had swept round until she was parallel with the column of ships but moving in the opposite direction and now powered down towards the rear of the convoy. But Thorburn was well aware he needed to give his main armament every chance.

'Half ahead, twenty knots!'

Falconer's calm reply came to him.

'Half ahead. Revolutions for twenty knots, aye, sir.' The Cox'n glanced at the seaman on the telegraph and the indicator revolved until it reflected the required speed.

Down in the engine room, Lieutenant (E)

Bryn Dawkins R.N.R., the one time Petty Officer who'd received his promotion to Chief Engineer just before joining *Brackendale*, saw the telegraph pointer move and he throttled back.

The bow-wave slackened as the ship reduced speed, still driving ahead but less frenzied.

An enemy shell whipped across the bridge and flew over the stern. Thorburn sucked air through clenched teeth. Close, too close. He looked about, assessing his position. Two freighters badly damaged, a third about to be engaged. But there was no doubting the direction from which that shell came. He raised his glasses to focus beyond the bows, searching down towards the rear of the convoy. The flare still hung bright and he used it to find this second warship. *Brackendale's* 4-inch guns fell silent, only the Pompom and Oerlikons continuing the fight.

Then a sparkle of flame stabbed at him from down the convoy and he gave a mirthless grin.

'You bastard,' he muttered, and concentrated on the sleek, flying bow-wave.

Brackendale's main armament bellowed again, the next lumbering merchantman taking punishment. Tracer erupted from its wheelhouse and shells ricocheted wildly. Thorburn ignored it all, closed his mind to everything but a single grey shadow. Know your enemy was a maxim of dual purpose, and in this case it was vital to establish enemy strength. He knew he had a destroyer somewhere out to the head of the convoy, but what exactly was this newcomer?

A pair of shells hit the sea, waterspouts lifting, and another shell near missed the starboard bow, shrapnel rattling the side plates.

He leaned to a pipe. 'Guns!' he called.

'Guns, sir.'

'Something dead ahead. What can you see?'

There was a pause, and then Carling reported. 'Destroyer type. Can't see enough to identify.'

There was a shout from abaft the bridge. 'Enemy ship! Red one-seventy, Range four-thousand.'

Thorburn whipped round to face astern and steadied his glasses beyond the port quarter. He found it immediately, bow wave creaming as it raced in towards *Brackendale*. It was the leading escort he'd seen earlier come to join the fun.

Thorburn rubbed his jaw. Now they'd both located him, one ahead, one astern, and that made him piggy-in-the-middle. And he couldn't be sure of any others. This far from home on an enemy coast, with a possibility of being caught in crossfire, well . . . , he'd fulfilled his orders, discretion might be the better part of valour.

'I'm not going to hang around, Guns, we'll set course for home. See if you can finish that merchantmen.'

'Sir!' Carling said, and the guns crashed again.

To the wheelhouse, Thorburn gave the order. 'Hard-a-port!'

'Hard-a-port, aye aye, sir.'

Brackendale heeled into the turn, her starboard waist momentarily awash, gallons of water sluicing down the decks. Mid-turn the solitary starshell blinked out and darkness closed in on the skirmish. Beneath the bridge the pair of fo'c'sle guns ceased firing, unsighted by the turn away, but on the quarterdeck, under Carling's guidance, the after guns gave the target another five salvos before the 'cease fire' sounded.

'Midships . . . , steady.'

'Wheel's amidships. Steering three-five-oh, sir.'

Almost due north, Thorburn thought, that would do for now. 'Very well,' he said. 'Full ahead together.'

'Full ahead both, aye aye, sir.'

Brackendale surged out into open water and Thorburn turned to check astern. The evidence of her attack was plain for all to see. Three of the convoy's ships were well alight, the lurid, dancing glow of orange flames reflected in the sea.

Thorburn nodded and allowed himself a tight grin.

'Bloody marvellous,' he said under his breath. He might well have inflicted more damage but given the spread of the escorts he thought enough was enough. He'd definitely succeeded in carrying out the Admiralty's orders. The Germans would think long and hard before sending another convoy down that coast without better escort. And as the Royal Navy had already discovered, small warships were at a premium. It wasn't easy to conjure them up at short notice.

Brackendale slammed into a steep wave and buried her bows, corkscrewing wildly. The mast described a wicked arc from port to starboard. The crew scrambled to secure their footing, reaching for hand holds. A deluge of flying spray hit the bridge, soaking the occupants.

Thorburn grimaced, accepting the need to slow her down, and leaned to the wheelhouse pipe.

'Half ahead both, Cox'n,' he snapped. 'Revolutions for twenty knots!'

'Speed twenty. Aye aye, sir.'

Well astern a second starshell cracked open above the convoy, drifting, and Thorburn gave a wry smile. *Brackendale* had already moved far enough away to be outside the broad oval of light, and every passing minute improved their chances.

Armstrong appeared at his side. 'I make it three, sir.'

Thorburn pushed the cap off his forehead and grinned. 'I think our calling card was duly delivered, don't you?'

'Indeed I do, sir. We also seem to have escaped their attention. For now, anyway.' He hesitated. 'I'd better check for casualties and damage.'

'Yes, do that, Number One. Let me know.'

Armstrong nodded and turned for the ladder, and Thorburn looked round. 'Set course for home, Pilot.'

'Very well, sir,' Martin said and moved to the wheelhouse pipe. 'Port five.'

The Cox'n's reply was faint up the pipe. 'Port five, sir.'

'Midships.'

'Midships, aye sir.'

'Steer two-eight- five.'

'Steer two-eight-five degrees, aye aye, sir.'

Thorburn heard the orders, took note, normality returning, and then stepped over to the bridge-chair. 'Time?' he queried.

'02.55 hours, sir.'

'Thank you. We'll be home before daylight?'

'All things being equal, we will, sir.'

'Good,' Thorburn said. 'And well done, Mister Martin. We'd have been aground without your guidance.'

Momentarily taken aback by the compliment, Martin let the darkness hide his smile. The praise was unexpected and in one aspect a small thing, but it carried with it the mark of a man who could remember others even in the midst of battle.

'Thank you, sir,' he said to the back of Thorburn's seated figure, and getting no response, let it be. After all, a Captain had more to dwell on.

Doc Waverly had returned to his 'office' as soon as the first shot was fired. He waited in expectation of an urgent call, or for a wounded crew member to be brought in. As Surgeon-Lieutenant this was his primary role and one to which he was well adapted. His civilian career had led very neatly to the repair of terrible injuries, and he was well aware that above all else his exemplary skills had saved many a life.

The telephone rang, answered by one of his attendants. A stretcher case with a shrapnel injury was on its way.

In *Brackendale's* engine room, Lieutenant Bryn Dawkins stood watching the telegraph as he waited for the next alteration of speed. The overwhelming thunder of the guns overhead had ceased, the physical expression of which meant all those in the engine room had cringed at the violent hammering their eardrums had received in such a confined space. It seemed the worst was over.

At thirty-eight years of age the red haired Welshman, vastly experienced in all things mechanical, proudly maintained a hands on approach to his life's work. That work, deep below the waterline, was one of heat and noise, of glistening dials, and the never ending need to resolve whatever new mechanical issue arose. A rivulet of sweat trickled down the heavily lined face, was ignored, and left to fall. Whether it was the two Admiralty 3-drum boilers, or the Parsons geared turbines delivering 19,000 horsepower, the rotating shafts must not be allowed to falter. In battle the twin propellers that thrust the destroyer through the water were the be all and end all of a Chief Engineer's existence. The Captain relied on Bryn Dawkins to supply that propulsion and the Welshman would not be found wanting.

He wiped his hands on a piece of waste cotton and watched the Stokers go about their business. None of them signalled that he was required and, for now, the needle of the telegraph remained static.

Well astern of *Brackendale's* wake, Korvettenkapitän Wolfgang Herzog, cursed. He cursed the Gods and cursed the fools under his command, but mostly he cursed the Royal Navy. Why could they not accept their war would soon be over? No . . . , they had to stick their noses into Kriegsmarine business, where they no longer had an automatic right of way. He cursed again, a bitter monologue aimed directly at Churchill, and shook his head. Three merchant ships out of action and all he had to show for his efforts was an Englander on the run. As bad as it was a faint smile crossed his face. It was rumoured the *Bismarck* would soon put to sea. For Herzog it couldn't come soon enough.

CHAPTER FIVE .. RESCUE

To the west of the headland at Dungeness the five German E-boats had been rewarded. They'd found the convoy trailing along in the wake of the minesweeper. The only visible close escort was a lone corvette holding station ahead of the nearest column of freighters. The Oberleutnant in command assumed there would be at least one other somewhere astern but neither of them caused him any real concern. Their maximum speed and poor armament when confronted by fast moving Schnellboats seldom if ever inflicted any damage on a well handled flotilla.

The Oberleutnant, convinced of the convoy's vulnerability, gave the signal to attack at will and the five boats, with their lethal load of ten torpedoes, surged towards the relatively unprotected convoy. With each boat powered by three Daimler Benz MB 501 marine diesel engines, they throttled up to almost eighty kilometres an hour, and the plodding merchantmen succumbed to the inevitable.

Six torpedoes found targets and within minutes ships were floundering, engulfed by fire, sinking. As quickly as they'd struck the E-boats turned away and melted into the darkness, leaving carnage in their wake.

Lieutenant-Commander Charles Rutherford

in H.M.S. *Cheriton* managed to fire a few salvos from her 'A' and 'Y' mounts. As a deterrent it proved to be useless and the fast moving E-boats replied by raking the ship with their rapid-fire Flak canon as they wriggled clear. From *Cheriton's* fo'c'sle to the waterline, 37mm rounds punched holes in the warship's thin plating. A gunner died, almost torn in half, and two were badly wounded. For the German officer commanding the flotilla it had been a superbly timed attack and he happily led them home to Calais.

By the time *Cheriton* and *Cornflower* arrived on scene they were reduced to rescuing survivors. Those they pulled from the sea were cold and shocked, and covered in oil, coughing and gasping to clear their lungs. Some had broken limbs, others open wounds, a few with terrible burns.

Through no fault of their own the escorts had suffered the indignity of having to fend off a determined attack without being able to offer any really effective resistance. Attempting to fight off a fast moving force of E-boats always put them on the back foot. And this time, low on the waterline, *Cheriton* had sustained enough damage to cause the destroyer to lose power. Accordingly, Charles Rutherford ordered *Cornflower* and the minesweeper to assume responsibility for the remaining passage to Southend-on-Sea and signalled the Admiralty that *Cheriton* was sailing under reduced speed.

He watched as the remaining ships gradually pulled away and shook his head in frustration. He swore to take revenge on the Germans and prayed to be let loose in more advantageous circumstances.

In the end, only fourteen merchant seamen had been rescued from the bitter sea. The convoy lost five of the six freighters hit, including three of the desperately needed colliers. Unhappily, shortly before dawn, and with the North Foreland at Folkestone a stone's throw off her port beam, the old three-thousand ton S.S. *Apollo Star*, her holds full of grain, lost the battle to stay afloat and sank in fifteen fathoms. On this occasion, forewarned of their struggle to stay afloat, luck was with them. Her captain and the entire crew were rescued by *Cornflower*.

In London, hidden in the bunkers deep beneath the Admiralty buildings, an array of duty Telegraphists acknowledged the never ending flow of incoming signals. Whether from ships in the North Atlantic or localised traffic defending the English Channel, each message was recorded and filed according to its nature. Well before daylight senior Admiralty officers became fully aware of the night's tally. And the simple truth was hard to deny. Six to three in favour of the Germans, and another much needed escort destroyer temporarily out of action. The pendulum had again swung away from the Royal Navy's grip on that narrow strip of sea.

In the German occupied French port of Cherbourg, at the Kriegsmarine's Headquarters for Western Operations, Admiral Frederic Thomas Blomberg, Knights Cross, sat in a large leather armchair and contemplated a fresh directive from Grand-Admiral Erich Raeder. Blomberg was instructed to reinforce his naval presence in Cherbourg and thereby increase operational capability in preparation for the imminent arrival of a vessel called the *Castillo de Maria*. It carried an important consignment and was attempting to run the British blockade of French ports. An escort of at least three destroyer type units would be required to rendezvous with the *de Maria* at a point one-hundred kilometres to the west, and then ensure her safe arrival into port.

He read the orders once more, rubbed his heavy jowl and called over his shoulder. 'Müller.'

Assistant Executive Officer to the Admiral, Fregattenkapitän Peter Müller, looked up from his files.

'Herr Admiral?'

'I am told we are short of offensive capability here in Cherbourg. Raeder wants more. You will find another two and detach them immediately.'

'Jawohl, Herr Admiral,' Müller said, picturing his current dispositions. 'I could reduce one of the flotillas in Brest. We could spare a minesweeper, and there is a destroyer escorting a convoy, the *Puma*. It will shortly enter Dunkirk. That too could be detached, transferred away from escort duty.'

Blomberg raised his chin to stare at the ceiling, hands entwined over his expansive waist. 'Who commands the *Puma*?'

Müller reached for a file and ran a finger down a column. 'Korvettenkapitän Wolfgang Herzog.'

'Mmm,' Blomberg mumbled and rubbed his forehead. He thought it over and eventually gave a reluctant nod. 'If that is what we must do, so be it. The Grand-Admiral is not to be denied.'

Müller rose from his chair and clicked his heels. 'But of course, Herr Admiral. I see to it now,' he said and slipped out of the door.

Admiral Fredric Thomas Blomberg gave a thoughtful smile and drummed his stubby fingers on the walnut desk. Always better to obey the latest order and worry about how it would affect future operations when the need arose. He straightened in the chair and reached for his pen. Official authorisation would be required.

Korvettenkapitän Wolfgang Herzog led the remnants of his convoy into Dunkirk's ruined harbour and duly berthed the *Puma* alongside the Kriegsmarine's designated refuelling dock. Within minutes of his arrival a messenger came aboard ordering him to report immediately to Kapitän-zur-See Klaus Schröder, the Kriegsmarine's Area Commander for Northern French ports.

Leaving his ship to be replenished under the watchful eye of his First Officer, Herzog shrugged into a leather coat and strode off towards the half demolished old pre war office. Daylight brought a dusting of snow and he took great care with how he placed his feet. The breeze strengthened and he turned up his collar, his chin tucked away from the icy gusts. At the end of the dock he turned for the old brick building, picked his way through a jumble of strewn masonry and slowed to return a guard's salute. The oak door was opened and he stepped into the warmth of a large, wood-panelled outer office. He ignored the curious glances, slackened his leather coat, and marched imperiously down the corridor to his left. At the third door on his right a young woman in Wehrmacht uniform stood waiting. He'd seen her around the last time he was in port, twice striking up a conversation that had culminated in her accepting his invitation for dinner at a fine French restaurant. Hanna had proved to be excellent company but he'd been disappointed when the evening had ended without the romantic conclusion he'd envisaged.

She gave him a warm smile, and offered to take his coat and cap. He gave her an appreciative smile in return, slipped out of the coat, and as she hung it on a rack he ran a hand down the small of her back and patted her backside.

The welcoming smile disappeared before she brusquely snatched away his cap and ushered him inside. He grinned at her annoyance, forgot it, and snapped to attention.

Kapitän-zur-See Klaus Schröder looked up from his desk and gave a thin smile. It was a cold smile, and there was little warmth in the grey eyes. Herzog felt the full force of a silent interrogation, but the words when they came carried no hint of animosity. 'Well, mein Jugend,' he said quietly, 'how do you explain the loss of ships?'

'The British took us by surprise, Herr Kapitän. They attacked through heavy snow and from inshore. I had no warning and before we could engage they were gone.'

Schröder raised an eyebrow. '*They*? They were gone? How many were there, Herzog? Three . . . , four?'

'I could not be certain, Herr Kapitän. At least two.'

'And they were obviously destroyers?'

'Without doubt. They cut through our columns at great speed and then . . . , nothing. No sign of where they went.'

Schröder stared at him. 'Mmm,' he mouthed, and rubbed his chin. 'Like ghosts, no?

Herzog could see Schröder wasn't convinced but decided not to elaborate. Instead he simply nodded.

Schröder studied him a little longer, shook his head in exasperation and looked down at his desk. 'No matter,' he said at length. 'You are relieved of convoy duties. I have a signal instructing you to report to Cherbourg. Admiral Blomberg is increasing the strength of the flotilla there and you have been chosen.' He leaned back from the desk. 'Questions?'

Herzog swallowed and cleared his throat. He'd had a good run recently, but this latest fiasco might well hamper his future prospects. Better to accept his new orders and walk quietly away.

'No, Herr Kapitän, no questions.'

Schröder nodded in dismissal. 'Good, then may I suggest you hurry, Herzog. Admiral Blomberg does not like to be kept waiting. Yesterday is not soon enough for a man of his temperament.' He gave a wicked grin and waved a hand in farewell.

'So go. . . . Go!

Herzog clicked his heels and spun away. The door opened and young Hanna stood waiting, cap and coat ready. But the accompanying smile was mocking, blatantly disrespectful, a glint in her eye. Ruefully, he reached out and took his coat, accepting the unspoken rebuke. He knew his authority on this station no longer counted, particularly when it came to how he treated the uniformed women and what favours he could no longer count on.

He turned down the corridor and headed for

the exit. Outside in the twilight world of a snow covered new day he hurried toward his ship. The sooner *Puma* slipped her moorings the better.

Lieutenant-Commander Richard Thorburn hauled himself up the starboard ladder and stepped on to the back of *Brackendale's* bridge. As the first hint of pre-dawn grey lit the eastern horizon, the small destroyer entered the outer reaches of the River Medway and he could see both Armstrong and Martin busy issuing helm orders to guide her into the 'safe' channel swept by the minesweepers.

Armstrong broke off to make his report. 'Approaching second portside marker buoy, sir. Course two-oh-five, speed six knots.'

'Very well. Carry on, please.'

Brackendale ran on, daylight emerging, the dark outline of land and buildings slowly taking shape, more apparent, a hint of colour returning to the snow dappled countryside.

Thorburn moved to the dropped bridge-screen and leaned his elbows on top, cradling his chin on his forearms. The icy wind of the previous hours had subsided and the inshore waters were almost flat calm, and standing there eyeing the foreshore, he marvelled at how serene it all looked. But then a pair of barrage balloons lifted into the air, disfiguring the placid calm, and further upriver more followed. An early morning patrol of three Hurricanes banked out for the channel, the noise of their engines quickly receding into the distance.

'Captain, sir!' The voice from behind was insistent, demanding attention. He turned to find Petty Officer Langsdale waiting.

'Urgent signal, sir.'

Thorburn took the pink slip and read through. "*Brackendale* to proceed Dover with all despatch. *Cheriton* in need of assistance." It was signed Captain (D).

'Acknowledge!' he snapped, handing it back and trying to recall exactly who had command of the destroyer. He gave it up and glanced round at red rimmed eyes. Tired or not, there was a job to do.

'Pilot.'

'Sir?'

'We're needed at Dover. I'll take the bridge.' He leaned to the wheelhouse voice-pipe. 'Cox'n?'

'Cox'n, sir.'

'We're going about. It'll be a bit tight. Understood?'

Chief Petty Officer Barry Falconer was only too well aware of the restricted channel in this part of the Medway. 'Aye aye, sir,' he answered firmly.

Thorburn straightened to check the narrowing body of water. 'Mister Martin, are we on an ebb tide?'

'Yes, sir.'

'Very well,' Thorburn said, and prepared to use the current to swing round. Timing, he knew, would be critical. The mud flats either side of the river awaited the smallest misjudgement and *Brackendale* had only just missed that port buoy. With an eye on the bows he bent to the pipe.

'Stop starboard.'

'Stop starboard, aye, sir.'

'Half ahead port. Ten knots.'

'Half ahead port. Revolutions for ten knots, aye aye, sir.'

Thorburn watched *Brackendale's* movement. 'Hard-a-starboard!'

'Hard-a-starboard, aye, sir!' The small destroyer hesitated, slow to respond, but reluctantly began to answer the helm, the bows falling away with the current. The turn was wider than Thorburn had bargained for and he called to the voice-pipe.

'Full astern starboard!'

'Full astern starboard! Aye, sir!'

He breathed in, eyes narrowed, waiting. The propellers found purchase, one pushing, the other pulling, opposite thrust, thrashing the water beneath her stern rail. The bows came round . . . , further . . . , until the portside was beam on to the power of the ebb, and a marker buoy floated past upstream. The mud flats threatened, closer, and Thorburn gripped the rail, grim faced. It would be touch and go.

And as the bows swung round beyond the mid-turn, his worst fears were realised. The ship grounded, rocking, then tilted to starboard, a grating sound coming from beneath her forefoot. She scraped noisily, and he prepared to put her in reverse. But as he leaned to the wheelhouse pipe *Brackendale's* momentum took her clear and she lurched upright, slithering awkwardly over the last of the cloying mud. And they were free.

Thorburn glanced at the sky. Thank God there'd been no Luftwaffe around.

'Stop starboard,' he ordered, and watched the bows coming round to finally head downstream. He checked her swing.

'Midships . . . , steady.' She settled, mid-channel once more. 'Half ahead together. Revolutions for ten knots.'

'Half ahead together, speed ten knots, aye aye, sir.'

Thorburn peered at his watch. Four minutes by his reckoning. He caught Martin's eye and winked. The navigator gave him a wry smile and nodded. They both knew the mud flats had almost claimed them but equally they chose to leave it unsaid. Precious time had been saved by making a risky manoeuvre, and it had paid off. Now to make the most of it.

'All yours, Pilot. Quick as we can,' Thorburn said, and stepped clear of the platform.

Martin took charge and following a stream of helm orders *Brackendale* finally made it out past Sheerness docks and into open water.

'Twenty-four knots, please, Pilot.'

The telegraph rang in the wheelhouse and in the engine room Bryn Dawkins caught the movement on the dial. A finger was pointed and a Stoker made an adjustment, and the spinning shafts increased revolutions.

Nose up, stern down, the small destroyer surged ahead, the snow covered roofs of Margate beckoning them on towards the North Foreland. An alteration of course took them due south for Broadstairs and they then mirrored the coastline down past Ramsgate, Pegwell Bay, Deal and Walmer Castle. With Dover Castle in sight Thorburn eased *Brackendale* into mid-channel and the lookouts concentrated their efforts on the waters ahead. But the warmth of a weak winter sun had brought a thickening mist; visibility reduced.

Thorburn had the speed halved to twelve knots and shortly after a voicepipe squawked.

'Guns-Bridge?'

He answered the pipe. 'Bridge.'

'*Cheriton* in sight, sir. Red-one-oh.'

'Very well,' he said, and snatched up his binoculars. He focussed across the port bow and quickly located the ship. Outwardly, he thought, as he gave her a brief once over, she showed no signs of damage. Certainly her superstructure was intact; the biggest concern had to be her bow-wave, or rather the lack of it. He noticed the mist thinning and glanced at the sky. Intermittent cloud had drifted in, ideal conditions for the Luftwaffe to cloud hop in search of a worthwhile target. And with *Cheriton* almost dead in the water *Brackendale's* anti-aircraft support might well be called into action.

A lamp flickered.

'*Cheriton* signalling, sir.'

'Go on,' Thorburn said.

'Reads . . . , "c . o . . n . . . , tam . i . . , contaminated fuel oil. Five knots." End of message, sir.'

Thorburn grimaced. This was a new 'Hunt' class destroyer wallowing around mid-channel. Way too much of a temptation for the Luftwaffe.

To the signaller he said, 'Acknowledge.' The shutter clattered briefly.

Thorburn pursed his lips and gave orders for *Brackendale* to swing round *Cheriton's* stern and take station off her starboard beam. That would place his small destroyer a couple of cables length out towards the enemy coastline with a reasonable chance of intercepting any incursions by the Luftwaffe.

With the manoeuvre almost complete a call from Armstrong caught his attention. 'Sir!'

With the ship just gliding into position Thorburn looked up from the chart table.

Armstrong was pointing over the port side at *Cheriton*. 'I think that probably says everything.'

Thorburn nodded. Her starboard side had taken a number of hits on the waterline near No1 boiler. If she'd suffered penetration of her fuel oil tanks that would explain the contamination.

Salt water could take hours to clear.

'Looks like it'll be a long day ahead, Number One.' He looked again at the chart and pushed the cap back off his forehead. The nearest dockyard suitable for repairs had to be Sheerness.

Armstrong raised his eyes to the heavens. 'Really? God help us.'

Thorburn swivelled a pair of brass dividers along a roughly sketched line, and swore. 'Be dark before we make Sheerness.' He closed the dividers, settled his cap, and then joined his First Lieutenant in the port bridge-wing.

'I think,' Thorburn said slowly, 'we might ask them how the repairs are going.'

Armstrong gave him a rather old fashioned look. 'If you think that's helpful, sir.'

'I do. If they can clear the lines to just one of the boilers, then they can draw uncontaminated fuel from the port side tanks. With luck they might get fifteen knots.'

'Of course, sir, and much better than us playing nursemaid all day.'

Thorburn gave him a sideways glance, but saw no hint of a smile. He wondered if it was really worth badgering *Cheriton's* captain.

From *Cheriton's* bridge a lamp flickered.

'Read it, Yeoman.'

'From *Cheriton*, sir,' he said formally. 'Reads, "Have stripped and cleaned lines to No-1 boiler.' There was a pause. 'Injectors and sprayers to be checked. Lines clear. Thirty minutes to trial run."

Message ends, sir.'

Thorburn grinned at Armstrong. 'Someone was reading our thoughts.' To the signalman he said, 'Acknowledge.'

The lamp clattered briefly and Thorburn moved to the bridge-chair, sat and jammed a boot against a bracket. It was worth the wait if *Cheriton's* engine room could get it to work.

CHAPTER SIX . . HELL'S CORNER

'Enemy aircraft! Green two-oh, angle of sight-twenty degrees.'

Thorburn sprang to his feet. 'Action stations!' he shouted, and lifted his binoculars. The alarm shrilled and men scrambled for their places.

'Full ahead both!' he called down the pipe, and then found the distant formation of black dots high beyond the starboard bow. With the bows of both destroyers pointing north-east towards St Margaret's Bay it was important that he create a moving anti-aircraft shield to both defend and draw fire from *Cheriton*.

'Guns - Bridge!'

'Bridge,' he answered.

'Looks like Stukas, sir. I count twelve, no visible escort.'

'Very well. Open fire when ready.'

'Aye aye, sir,' Carling said, and Thorburn watched as the fo'c'sle guns elevated to starboard.

Brackendale increased speed, bow wave rising, her sharp stem knifing the sea.

Thorburn couldn't let her run too far and bent to the pipe. 'Starboard thirty.'

'Starboard thirty, aye aye, sir.'

Beneath his feet the ship heeled to port and Thorburn balanced, right knee bent. The cold dampness of a fine spray settled on his face and he licked his lips. The small destroyer's head came round towards mid-channel, circling back to run parallel with *Cheriton's* feeble wake, but now travelling in the opposite direction. He saw there was nothing wrong with *Cheriton's* guns. They elevated and trained, steadied on the fast closing shapes.

'Midships!'

Falconer acknowledged. 'Midships, aye.'

Brackendale swung upright, her guns traversing round to follow the enemy astern. With the rapid turn the bombers now trailed off their port quarter and Thorburn waited before circling again to run back alongside *Cheriton*.

'Hard-a-port!'

'Hard-a-port. Aye aye, sir!'

Again *Brackendale* heeled this time to starboard, hard over, powering out and round ready to face the enemy.

'Midships . . . , steady!'

'Midships, sir. Steering oh-four-five degrees.'

'Very well,' Thorburn acknowledged, and raised his binoculars. The bombers were in two groups of six, a loose formation, and as he watched the leading Stuka dropped a wing.

Armstrong voiced their thoughts. 'Here they come.'

Thorburn snatched a glance at Labatt's Pompoms, the four barrels almost at maximum elevation. Labatt himself shielded his eyes from the glare and followed the bombers as they swept wide towards Dover and then, at a thousand-feet, came winging back towards an almost stationary *Cheriton*.

Thorburn stepped up onto the compass platform. The Stukas had seen his move and countered by heading for the castle before returning to the attack. It placed *Brackendale* at a disadvantage by being on the wrong side. He allowed himself a momentary glance at the sky inland above the Kent coast. 'What wouldn't I give for a few Spitfires,' he said.

Armstrong nodded and raised his glasses. 'I doubt anyone's told the RAF. We're only two ships.'

At that moment *Brackendale's* guns thundered into action. Explosive steel lifted skywards. The staccato bark of Labatt's four-barrelled Pompoms hammered at fast moving targets, and the 20-mm Oerlikons thumped rounds at the enemy.

Cheriton joined the mêlée, her 4-inch guns hurling lethal exploding balls of shrapnel at the first Stuka's run in. And the bombs began to drop. They plunged down, four from the wings and one from beneath the fuselage. Thorburn watched them arrow towards *Cheriton*, held his breath, and saw them all miss long. They erupted into drifting columns of foam, the sea speckled with shrapnel.

A pair of Stukas teamed up for the next

attack, and this time they came round from beyond *Cheriton's* stern and flew towards her bows. A torrent of shells blazed skywards, every calibre of gun blasting at the gull-winged enemy. Glowing tracer filled the air, converging on the dive bombers, but still they came. Thorburn knew he must bring his ship across *Cheriton's* bows to stay close, keep his gunnery within range. He bent to the voice-pipe and snapped an order.

'Port twenty!'

'Port twenty, aye sir!' Falconer acknowledged, and *Brackendale* heeled to starboard. The 4-inch guns crashed in unison and Thorburn coughed at the acrid smoke, eyes watering. The Stukas increased their angle of attack, and then, when it seemed they must surely crash onto *Cheriton's* quarterdeck, released their bombs and pulled away. How they managed to survive that much anti-aircraft fire Thorburn was at a loss to explain. Columns of water marked the misses, but then, not unexpectedly, he saw one bomb find the target. It struck *Cheriton* between the depth charge rails and 'Y' gun, but astonishingly failed to explode. Thorburn shook his head. Pure luck.

He snatched a glance over the funnel on the port side and found the other flight of six Stukas silhouetted against the blue sky.

Armstrong shouted a warning. 'Three coming in. Port bow!'

Thorburn spotted them commencing their dive and leaned to the wheelhouse pipe. 'Dive bombers, Cox'n. I'll be throwing her about.'

'Aye aye, sir.'

The high pitched wail of Stuka sirens caught their attention, the bombers plummeting down in a vertical dive. Thorburn could see someone manning the bow-chaser, tracer arcing skywards. Spent shell cases cascaded to the deck, the 'pom-pom - pom-pom' clearly audible over the general din.

'Hard-a-starboard!' he snapped at the pipe, and *Brackendale* veered north towards Dover. Hardly had the turn commenced when Thorburn countermanded the order.

'Hard-a-port!'

The small destroyer lurched upright, centred, and changed direction south. Thorburn grimaced in concentration. *Brackendale* had just described an 'S' shaped evolution and yet the Stukas clung to his stern.

'Midships!' he called, and waited for the bombs. Then a bright orange flash ripped apart the foremost Stuka and debris rained down to the waves. The second Stuka veered right as it released, and the sea erupted off the starboard waist. The last Stuka took a stream of tracer and pulled out early, racing away at sea level.

'Spitfires! Green one-hundred!'

Thorburn turned and grinned. 'Cease fire!' he shouted. 'Cease fire!'

Carling heard him. 'Check, check, check!' he called, and the 4-inch guns fell silent. The secondary armament, Pompoms and Oerlikons were the last to stop. The Spitfires peeled out of formation in pairs and attacked from above and behind. German pilots saw them late and tried to scatter, to no avail. The British fighters, each armed with eight Browning .303" machine guns, tore into the fleeing Stukas and immediately began inflicting casualties. Green and scarlet tracer flashed between opponents but the overwhelming advantage was with the Spitfires, their sheer weight of firepower proving irresistible. Two Stukas attempted to dive away for the French coast. They were caught, riddled with bullets, and smoking badly crashed into the sea. Another caught fire alongside the port fuselage and the pilot inverted the aircraft to parachute for safety. Yet another exploded in mid air, a wing spinning away and the tail plane folding. It fell as might a feather, tumbling and swaying and circling, before splashing violently into the waves.

Two Spitfires latched onto a fleeing Stuka and a four second burst obliterated the aircraft. The closest Spitfire almost collided with the flying debris but, banking hard, managed to avoid the worst.

Unseen above all their heads a lone, damaged Stuka made it to the safety of the clouds and disappeared from view.

The Spitfires returned from their exploits and regained formation, and as far as Thorburn could tell none seemed to have suffered any damage. The leader waggled his wings and with the winter sun glinting off their cockpits, they roared away towards Dover and the airfield not far inland.

'Half ahead both. Speed ten knots,' Thorburn ordered. 'Damage reports, Number One?'

'Nothing so far, sir, and no casualty reports either. I'll make certain,' he said and reached for the bulkhead telephone.'

Thorburn pursed his lips and glanced around for *Cheriton*. She appeared to be intact but looking at her in the entirety he wondered just how long her casualty list was?

'Port ten,' he said.

'Port ten, aye aye, sir.'

Brackendale came round past *Cheriton's* stern rails and he brought her parallel to the destroyer's starboard side.

'Slow ahead.'

He saw movement on her bridge. A megaphone was raised.

'Ahoy, *Brackendale*!'

Thorburn motioned for his own speaker. 'Lieutenant-Commander Thorburn. At your service.'

'Good morning to you, Rutherford here. Glad to have you alongside. Thought we might try for Sheerness. Any objections?'

'None whatsoever, my thoughts exactly,' he said. 'Can you give me your speed?'

There was a short pause as Rutherford conversed with someone behind him. Then the megaphone was raised again.

'My Chief says four or five knots, but he's working on No-2 boiler. When he clears that we'll be more like fifteen.'

'Very well. I thought I'd take station off your starboard quarter?'

'Couldn't ask for more,' Rutherford boomed. 'Just the ticket.' The megaphone disappeared and Thorburn looked round at Sub-Lieutenant Martin. 'Put us two cables off her starboard quarter, Pilot. No need for anything showy, just let her drift back.'

Martin nodded and gave an order to the wheelhouse. 'Starboard five.'

Armstrong returned to report. 'Three casualties, sir All with the Doctor. Minor damage only.'

'Very well,' Thorburn nodded.

Then Armstrong asked *the* question. 'Defence stations, sir?' Eyes and ears around the bridge waited, expectant.

Thorburn took an exaggerated glance at the sky. It didn't do the Ship's Company any favours to keep them at Action Stations longer than necessary, but another thirty minutes wouldn't harm.

'Not yet, Number One. Some of our little

friends might be back.'

Armstrong nodded and gave an overly loud reply, for effect. 'Maintain Action Stations. Aye aye, sir.'

Thorburn moved to his chair and planted one worn boot back on the pipe bracket. The sun was well up now, just another day in the English Channel, and one more skirmish at Hell's Corner. Luck had been with them this time and *Cheriton* had got away with it. Too often during the last few months this part of the narrow sea had proved a death sentence for those in trouble. Not that they were out of the woods yet. There was still a long way to go. More than anything Thorburn wished *Cheriton's* Chief Engineer all the luck in the world.

The passage to Sheerness eventually took nine hours and Thorburn was only too pleased to formally release *Cheriton* into the hands of the dockyard. Lieutenant-Commander Charles Rutherford thanked him by loud-hailer and the pair parted company. *Brackendale's* crew had been without a break for too long and with night upon them Thorburn was only too pleased to find their mooring on the River Medway and settle down for a well earned rest.

CHAPTER SEVEN .. GUN BOAT

In Captain Pendleton's outer office, an attractive young Wren officer finished typing an order and quickly checked for errors. She then placed it in her out-tray for signing, rose from the chair and walked to the window.

Second Officer Jennifer Farbrace pursed her delicate lips and in the half light of a grey morning, she stood and scrutinised a number of warships moored out on the River Medway. A slight frown disturbed the gentle curve of her elegant eyebrows until she finally located the one small destroyer she was seeking.

Brackendale swung to her mooring near the far bank and Jennifer reached for a pair of binoculars. Bringing them into sharp focus she swept from the fo'c'sle to the stern depth-charge rails and counted a total of four men on watch, two of whom were up on the bridge. The ship's motorboat lay tied up alongside the port quarterdeck ready to transport who or whatever was needed at short notice. There was no sign of damage to the destroyer and she breathed a sigh of relief. Lowering the glasses she gingerly replaced them on the window sill, careful to ensure the heavy, drawn-back curtain hid them from prying eyes. They were a pair she had secreted into the office by devious means and had become a vital part of her daily routine. The last thing she needed was for some young officer thinking they would make a fine addition to his seagoing rig.

She pushed aside a strand of hair and allowed a faint smile to lift the corners of her mouth. Richard had returned, and she felt a tingle of excitement at his near presence. Not that there had ever been anything serious between them, just a warm understanding that somehow their being in close proximity was enough. No embellishment needed. Of all the men with whom she'd had the opportunity to become romantically entangled, it had come as a pleasant surprise that the least obvious choice for a relationship was the one man who, initially, had paid her no attention at all.

A knock on the door revealed a messenger with mail and he placed a dozen or so envelopes on her desk. She scrawled her signature where he indicated and settled back behind the desk. Inserting an intricately embossed paper knife under the flap of the first letter, Jennifer slid it expertly along the seam, extracted the contents and hurriedly read it through. Dropping it into the Captain's tray, she reached for the next envelope and pushed all thoughts of Richard to the back of her mind. There was work to be done.

At the opposite end of Chatham's busy dockyard, near No-1 repair basin, an army

Lieutenant by the name of Paul Wingham marched step for step alongside the imposing figure of a tall staff officer on his right. That man was General Scott Bainbridge and the face of tanned leather had the most piercing blue eyes. A vivid white scar ran back across his right cheekbone. Scott Bainbridge was an officer from Whitehall tasked with 'getting things done', and his determination to achieve a good outcome when so ordered was what made him popular amongst Winston Churchill's closest advisors.

Lieutenant Paul Wingham, ex Sherwood Forester, had been called in at short notice from a training ground in the Scottish highlands and ordered to report immediately on arrival. But with the amount of bomb damage to the railways it had taken the best part of twenty-four hours to reach Chatham. As they strode on he took another furtive sideways glance at the General's weather-beaten profile, the scar on his left cheek prominent against the leathery skin. Not for the first time he wondered what the old war horse had planned for him this time? Wingham's first, and so far his only foray into enemy territory, had been a mission centred around the Cherbourg Peninsula and he'd been kicking his heels hoping for another opportunity. This seemed to be that moment and he noted their footsteps took them progressively nearer the quayside where a number of warships were undergoing servicing and repairs.

And still they walked on, with no word from Bainbridge, until they rounded the corner of a small red brick building.

'Here we are,' Bainbridge announced, and nodded in the direction of the water.

Wingham stopped in surprise, unprepared for the sight that met his gaze. There in front of him sat three Motor Gun Boats, each boat tied to the other.

He felt Bainbridge looking at him with an amused grin.

'Come on,' said the General, 'your carriage awaits,' and with that he strode over to a temporary companionway and clambered down onto the foredeck of the inboard boat.

A Petty Officer saluted from the cockpit and Bainbridge called to him.

'Lieutenant Kendal?'

'Tied up outboard, sir,' he replied, pointing to the third boat.

The General returned the salute. 'Good man,' he said, and stepped gingerly across the rocking deck. Taking a moment to recover his balance he moved swiftly across to the middle boat, and then stepped just as quickly onto the deck of the outlying gun boat.

A Royal Navy Sub-Lieutenant appeared on the bridge and gave the General a smart salute.

'General Bainbridge, sir?'

'Correct,' the old warhorse said, acknowledging the salute.

'I'm Garret, sir. The Skipper's expecting you. If you'll follow me I'll show you where.'

'Then lead on, Mister Garret,' Bainbridge said, and rubbed his hands in anticipation.

Wingham smiled, Bainbridge was obviously enjoying the encounter; and he had to admit it wasn't every day a man stepped aboard these sort of power boats.

Garret led them down the side of the boat and then ushered them up to the flying bridge. Wingham waited for the General before making his move to follow. A Petty Officer pointed to a short set of steps. 'Just watch where you put your feet, sir,' he said with a grin, and Wingham smiled in return. The advice was totally unnecessary, just an old sea dog invoking his rights over the clumsy efforts of a landlubber. He emerged into a small space where the boat's captain would command the crew in action. He was greeted by a tall, fair haired officer with an outstretched hand.

'I'm Craig Kendal, the skipper of this tub.' He grinned and winked. 'See you managed the steps all right. Wingham isn't it?'

'It is, yes. Glad to meet you,' he said, acknowledging the greeting.

'Good to have you aboard,' Kendal said and gave Wingham another broad grin. He turned to General Bainbridge and gestured below. 'Let me show you our so called wardroom.' He led them down to a small compartment with a central table surrounded by bench seats. 'Here we are,' he laughed, 'not as roomy as some but it'll do.'

Wingham sat and for the first time it began to dawn on him how all this might be about to impact his immediate future. When they were finally settled he waited for Bainbridge to speak, and the General cleared his throat.

'I brought you here to familiarise yourself with a Gun Boat. Lieutenant Kendal has volunteered to take you on your next operation.'

Wingham raised an eyebrow. 'Operation, sir?'

Bainbridge chuckled, ran a finger over the scar on his cheek and looked at Kendal.

'Straight to the point.' The smile evaporated and he spoke softly. 'How would you feel about going back to Alderney?'

Wingham nibbled his lower lip. Before the Germans invaded the Channel Islands it had been his home. Born and bred. 'Why, sir?'

'Offensive reconnaissance.' The General challenged him with narrowed blue eyes. 'Will you go?'

Wingham gave it a moment of thought and slowly nodded. 'Yes, sir. I can do that. Just me?'

Bainbridge raised a hand, fending off any more questions.

'I'll explain all later. Right now we're going to get a guided tour of this boat. Once you're acquainted with the basics we'll adjourn to a rather more spacious office ashore.' He looked at Kendal and rubbed his hands in expectation.

Wingham glanced at the Skipper who in turn gave a non-committal half smile and rose to his feet. 'In that case,' he said, 'I'd be honoured to show you around. If you come with me we'll start at the sharp end.'

With Kendal leading they filed out and made their way forward. The first thing Wingham recognised was a tiny wireless room, more properly called the 'R/T' according to Kendal. That was followed by an accommodation space for the crew, then a claustrophobic storage compartment, and finally into the 'sharp end' which Kendal explained was their kitchen but in Navy parlance was known as the galley. They then reversed direction and had a revealing fifteen-minute session with the three Packard engines. For Wingham, having only ever seen a power boat on the surface from a distance, it was an enlightening forty minutes, and all too quickly he found himself back on dry land and making his way towards an austere looking, single-storey dockside building.

He dutifully followed the two officers inside and prepared himself for an explanation.

Bainbridge took them along a corridor past a number of busy offices and at the far end opened an unmarked door into a medium sized room. It contained a small desk and a large map table, and Wingham respectfully moved to one side as the General walked to the desk. Kendal stopped to look at the maps, resting his hands on the edge, staring down at some highlighted features.

Bainbridge flicked through some paperwork, dropped his cap on the desk and looked up. 'Grab a chair, gentlemen, and I'll give you a brief rundown.'

Wingham pulled two chairs out from the corner, pushed one to Kendal and sat opposite the General's desk.

Bainbridge rubbed the scar on his cheek and looked at each of them in turn.

'The War Office,' he began, 'in conjunction with our Intelligence Services have decided to mount a small raid on Alderney. We understand that the German 216th Infantry Division are the unit assigned to the Channel Islands and information received indicates the Islanders are being treated reasonably well. But Alderney is different. Unlike the others, none of the residents remained, completely evacuated.' He caught Wingham's eyes. 'I believe you were on the last boat to leave?'

'Yes, sir.'

It appears the Germans have set up two different types of radar station, one to the north and a second installation to the south . . . , we think. Importantly from our point of view, the station in the south is rather unusual. We believe it can detect aircraft out to a range of thirty miles but much more accurately than the one in the north. Our intelligence people thought it was still in the planning stage but aerial reconnaissance has made them doubt their original hypothesis. Whatever the reason we intend to attack it, retrieve any ciphers and documents we find, and destroy it.' He paused and fingered the scar on his cheek, gathering his thoughts.

'At the same time, if the reports are correct about the northern station we intend to make a mess of that too. The biggest issue facing us was how to get a raiding party in there, bearing in mind the Germans have a permanent garrison based nearby in case of possible assault.'

'We decided on a Gun Boat, and some of the Special Service chaps you've been training with.' He hesitated and smiled. 'That of course, is after we've been kindly given a lift across the water.' He turned away and paced the floor, chin buried on his chest. When he looked up it was to meet Wingham's eyes.

'One other thing. There'll be a couple of destroyers in attendance, and the Admiralty said I could have one by the name of *Brackendale*. You might remember she's captained by a chap called Thorburn?'

Wingham smiled. 'Yes, sir, I most certainly do.' He thought back to the previous year and his first job working for the General. Richard Thorburn had become a trusted friend. It would be good to know he was somewhere close by. 'But why destroyers, sir?'

'The Kriegsmarine,' Bainbridge said. 'They put

out regular patrols from Cherbourg. We don't want any interference with your mission.'

Wingham half raised a finger. 'If I may, sir?'

'Go ahead.'

'Do we have a date, yet?'

'Unless Commander Kendal has any objections, the sooner the better?'

Kendal shook his head. 'No objections, sir. Ready when you are.'

'In that case let me show you the map,' Bainbridge said, and walked round to the big table. He swivelled it round for them both to see and looked up at the ex Sherwood Forester..

'You're the expert, Wingham. Where can we make landfall?'

Lieutenant Paul Wingham looked at the familiar outline of the island he called home and immediately pointed to the south. He knew that section of the coast as well as any man alive. It had been his playground from the age of seven.

For the next hour, a scarred old General and two young Lieutenants talked through the advantages and pitfalls of raiding the Nazi held island of Alderney. As they firmed up a plan of action Wingham guided their every decision, happy to be usefully involved in the preparations for a return to his island home.

CHAPTER EIGHT . . 'NEED TO KNOW'

It was lunchtime before Second Officer Jennifer Farbrace had cleared her desk of the last batch of mail. She dined with two of her Wren colleagues and on returning to the office she once again moved to the window to stand and watch the busy harbour. It was a moment to enjoy. The sun shone, the river lay calm and she looked forward to the evening briefing with delight.

It was on the stroke of one when she took a call from an outside line. 'Captain Pendleton's office,' she said.

'With whom am I speaking?' It was a man's voice, cultured, full of authority, vaguely familiar.

'Second Officer Farbrace, sir.'

'Ah yes, of course . . . , the long suffering Jennifer.' There was a dry chuckle. 'Well, I don't know if you remember dear lady, but my name is Bainbridge, General Scott Bainbridge. Need a chat with the Captain.'

Jennifer swallowed, wary. She most certainly knew who was on the other end of the line and, politely old world with his charm he might be, in her experience it didn't bode well.

'I'll put you through, sir,' she said, and pressed a button.

Pendleton gave his usual gruff response. 'Yes, young lady?'

'I have General Bainbridge for you, sir.'

Pendleton cleared his throat and gave a short laugh. 'Do you indeed? Very well, put him on.'

Jennifer flicked a switch to scramble the line and transfer the call, sat back and nibbled pensively at her bottom lip. Minutes earlier her day had been filled with anticipation, the excitement of seeing Richard. But that one telephone call had her immediately wishing he were anywhere but here.

General Scott Bainbridge from the War Office spelt trouble with a capital 'T' and she frowned at the thought.

Pendleton heard the click of a connected call, but before being able to say a word, was silenced by a verbal tirade.

'Hello, James! Scotty here. How the devil are you?' Keeping well I trust? Something's cropped up, need some destroyers. The Admiralty said *Brackendale* might well be one of the candidates, if she's still available?'

Pendleton listened to the rapid flow of questions, waiting to get a word in edgeways. He grabbed his opportunity.

'Good afternoon, General. I do believe *Brackendale* is a possibility. And I might be able to call on another but she's not actually part of my flotilla. She's temporarily out of action. Anything else I can do?'

'Damn and blast,' Bainbridge snapped. Silence followed and Pendleton was just about to make a query when the General spoke again. 'Best laid plans . . and all that, eh, eh? Right . . . , who else have you got?'

'Be helpful if you could fill me in.'

Bainbridge hesitated. 'Well . . . ,' he said, ' I don't want to say too much. Suffice to say we have a little expedition in mind. And the chap in the Admiralty expressed his opinion that two destroyers would be ideal for what we have in mind. Look . . . , how about this afternoon? I could be at your office for three.'

Pendleton gave a wry smile.

'Yes,' he said, 'we could do that. I take it this 'little expedition' is pretty much fait accompli?'

'Indeed, of course. Very much so. Be just like old times.'

'In that case,' Pendleton said, ' I look forward to seeing you at three.'

'Splendid, James. Three o'clock.' And the line went dead.

For a moment Pendleton stared into space, then he thoughtfully dropped the receiver onto its cradle.

In the outer office Pendleton's strident baritone interrupted Jennifer's thoughts. 'Miss Farbrace! A moment, if you please.'

She came to her feet, smoothed her skirt, and

stepped briskly across to his office. She popped her head round the open door.

'Sir?'

'Contact Sheerness and find out when *Cheriton* will be back here.'

She made a note and gave him a raised eyebrow.

Pendleton frowned, guarded. 'What?'

'There was talk about fitting a new fuel tank, sir.'

'I think not. I'm sure they can patch the original, more than good enough.'

'Yes, sir,' she said, not willing to press the point. 'I'll give the dockyard a call, find out.'

'Good,' he said, smoothing his beard. 'And get a message to *Brackendale*. Have Thorburn report to me at 15.00 hours.'

'Yes, sir.'

'By the way, that *Cheriton* . . . , who's her captain?'

Jennifer frowned in thought as she tried to remember his name. The ship wasn't part of Pendleton's flotilla.

'Sorry, sir, I'm not certain. I'll find out.'

'Very well, and when you do I want to know the exact state of repairs.'

'Yes, sir.' She paused, one delicate eyebrow raised. 'Anything else, sir?'

'No . . . , thank you. That'll do for now.'

She backed out, closed the door and stepped lightly across to her desk. Richard would be here this afternoon; the hour couldn't come soon enough.

Jennifer reached for the telephone and rang the switchboard. When the Wren answered she instructed her to make enquiries as to *Cheriton's* fitness for duty. 'Also,' she asked, 'find out the name of her captain?'

'Oh, don't you know, ma'am? He's very dishy. It's Lieutenant-Commander Charles Rutherford, ma'am.'

Jennifer blinked and said, 'That's enough. I only needed his name.' She replaced the receiver and for a moment smiled, then shook her head in disbelief. She had met this Charlie Rutherford once, at a wardroom party aboard a cruiser. From what she could remember he was a rather outgoing young man, spirited, very enthusiastic. Her telephone rang within minutes.

'Pendleton's office.'

'*Cheriton* is running engine trials now, ma'am. The fuel tank had not been damaged, it was pipework and a pump they've replaced, and they've patched up some holes.'

'Thank you,' she said, and smiled. Richard Thorburn and Charles Rutherford, what a pair. She settled into her chair, and began typing the two official signals.

Richard Thorburn had been awake since six that morning and now ploughed through his official operational report for Pendleton. A tap on the cabin door revealed the earnest face of his steward.

'Time for lunch, sir?'

'Is it really?' Thorburn asked, and glanced at his watch. It showed almost one o'clock. 'Yes, alright. What's on the menu?'

'Tinned sausage, sir.'

Thorburn raised an eyebrow. 'My . . . , a veritable feast.'

Sinclair looked doubtful. 'If you say so, sir. Will you eat here or in the wardroom?'

Thorburn looked at the unfinished report and sighed. 'It'll have to be here.'

'And a mug of tea?'

'Marvellous, thank you.'

Sinclair bobbed his head and backed out of the door, leaving Thorburn to resume where he'd left off. If there was one thing he could really do with, it would be a 'writer' to deal with all the paperwork. He might have to make a quiet suggestion to Falconer, see if the Cox'n could make a recommendation.

A heavy knock on the door and Armstrong stuck his head in. 'We've been allocated a berth to re-ammunition, sir. But strangely not until 17.00 hours. Be almost dark by then. It's normally mid-afternoon for a night patrol.'

'Mmm . . . , they'll undoubtedly have their reasons. Have the crew eaten?'

'Port watch, yes, sir. Starboard watch having theirs now.'

'Very well. I'll be up in a while, just trying to finish this damned paperwork.'

Armstrong grinned. 'Aye aye, sir,' he said, and then hurriedly stepped aside as Sinclair appeared with a covered tray. The steward slid it carefully onto the desk, whipped off the cloth and hovered expectantly.

Thorburn removed the polished dome from the plate, eyed the sparse meal, and reached for his mug of tea. 'Just the ticket,' he said, taking a mouthful.

'Will that be all, sir?'

'Yes, thank you, Sinclair,' he said, and a moment later, with Armstrong departed, he was alone in his cabin.

He made a last entry in the report referring to *Cheriton's* timely arrival at Sheerness and then after a quick read through, signed it off. He dropped the folder into his briefcase and reached out to his 'in-tray'. The first sheet of paper was entitled 'Engineering Spares' and included a long list of items the Chief was adamant he couldn't do without. Picking up his knife and fork, Thorburn began to chew while reading down the meticulously itemised list.

He finished the meal, lit a cigarette and took another mouthful of tea.

A knock on the door interrupted him as he was about to sign.

'Come,' he called.

It was the First Lieutenant again, a quizzical

look on his face. 'Signal, sir.'

Thorburn finished adding his signature to the long list, and then reached out a hand. He acknowledged the message with a faint smile and handed it back. 'Time to dig out my best bib and tucker.'

Armstrong nodded, frowning. 'Mid-afternoon, sir, bit unusual. Any idea why?'

Thorburn slowly shook his head and rubbed his jaw. 'Your guess is as good as mine. Probably explains why re-ammunitioning is at five. Or . . . , it might be he's just impatient for my action report.'

Armstrong tugged an ear, tilting his head in disbelief. 'And pigs might fly.'

Thorburn gave a tight laugh. 'You're being very cynical, Number One. I'm sure Captain (D) has good reason. And more to the point, on a 'need to know' basis, probably not something a mere First Lieutenant should be privy to.'

Armstrong grinned and gave a deep, exaggerated bow from the waist. 'Pardon my insolence, sir. I am but a humble servant.'

Thorburn assumed an air of gracious generosity. 'Indeed . . . , indeed, your apologies accepted.' He dropped the pretence. 'But off the record, I haven't a clue. If it's any consolation, you'll be the first to know.'

Armstrong glanced at his wristwatch. 'It's one-thirty, sir. Motor-boat in an hour?'

'I think so, yes.' Thorburn leaned back in the

chair. 'And ask the Chief if he can scrounge some of those spares he's after.' He pointed to the long list. 'Looks like we're running short of everything.'

Armstrong nodded and straightened to his full height. 'Very well, sir. If there's nothing more, I'll have the boat's crew stand by and inform the Chief.' He turned for the door.

'And ask Sinclair to sort my shore-going uniform. It might need some special care and attention.'

He heard a parting, 'Aye aye, sir,' as the door closed, and then reached for another cigarette. He struck a match, eyes narrowed, thinking. If *Brackendale* had been selected for routine night patrol the briefing would have been at 17.00 hours, but if the Dunkirk deployment was anything to go by, who knew what might come of this next meeting. A tendril of blue smoke coiled from the cigarette and a smile tugged the corners of his mouth.

Never a dull moment with Pendleton in charge.

CHAPTER NINE . . ISLAND SECRETS

It was five to three when Thorburn slipped into Pendleton's outer office. Jennifer glanced up, frowning at the intrusion, but immediately replaced the furrowed brow with a warm welcoming smile.

Thorburn grinned and then gave her a deliberate wink. 'Miss Farbrace,' he said very formally. 'Reporting as ordered.'

She came to her feet, smoothed her skirt and moved out from behind the desk. She came close and Thorburn caught the delicate fragrance of her perfume.

'Not a moment too soon, Commander,' she said, her voice carrying, loud enough to be heard in the next office. She smiled and ran a pink tongue along perfectly straight, white teeth. 'I'll let the Captain know you're waiting.' She touched the fingers of his hand, squeezed them and turned away for Pendleton's office. She knocked, opened the door and peered in. Thorburn admired the view.

'Lieutenant-Commander Thorburn's arrived, sir.'

'Ahh . . . , send him in. Send him in.'

Jennifer pushed the door wide and stood aside. 'You can go in now, Commander.'

He walked forward and brushed past, pausing

just long enough to give her a whispered, 'Thank you.'

And then he was inside the warmth of Pendleton's office.

'Richard, m'boy,' the Captain beamed, and gestured towards the big window. 'you know Rutherford. He's *Cheriton*.'

Rutherford turned from the tall window where he'd been staring out at the river.

Pendleton made the formal introduction. 'Charles . . . , Richard Thorburn.'

For a long moment Thorburn was caught by surprise. Sheerness must have worked wonders. 'Charles,' he said, somewhat taken aback, 'have they actually turned you round already? That's not like any dockyard I know.'

Rutherford's infectious grin lit the room. 'Indeed they have, Richard. But as you know, I've only got me a small destroyer, easier to repair. Come to think of it,' he added wickedly, 'she's a bit like yours . . . , little.'

Thorburn laughed, quick to concede the point. The 'Hunt' class were definitely on the small side.

Pendleton chuckled waving at the chairs. 'Have a seat, have a seat.' He turned to the big desk and reached for a pack of Senior Service. 'Cigarette,' he offered, waited while they both took one, and selected one for himself. Thorburn drew smoke and sat contentedly, the flames dancing in the large fireplace spreading a welcome glow to the room.

'Now,' Pendleton began, making himself comfortable behind the desk. 'I called you in because I've received a rather important request. You're both wanted men, you know . . . , wanted men.' He glanced at his wristwatch. 'Any minute now.'

There was a commotion in the outer office quickly followed by Jennifer's voice. 'The Captain's waiting for you, sir.'

The door swung wide and Jennifer made her introduction. 'General Scott Bainbridge, sir,' and she stood aside to let him enter

The General strode in, ignored Pendleton, and reached out to shake Thorburn's hand. 'We meet again, how are you Commander?'

Thorburn accepted the handshake and met the penetrating eyes. There were no overt signs of ill feeling, even though Thorburn had not always been the General's flavour of the month. At the same time he found he wasn't surprised that Bainbridge had resurfaced.

'I'm well, thank you, sir,' he said evenly.

'And your shoulder?'

'Healed nicely,' Thorburn lied. Outwardly the shrapnel wound to his shoulder blade had faded to a jagged scar, but it could still stab him painfully and without warning.

Bainbridge nodded and turned to Rutherford, vigorously shaking hands. 'And you, Commander, I trust you're well?'

Rutherford nodded. 'Yes, sir.'

'Ship okay? Hear you had some trouble.'

'She's fine now, sir.'

The General coughed and cleared his throat. He turned back to give Thorburn a more considered appraisal and for a moment stood very still, his deep set eyes probing, searching, and then he seemed to nod his approval.

'Right!' he said suddenly, breaking the silence. 'Shall we get on and I'll explain why I'm here.' He raised an eyebrow to Pendleton. 'May I?'

Pendleton waved a hand. 'Of course, General.'

'Right,' Bainbridge said, and hesitated. 'Probably be as well to have Miss Farbrace take notes,' he added, and only then did he walk over to the large wall chart.

Pendleton called Jennifer and she duly took her place at the end of his desk, crossed an elegant leg, and notebook in hand sat with pen poised.

Bainbridge reached across the chart and prodded an area off the north-west tip of France. 'The Channel Islands,' he began, 'I doubt that you're aware but the Germans are beginning to fortify the island of Alderney. Thus far, we've not made any attempt to interfere with that ambition.' He turned back from the chart and looked directly at Thorburn. He cleared his throat, his Adam's apple bobbing. 'The thing is, gentlemen, although we have no intention of disrupting those specific exploits any time soon, something's cropped up that demands our attention.' He glanced at Jennifer scribbling furiously on her pad.

'Forgive me Miss Farbrace, I'm running off at the mouth. Do you need a moment?'

Jennifer had her lips compressed, concentrating, but shook her head. 'No, sir,' she said, and with an exaggerated flourish, finished writing. She looked up, head tilted, eyes wide, expectant.

Thorburn couldn't keep the smile from his face and covered it with a thoughtful rub of his jaw.

Bainbridge continued. 'Our attention has been drawn to a couple of objects that we feel are of utmost interest. One here at Fort Tourgis,' he said, tapping an area near the north-west coast, 'and this one up here near Fort Albert,' he added, pointing to the north-east headland of Braye Harbour and circling it with his finger. 'We think one or or both are being used in a similar fashion to our Home Chain early warning system of Radio Detection and Ranging equipment. We believe they may be two interlinked systems, one of which we are reasonably sure is called Freya. Our intelligence people have a passable understanding of how that works. Like ours, Freya is used for long range aircraft detection.' The General paused and studied the map, then looked round again.

'The difference in this case is the discovery of a second installation, similar but different.' He smiled acknowledging how odd it sounded.

'If we're right this could be a short range equivalent to Freya that can pinpoint more accurately the range, height and numbers of aircraft involved. Combine the two elements and the Germans can warn their fighter squadrons in plenty of time to intercept our bombers.' He paused to look down at his feet. Then he glanced up and continued.

'So we ordered a couple of low level photo reconnaissance flights over Fort Tourgis. When our intelligence people studied the results they concluded that the Germans are indeed possibly operating a new system. Working in tandem the two installations could achieve a greater field of operation.' He stepped away from the chart and tugged at his nose.

'Now it just happens that we've a chap who knows Alderney like the back of his hand. It's our good fortune that he's volunteered to go back.' He smiled. 'Believe it or not but one of you is well acquainted with him.' He smiled at Thorburn.

'Chap called Wingham.'

Thorburn grinned. Paul Wingham had been instrumental in the success of *Brackendale's* last covert deployment and he and Thorburn had quickly struck up a genuine friendship.

'The intention,' Bainbridge went on, 'is to mount an offensive reconnaissance and gather all the information we can. We then destroy the facilities before withdrawing from the island.'

'If I may, sir?' Rutherford interrupted. 'Who's 'we'?'

'A section of twelve men including Wingham. I've put him in command for obvious reasons. Two of the men are Royal Engineers and then there are two chaps from the R.A.F. They'll be operating as two, six man sections, each section tasked to raid one of the installations. An M.G.B. will take them across from Weymouth, or more specifically, Portland. Lieutenant Wingham is with Lieutenant Kendal now. He's the Gunboat's skipper.' He glanced at Pendleton. 'He's in what I believe you call No-1 Basin.'

The Captain nodded. 'Correct.'

Thorburn looked from the General to Pendleton. 'And so what's our role, sir?'

Bainbridge gestured towards Pendleton who sat forward from his chair.

'You'll be mother hen, so to speak. I recommend you station *Brackendale* north of Alderney and wait there for Lieutenant Kendal to withdraw and join you. *Cheriton* will ensure there is no interference from the patrol boats deploying from Guernsey. When all's done you rendezvous and make your way back to Portland.' He grinned, and businesslike, rubbed his hands together. 'Unless there are any serious objections, you sail for Weymouth this evening, six o'clock. The raiding party will travel down in Lieutenant Kendal's boat. That'll give them a chance to familiarise themselves with their surroundings.' He stroked his beard, eyes twinkling. 'If all proceeds as expected, there will be a final briefing in Portland tomorrow afternoon and if there are no issues you sail for Alderney after dark.'

Bainbridge took over. 'This will be a new experience for all concerned. We've not used either an M.T.B. or an M.G.B. until now. It was thought that the engines would be too loud close inshore but I was advised that using only a single motor on its own makes the boat almost undetectable. I've now heard it. Impressive.'

Thorburn lifted a finger. 'Where will they make the landing, sir?'

'There's a cove to the south called Telegraph Bay and Wingham assures me that with care a Gun Boat can deliberately beach nose first in shallow water. Push comes to shove they'll have dinghies on board just in case.'

Pendleton coughed and cleared his throat. 'Yes, and the cove is subject to tidal forces. Lieutenant Kendal has been brought up to date with the latest tide times and planning has been adjusted accordingly. And that, gentlemen, just about brings us up to date.' He turned to Jennifer.

'Miss Farbrace! A pot of tea would be very welcome.'

'Right away, sir,' Jennifer said, and disappeared out to her office. She must have been expecting the request and prepared everything beforehand because in a very short space of time Thorburn watched her elbow a tray of cups and saucers through the door. He offered to help and she smiled her thanks. He placed the tray on Pendleton's desk while she hurried back out and brought in a large silver pot of tea.

'Shall I pour, sir?' she asked, knowing what the answer would be.

'Please do,' Pendleton said, and selected a cigarette before offering his pack. Bainbridge chose one, nodded his thanks and moved back to the window. A tendril of smoke wafted over his shoulder. Thorburn struck a match and with his and Pendleton's cigarettes both alight he stepped closer to Jennifer.

She smiled, placed the tea strainer on the next cup and carefully finished pouring. Then she looked beyond him at the General. 'Sugar, sir?'

'One please. Thank you.'

She added a lump with the tongs, poured a drop of milk, stirred, and handed it to Thorburn. She nodded in the General's direction. 'Off you go,' she said, and turned to pour a cup for Rutherford. Pendleton inhaled smoke and waited his turn.

Bainbridge had continued to stand and smoke with his back to the room.

'Tea, sir?' Thorburn prompted to attract his attention.

'Thank you,' he said, and eyed Thorburn over the rim of the cup. 'Hope you didn't mind me volunteering you for this little jaunt. I know what happened last year wasn't all that it might have been, but I heard through the grapevine that you quite enjoyed our last little shindig.'

Thorburn grinned. 'I have to say, sir, my enthusiasm almost got me killed. But you're right, I do quite fancy another crack at 'em.'

The old warrior gave him a wicked grin. 'Good,' he said with genuine pleasure. 'I don't think you'll be disappointed.' He turned into the room. 'You hear that, James. Thorburn here can't wait to have another crack at Jerry.'

Jennifer looked up, eyes wide, her delicate brows knitted into a worried frown.

Pendleton laughed and stroked his beard, eyes twinkling. 'Guessed as much. Always pestering me for another assignment.' He stubbed out his cigarette and addressed both Rutherford and Thorburn.

'Tonight, gentlemen . . . , you cast off tonight, 18.00 hours. You will receive your orders by messenger before sailing and should make Portland in time for breakfast.'

It was 16.30 hours before the meeting finally broke up, Pendleton and Bainbridge remaining behind to thrash out some further minor details. Jennifer cleared the crockery and took the tray through to the small scullery, returning to her desk just as Thorburn was about to follow Rutherford out into the corridor. She wasn't about to let him go without a word.

'Richard,' she said quietly, but with a degree of insistence. 'Look after yourself out there. I want to see you again.'

Thorburn glanced over his shoulder and she felt the warmth of one of his broad grins. 'I can promise you I'll do everything in my power to come back in one piece. So how about you book us a table for Saturday evening? I should be back by then.'

Jennifer smiled in return, excited by the prospect of an evening shared. 'That would be lovely, Richard. Eight o'clock?'

'Whatever you think best.' He bowed slightly from the waist, smiling. 'Your servant, ma'am.' And with that he was gone.

She slumped into her chair, warmth coming to her cheeks, and for a moment fiddled absentmindedly with an A4 sheet of foolscap. He'd welcomed her suggestion, now it was just a matter of where?

'Miss Farbrace!' Pendleton called. 'A minute if you please, young lady.'

'Yes, sir,' she said, and picked up her note pad. They weren't done yet.

Nine miles off the west coast of Portugal and pushing steadily north through the dark waters of the Atlantic Ocean, the *Castillo de Maria* was on schedule to enter the Bay of Biscay as prescribed.

In Cherbourg a flotilla of small warships were

making preparations to meet her west of the Channel Islands. They were to form an escort and shepherd the old steamer into port where her precious cargo of gold and tungsten could be unloaded.

CHAPTER TEN . . PORTLAND

Half an hour prior to *Brackendale's* estimated time of departure, a bridge messenger brought a buff coloured, foolscap envelope to the Captain's cabin. Thorburn slipped a paper knife under the sealed flap and carefully extracted the contents. He found himself studying a typewritten copy of orders marked 'SECRET', with a highlighted reminder that they be returned to Admiralty House before departure.

Under the heading of Operation "BUTTERCUP" the men and ships allocated to the raid were itemised and individual personnel listed (a) for 'in-command' and (b) 'execution of specific tasks'. Timings were 'loose' but dictated mainly by tide and darkness. The overall objectives of the raid were laid out as: the retrieval of any and all documentation found and the destruction of those items deemed significant to the operation of each station.

The orders were signed and dated and Thorburn smiled at the rather impressive printed detail that revealed both Captain James Pendleton and General Scott Bainbridge as Senior Officers Commanding the Operation. He dropped the papers onto his table and called the bridge to ask for the First Lieutenant. A tap on the door followed.

'Come,' he said.

The questioning face of Armstrong peered in.

'You wanted me, sir?'

'Yes, come in, Bob. Have a seat.'

Armstrong slid himself onto a chair.

Thorburn pushed the papers across the table. 'Read and digest,' he said. 'Those orders have to be back ashore before we sail.'

At the allotted hour *Brackendale* cast off her moorings and manoeuvred carefully sternfirst away from the old granite quayside. Once the ship was clear Thorburn handed over the navigation to Martin and turned to watch *Cheriton's* shadow ease out into the Medway's ebb tide. Her head came round until her stem entered *Brackendale's* wake, and then with the night having closed in the two small destroyers floated downstream to join forces with the M.G.B. As dark as it was the small boat nonetheless exited the repair basins at a brisk pace before throttling back south of the Salt Marsh and then leading them east to the mouth of the river. Once out in the Channel's open waters Lieutenant Craig Kendal increased revolutions to twenty knots and made for the North Foreland. Rounding the headland at Margate he pushed on down the coast for Broadstairs and finally set course for Weymouth.

On *Brackendale's* bridge, Thorburn eased himself into his chair and planted a boot on the pipe bracket. The hardly discernible outline of Dover Castle's high, snow-carpeted battlements drifted past and the ship began to sway as she met the influence of long rollers. The night air was cold, bracing, and after a while he shifted position.

'Time?' he inquired.

'19.45 hours, sir.'

Thorburn nodded in the darkness. That was Martin, alert as ever. 'Thank you,' he said, and rose to his feet. He stretched and stepped over to the port wing to look aft where he found the faint sheen of *Cheriton* following in line astern. He moved to the bridge-screen and raised his old Barr and Stroud binoculars. Beyond the bow, no more than three or four cables length off *Brackendale's* stem, the Motor Gun Boat danced gracefully on ahead. He let the glasses hang on his chest and cast an eye over the lookouts. They all faced outboard concentrating on their own sectors, attentive, absorbed in their duties. Reassured that all was well, and that as Captain he was probably an unnecessary fixture at this particular time, he made a move for the ladder.

'I'm going below, Pilot. You have the bridge. Call me if you think fit.'

Martin stiffened at the compass binnacle. 'Very well, sir.'

Thorburn noted the confirmation and stepped onto the first rung. A few hours peace and quiet would do him the power of good. As much as he felt the need to be available no good ever came of overdoing one's time on the bridge. That's why there was always an Officer-of the-Watch . . . , to share the load.

He was sound asleep within minutes of his head touching the pillow.

It was daylight the next morning when Lieutenant Robert Armstrong stood and watched the fo'c'sle party secure the lines to the quayside bollards and snake the excess into neat coils. He personally walked to the starboard bow and checked the 'spring wire' for tension. Satisfied that all was as it should be he raised a hand to the bridge. Thorburn acknowledged and only then did Armstrong turn away to take another look at Portland's Royal Navy quayside.

He was thankful *Brackendale* had been able to enter in full daylight. There were ships moored all across the bay and many more tied up to the piers and docks that served as welcoming berths for tired vessels seeking shelter. *Cheriton* was in the process of tying up astern.

The Leading-Seaman reported to his First Lieutenant. 'All secure, sir.'

'Very well,' he said. 'Carry on.'

'Aye aye, sir.'

Armstrong moved to the bows and craned his neck to look down the length of the hard. Kendal's gunboat had tied up to a short jetty farther along and the raiding party were out of the boat smoking, probably enjoying the firm footing beneath their feet.

He heard Thorburn's raised voice at the wheelhouse pipe. 'Finished with main engines.'

The faint tremor in the deck plates faded and a gangway rattled into place between quarterdeck and quayside. An odd temporary quietness descended over the small destroyer, broken only by the screeching call of gulls.

Down on the quayside a shore based Petty Officer marched into view, saluted, and called up to Armstrong. '*Brackendale*?'

Armstrong retuned the salute. 'Correct. What can I do for you?'

'Your Captain is requested to attend the dock office at 15.00 hours.'

'I'll let him know. Where's the office?'

The Petty Officer pointed back along the quayside to an unpretentious wooden building about three-hundred yards distant. 'That's it down there on the right, sir.'

'Very well, thank you. He'll be there.'

The Petty Officer saluted. 'Sir,' and marched on towards *Cheriton.*

Armstrong touched the peak of his cap and made his way aft off the fo'c'sle and into the lobby leading to the wardroom and the Captain's cabin. A quiet knock resulted in the familiar, 'Come!' and he entered to inform Thorburn.

Sub-Lieutenant George Labatt dismissed the

hands on the quarterdeck and moved over to the port rail. This was his third time in Portland and although his two previous visits had been as a Midshipman aboard a training ship, he found it useful in identifying certain landmarks. But things had already changed since his days at Dartmouth along the coast. Out on the breakwaters an array of anti-aircraft guns had appeared and Breakwater Fort bristled with artillery. The constant movement of ships caught the eye. Escort destroyers, sloops, corvettes, tugs and minesweepers, all either heading out for the Channel or returning to take up a mooring. As far as the harbour facilities went it was almost unrecognisable.

And there again his previous visits had not been blessed with the sight of a 5,000 ton cruiser moored within the Inner Harbour. As he leaned on the rail and admired her lines, Petty Officer Langsdale came to stand at his shoulder.

'Grand sight, eh, sir? That cruiser is the *Vibrant*, eight six-inch guns. I served on her for eighteen months, China station. She was built up the coast at Portsmouth, and if memory serves me right, she was commissioned in '37.' He pointed across the water. 'And that Fleet destroyer, that's the *Kingfisher*. She was at Sheerness until a month ago.'

'Wonder why she's down here?' Labatt asked thoughtfully.

'Your guess is as good as mine, sir. Might be on

her way to Belfast.'

'Or Liverpool,' Labatt volunteered.

'Might be, sir,' Langsdale agreed, and sauntered off to the starboard side.

'All right, Sub?'

He turned to greet 'Doc' Waverly who struck a match and held it to the bowl of his old walnut pipe. Blue smoke drifted.

'Yes thanks, Doc. But this place has changed a bit.'

'Since when? In the days of your ill gotten youth?' Waverly chuckled.

Labatt grinned in turn and nodded. 'Yep, I was too young to know any better. There were some lovely girls.'

'I should think it's mainly Wrens now,' Doc said, and pointed the stem of his pipe shorewards. 'You'll find a few in there. That office building is bound to have a typing pool.'

'Won't have time for that. Have to get sorted for tonight. Anyway, I'm seeing a young lady in Chatham.'

'Are you indeed? Anyone I know?'

'I doubt it . . . , and I've said more than enough on that subject. I'd better see to the Bowchaser. "Guns" likes to have it inspected after a run.'

Waverly grunted his approval. 'Don't let me stop you,' he said and puffed smoke.

Labatt nodded and headed for the fo'c'sle. He liked old Waverly, affable, easy going, not at all what you might expect from a surgeon. But he'd also seen him at work, not something to be recommended if you didn't have a strong stomach.

He reached the starboard ladder to the fo'c'sle, bounced up to the deck and quickly made his way along the guard rail toward the single Pompom. He gave it an unhurried 'once over' to check for any obvious signs of damage and then he reached up to remove the canvas sleeve protecting the barrel. The gun metal was dry, devoid of salt residue and in good condition. A more considered examination of the breech followed and then he slipped the sleeve back into position. A final check on the ready use ammunition locker, and satisfied that the Bowchaser would do all that was required when called back into action, he returned to the bridge in search of 'Guns' Carling.

In Braye Harbour on Alderney's north-west coastline, three German Schnellboats lay moored in the sheltered waters behind the long Victorian breakwater. Although the torpedo boats were maintained and operated by a small contingent of sailors from the Kriegsmarine, the young naval officer in charge of the flotilla found himself answering directly to the Wehrmacht's Commanding Officer, a Major Hans Günther Zeigler. In addition to the few sailors, four-hundred and fifty soldiers manned the island's as yet minimal defences. But plans were in place, personally signed off by Hitler, to turn Alderney into one of the most heavily defended areas under German occupation.

For Major Hans Zeigler the day dawned bright and he washed, shaved and dressed before deciding the day would be spent on an inspection of Fort Tourgis. Some new piece of technical wizardry was to be tested and it might prove to be a pleasant distraction. A final check in the full length bedroom mirror and he gave his reflection a thin smile. Fair haired, level blue eyes and a dimpled square jaw, his image boasted of the true Arian race. The uniform still fitted perfectly, and the Iron Cross (First Class) pinned to his breast pocket informed all those with whom he came into contact that Major Zeigler was not a man to be trifled with. He turned sideways to admire his stance. Many a staff officer would envy the flat, well muscled stomach. Placing his cap at a jaunty angle, he settled the Luger at his waist and headed downstairs. From the kitchen the cook brought his meal to a small dining room and he tucked into a hearty breakfast. There were two freshly baked bread rolls, a large grilled bratwurst sausage and two extra large fried eggs, all washed down with a steaming pot of black coffee.

When he was done the cook cleared the table and Zeigler wandered outside to find a spot in the weak winter sun. He perched on a low stone wall, lit a cigarette and looked out at Braye Harbour and the long breakwater. He didn't profess to know much about the sea but he felt certain this bay would not be suitable for an armed landing. And the British would know in detail how futile it would be to try and retake the island. After all, they were the ones who fortified it in the first place. He studied the glowing end of the cigarette and frowned in thought.

Not so long ago he had been a well recognised member of Germany's Embassy in Buenos Aries and it had been an exceptional posting. At thirty-two he was married, and had one child, a boy. His wife, the beautiful Argentinean born Ingrid, had a sister called Sofia who lived with her children in a grand hacienda. Zeigler had recently been reminded that her husband Carlos, the Capitán of an old tramp steamer was shortly due to arrive at Cherbourg. Ingrid had immediately insisted that he stay with them while he was in France. It would give her the opportunity to catch up on all the news from Argentina. Zeigler had been reluctant to tell her that Carlos had become a blockade runner and might not actually make it to port in one piece. He thought it best not to dash her hopes. The recall to the 216th Infantry Division in Germany and his subsequent detachment to Alderney had come with the tantalising prospect of a promotion to Colonel.

He finished the cigarette, crushed it under his heel, and then made his way down the slope to a hut on the breakwater quay. A soldier saw him coming and stiffened to attention before saluting.

Zeigler acknowledged the salute and gestured toward the hut. 'Is Roeder inside?'

'Jawohl, Herr Major!' the man snapped in reply, ramrod straight.

'Then fetch him for me,' Zeigler prompted.

Before the man had time to react the battered wooden door was tugged inwards and Corporal Sven Roeder stepped out and saluted.

'I heard, Herr Major.'

'I intend to visit Fort Tourgis. You will accompany me. The walk will do us good.'

'Of course, Herr Major. At what time?'

Zeigler stared at him and frowned. 'Now, Roeder, we go now.'

The Corporal blinked, half shook his head and then nodded. 'Ahh, one moment, Herr Major, my gun,' he stammered, 'I need my gun.' He lunged back inside and reappeared slinging an MP40 sub-machine gun over his shoulder.

Zeigler smiled at the man's enthusiasm. 'You don't feel a little over dressed with that?' he asked.

'I am your escort, Herr Major. It is my duty to see you are not harmed. What if the British come today, while we are out walking? No, it is better this way.'

Zeigler grinned and conceded the point. 'In that case I now feel we are more than ready. We will take the coastal path to Fort Tourgis. There should be thirty men on duty there. We'll see if they are awake. Also a unit of radio people will be trialling a new piece of equipment. I am expected to give my opinion.' He patted the Luger at his hip. 'So, on you go, Roeder, I do not have all day.'

The soldier who first saw Zeigler's approach watched them go and relaxed. Bastards, he thought, they were both bastards and he had no time for either of them. They were the same as all men in command, with high opinions of themselves, and were only too fond of getting other men killed. They would point and shout and threaten and swear, and all the while they would make sure they were not exposed to unnecessary risk.

He spat. That's what he thought of so called leaders of men.

It was 14.45 hours in Portland when Richard Thorburn strode down *Brackendale's* gangway and waited for Charles Rutherford to join him.

'Charles,' he said, by way of a greeting. 'Do we know who's taking this briefing?'

'No,' said Rutherford, 'I thought you'd have been told.'

Thorburn shook his head. 'Not a clue, and more to the point, I was led to believe it would just be a formality. Dot the i's and cross the t's so to speak. Then wait for darkness and when Kendal gives the word, push off.'

Rutherford pointed ahead. 'Guess we'll know soon enough, that's the dock office.'

A solitary Marine acted as sentry and also asked for I.D. cards. Rutherford raised an eyebrow to Thorburn. This sort of security was normally reserved for something important. The sentry stood aside and Thorburn entered, Rutherford on his heels. The room already contained a number of service personnel, most of them belonging to Wingham's raiders. A veil of cigarette smoke hung heavy at the ceiling. A couple of vacant chairs were available and the two of them sat.

A side door opened at the far end of the room and men stiffened in their chairs. A nondescript man in a grey suit stepped onto a slightly raised platform, placed a briefcase at his feet and peered over the assembly. A senior officer from the Royal Air Force hovered in the background.

'Gentlemen,' he began, 'I'm Brigadier Patterson, and what I have to say specifically involves those of you who will be going ashore.'

He paused to scan his audience. 'Lieutenant Wingham?'

Thorburn saw a hand appear from near the front. 'Sir.'

'There's been a change of plan.' He turned towards the door and beckoned for someone to join him.

A short, bespectacled army Lieutenant came forward and stood to one side. Thorburn thought he detected a Royal Corps of Signals cap badge. He looked somehow out of place, awkward in his ill fitting uniform, too big for the man inside, as if seldom worn.

Patterson gestured with an outstretched hand. 'This is Lieutenant Ratcliffe. He's rather a boffin when it comes to radio waves and such like. Whitehall are convinced he will be extremely useful and he's volunteered to join us, lend us his expertise.' Patterson paused and smiled at his audience.

'He'll be better able to separate the wheat from the chaff so to speak. Don't want to destroy something we might need, eh?'

He looked again at Wingham. 'You would be well advised not to let this officer stray too far from your sights. He really is rather exceptional and it would be good if he survives this little foray.' He glanced at his wristwatch.

'One other thing. If the opportunity arises . . . ,' An interruption of raised voices from the side door stopped him mid sentence. 'What is it?' he demanded.

A Petty Officer came forward offering the Brigadier a message slip. 'Urgent signal, sir. Just in.'

Patterson took it, read through and handed it back. He looked up, searching.

'Commander Thorburn?'

Thorburn felt a twinge of apprehension. 'Sir,' he answered, raising a hand.

'*Brackendale* has been reallocated and will now take up a defensive station close to the Cherbourg Peninsula. *Cheriton* is to patrol between Jersey and Guernsey. Your new coordinates are with this Petty Officer.'

Thorburn frowned but acknowledged the change with a, 'Yes sir.' It sounded as though 'mother hen' was no longer part of the plan. He leaned closer to Rutherford. 'Something's up. Let's hope they know more in the Signals Office.'

The Brigadier raised his voice. 'Well that's it gentlemen. If all goes to plan, I'll see you tomorrow morning.'

At the front, Paul Wingham had a question. 'Sir, you were saying something about "if the opportunity arises". Before you were interrupted?'

'Ah, yes, my mistake. Getting forgetful,' Patterson said. 'If you get the chance, a couple of prisoners wouldn't go amiss. For questioning, back here. Mind you, that's only if you get the chance. Don't push your luck.'

He bent to retrieve his briefcase and made for the exit, leaving the entire raiding party upright in their seats.

Thorburn stood and immediately strode forward to waylay the Petty Officer. He caught up with him just as he was about to leave and stepped into his path.

'That signal, I'd like to see it?'

The Petty Officer gave a quick salute and

offered the slip. 'Of course, sir.'

Thorburn touched the peak of his cap and took the signal. It was plain enough. The message was timed at 15.20 hours, on the 28th January 1941, and ordered him to disregard previous instructions. The new orders required *Brackendale* to take defensive station five miles northwest of the Peninsula until contacted by the Gunboat. Likewise, *Cheriton* was also reassigned as the Brigadier outlined. The signal was authorised by Captain (D).

Rutherford had arrived at his shoulder. 'That's clear enough,' he said, and Thorburn handed it back to the Petty Officer.

'That was it?' he asked. 'Nothing else?'

'No, sir. I was on duty when it came in. That was all.'

'Very well, carry on.' They exchanged brief salutes and the Petty Officer marched off.

'Richard?' came a voice from behind and Thorburn turned to find the familiar, rugged face of Paul Wingham offering his hand. They shook warmly and Thorburn clapped him on the shoulder. 'You old bastard,' he grinned. 'I heard you were involved.' He nodded towards the rest of the raiders. 'And look at this lot. Not a pretty sight.'

Wingham too grinned in response. 'Maybe not, but I'd rather have them with me than against. We've been training in Scotland. Hard as nails that lot.'

Hovering close behind Wingham, the newly joined Signals officer stood ill at ease and Thorburn offered his hand. 'I'm Richard Thorburn,' he volunteered. 'Your name again?'

'Tony Ratcliffe, sir,' he said quietly, and though he was short in stature and possibly a little uncertain of his new role, the handshake was firm.

'Glad to have you along. And don't worry,' Thorburn grinned, jabbing a thumb at Wingham. 'Stick to Paul here and you'll be fine.'

The man blinked behind his glasses and gave a tentative smile, probably a little apprehensive about his new found employment, but determined to carry it through.

Thorburn glanced at his watch and pursed his lips. 'We'd better get on, it'll be dusk soon.' There were general nods of agreement and they headed outside, to be greeted by a fine, persistent drizzle.

'Nice,' Rutherford said sarcastically, pulling a face, and turned up his collar. Thorburn smiled and pulled down the peak of his cap, and then nodded to Wingham, about to go their separate ways.

'Good luck, Paul. We'll have a drink when we get back.'

'Look forward to it,' Wingham said, his dark eyes smiling through the rain. For a long moment they held each other's gaze, and then parted company.

Thorburn hurried along the quayside,

splashing through puddles, his mind churning over the change of orders. Good or bad he thought, it wouldn't be long before a single, small overloaded gunboat and two of His Majesty's sleek 'Hunt' Class destroyers made their way back into the Channel and headed south for enemy held territory. A rueful smile played round his mouth. The waves of war seemed never very far away.

CHAPTER ELEVEN ..
TELEGRAPH BAY

Major Hans Zeigler stood under a large camouflaged tarpaulin and shook his head. He carefully watched three specialist technicians adjust their newly installed electronic paraphernalia. The entire system had been assembled on the flat bed of a wheeled trailer and powered up by a diesel generator. The receiver array, something he disparagingly thought resembled a large elongated frying pan, stood three metres in diameter and was supported by a solid steel frame. It sat on its own turntable. Through the clever use of ropes and pulleys the entire installation could be quickly obscured from aerial observation by a long canvas sheet painted to mimic the surrounding scenery.

What caused him to shake his head was the pathetically small visual end result of such a complex system of electronic surveillance. Whatever information was gathered then passed down the interlinked wiring before being converted into illuminated spots. Those pulses were displayed on a shimmering oval disc, some sort of 'screen', no bigger than a dinner plate, and two of the technicians spent all their time studying the screen and fiddling with control knobs.

Zeigler turned to the instructor in charge of the demonstration and nodded his thanks.

'Very impressive, Herr Kaufmann,' he lied. 'Very good. I am sure the Fuhrer himself would approve. You will keep up the good work, no?'

The man wore a large lapelled, pin striped grey suit and a brown Fedora hat which he never seemed to be without.

'Jawohl, Herr Major,' he said, gave a slight bow and courteously raised and lowered his hat. 'I thank you for your observation. All is in order. By daylight tomorrow this machine will be detecting everything within thirty-kilometres.'

'Then I will return to my headquarters and sleep well. I take it we will have timely warning of any attacking aircraft?'

'If that happens your radio office will be informed.'

Zeigler pursed his lips. The man seemed very sure of himself and just for once Zeigler wanted to believe that this contraption would provide him with a much enhanced level of security.

'Then I take my leave,' Zeigler said, and stepped outside the camouflaged awning. He glanced at his watch . . . , already gone four in the afternoon.

'Roeder!' he called and beckoned for the Corporal to join him.

'Come, we go.' He took a last glance at the old fort, the apparent permanence of the solid stone walls. They were still more than a match for small arms fire, but modern heavy artillery? Not really. He moved off at a brisk pace and picked up the path back to Braye harbour. Roeder trailed along behind and Zeigler smiled to himself. The men needed to maintain their fitness levels. He must reintroduce morning marches. Once round the island would be good. And then he came to a halt. He turned to look again at the fort and changed his mind. He and Roeder would stay the night here, at Fort Tourgis. Apparently the chef's culinary skills were worth sampling and it would be a welcome change from the view over Braye harbour.

Roeder came to a stop and looked questioningly at his superior officer.

Zeigler pointed at the old walls. 'We'll stay the night, see what it has to offer.'

Roeder pulled a face. 'Cold and damp they say. Good for the days of Napoleon but not for soldiers of the Third Reich.' He spat in disgust.

The Major grinned at the Corporal's vehemence. 'So I will see for myself. Come.' The grin broadened as he thought of the morning. He could take the garrison for the first morning run.

In Weymouth dusk was fast approaching and with the fading light Lieutenant Craig Kendal gave orders for Lieutenant Wingham to embark his raiders. They came down the jetty single file, without a word between them and began squeezing themselves and their weapons into the cramped quarters below. With two of his crew standing by on the mooring lines, Kendal glanced round the boat and smiled. Her seventy feet of main deck sported two pairs of 1/2-inch Lewis machine-guns, another pair mounted either side of the bridge, and two 20mm Oerlikon machine-guns, one on the foredeck and another on the quarterdeck. She'd recently been uprated in her power train from the original 3-shaft Napier petrol engines, to Packards, giving her a top speed of 38 knots. The combination of power and guns made for a formidable weapon. His smile lingered until the moment came when the Cox'n straightened at the controls, hand hovering over the throttle levers.

'Ready, sir.'

Kendal nodded. 'Start her up.'

With a grumbling cough the engines came to life, blue smoke swirling astern.

'Let go for'ard.'

The crew man unhitched the line and jumped onto the foredeck.

'Let go aft.'

A rope came inboard over the stern rail, and the crew man followed. Flaking the rope into coils he made certain the props were devoid of any obstruction. 'All clear, sir.'

Kendal settled his cap and took a careful look round the harbour. He could see that *Brackendale* and *Cheriton* had released from the quayside bollards, a slight shimmer of disturbed water beneath their stern rails. He checked the long breakwaters and took note of a number of ships at their moorings. Only then did he give the order.

'Slow ahead. Take us out, Cox'n.'

The boat grumbled to the snarl of engines, and then veered gently out from the jetty. The helm came over and with practised ease the Cox'n steered her away for the harbour entrance. He rounded a silent minesweeper and avoided a sloop swinging to her mooring.

Kendal looked over his shoulder. *Brackendale* and *Cheriton* were coming on in line astern, easing their way through the harbour's numerous moorings.

Pushing out between the towering breakwaters, the gunboat lifted to the waves, and leaving Breakwater Fort to starboard he turned to face the sea. The wind blew in from the southwest, driving the sea into a rolling chop, and he set the boat's speed accordingly.

'Half ahead, eighteen knots.'

'Eighteen knots, aye aye, sir,' the Cox'n said, and pushed forward on the three throttle levers.

In the engine compartment, Chief Motor Mechanic Ben Moore, watched closely as the engines throttled up. As the noise levels increased he grinned at Leading Stoker Wells and nodded. They were under way.

Kendal felt the surge of open water beneath the keel. The lightweight, plywood built power boat forged ahead, back in her natural element. 'Steer one-eight-oh, Cox'n.'

'Aye aye, sir. One-eight-oh degrees.'

The skipper reached for a hand hold and squinted into the spray, knees bent to absorb the thumping undulations. With darkness drawing in the raiders huddled in the Gunboat's cramped accommodation and waited for the word to come on deck.

The weather during the time it took to travel sixty miles south to Alderney was not kind to a Gunboat. And again, as the M.G.B. veered wildly to port, Craig Kendal reminded the Cox'n to hold steady. The throttles were not wide open but not far off, so bow up, stern down, the boat powered across the waves, skipping and thumping to each breaking crest, leaping the troughs. Of the destroyers there was no sign, having already separated to take up their new stations.

Kendal grinned to himself. For the crew of an M.G.B. this was what they lived for. They loved every moment of the exhilarating, wind-in-the-hair, bow wave flying acceleration of a wooden hulled speed boat, albeit in the guise of a Royal Navy Gunboat. As for his thirteen passengers, and the grin widened, maybe the bouncing, yawing ride was not as welcome as it might otherwise be. If you were on deck in the fresh air, then it was quite possible that the bouncing ride could be enjoyed. But cooped up in the confines of the small compartments below and with the cloying smell of petrol fumes wafting through the boat, then perhaps a man used to terra firma might find the trip a little less agreeable.

He turned to Able-Seaman Brian Piper. 'Ask Lieutenant Wingham to join me.'

'Aye aye, sir,' Piper nodded, and dropped into the cockpit to find the officer.

A minute passed before Wingham made it to the bridge and Kendal beckoned him close. 'Fifteen minutes, Paul,' he said raising his voice above the wind. 'You'd best get them ready.'

Wingham peered out over the bows, searching for the first sight of land, but only dark seas and an even darker sky met his gaze. He gave it up.

'Right, Skipper. Fore-deck as rehearsed?'

'Yep,' Kendal said. 'Quick as you can.' He raised his binoculars and through the gloom found a first glimpse of land. It looked to be the bluffs running down to the southern tip of the island.

'Paul!' he snapped, seeking confirmation.

Wingham turned back and stood at his elbow.

Kendal handed him the glasses and pointed ahead. 'Will that guide us down to Telegraph Bay?'

Wingham nodded, still taking in the familiar rocky outline of a headland he knew so well. 'Yeah,' he said. 'It'll curve away to the right, and you want the second cove, that's the one we're after.'

'Thanks,' Kendal said, and retrieved his

binoculars. 'You better get on.'

'I'm gone,' Wingham said, and made his way below. Kendal turned expectantly to the two bridge machine-gunners and raised an eyebrow, querying the possibility of nearby enemy activity.

One man's head turned, eyes narrowed, watching and listening. 'Nothing, sir.' The other gunner looked slowly round and shook his head. 'All I can see are the waves, sir.'

Kendal reduced speed, down to ten knots. The spray from the bows diminished and the boat rocked to the inshore waves. From either side of the boat the Raiders began filtering forward to take their places on the foredeck. They were shadowy figures, all wearing battle-dress uniforms, blackened faces, fighting knives in scabbards at their waists. Grenades hung from webbing straps, ammunition pouches bulging with spare magazines, the American made Thomson machine-guns slung over shoulders. One man wore glasses and as far as Kendal could see carried no weapon. Without a word they took their places. He saw Wingham kneel and check his kit.

'Standing rocks! Starboard bow,' the Cox'n warned.

'Port five.'

'Port five, aye.' The boat came out from the shore and Kendal gave the order to change engines. A muted grumble from the auxiliary replaced the snarling growl of the two turbo charged main motors. He glanced round for Piper.

'Get yourself up front and watch us in.'

Piper picked his way through to the bow and crouched to peer down at the water. Kendal estimated one-hundred yards and if Wingham was correct there should be no problems getting to within twenty. The raiders had split, six and seven, kneeling either side of the foredeck. Wingham knelt behind Able-Seaman Piper at the bows, unmoving, silent.

Kendal raised his eyes at the dimly seen high ground silhouetted against the night sky. If trouble was coming it would be from up there, a roving patrol, or a dog handler.

Piper raised a fist, clenching and unclenching, and then he waved the hand down, repeating the movement.

'Stop engine,' Kendal said, and in the ensuing silence the boat drifted to a grinding halt in two feet of water. He watched the men come to their feet and prepare to drop off the boat. Thirteen in total, all set to wreak havoc on two unsuspecting targets. He wondered how many would come back?

The two Royal Engineers were first over the side, each armed with a slim metal probe. The mining of beaches was common practice and a path must be cleared before the raiders could advance. The sand and shingle was duly probed; deliberate, unhurried. When it came to mine warfare the maxim of "more haste, less speed" was particularly apt. Two bands of tape were pinned to the beach either side of the cleared area and only then did the 'sappers' beckon them on. Wingham was first over the side and dropped with a splash into knee high water. He hurried forward, quickly covering the remaining yards to the beach. It was as he remembered, a mixture of firm sand and shingle, offering secure footing to the user. Staying well within the taped zone he went straight up to the base of the grass covered slopes and paused where the seldom used path wound its way up to the top. Looking back to the water's edge he watched as the boat reversed slowly out into deeper water. The Raiders were all ashore, hunched down on one knee and spread out at the base of the slopes. He caught sight of Sergeant Dave Cartwright with Ratcliffe in close attendance and signalled for them to move up the path. Five men followed, well spaced, weapons at the ready.

Wingham gave them distance before coming to his feet. He began to climb, glanced briefly over his shoulder to see his own section following, and as he'd done on so many occasions in his youth, he leaned into the slope and pushed hard for the top. His weapons and equipment, minimal though they were, made the climb tougher than he remembered and he was glad to crest the final rise. Cartwright's section were lying prone in a semi-circle, almost hidden in the darkness. His own men joined them.

'Anything?' Wingham whispered.

Cartwright shook his head. 'No . . . , quiet as the grave.'

'You happy you can find your way?'

Cartwright turned his face and his teeth glinted as he grinned. 'Well it's your map. You saying it might be wrong?'

Wingham shook his head and smiled. 'No, the map's fine. You just might not read it right.'

Cartwright mumbled something about rubbish map makers, still grinning. 'I'll manage. And you'll be back in three hours?'

'That's the theory.' He turned his attention to Ratcliffe. 'You come with me now. Let's make a move.'

At the same moment Sergeant Cartwright stood and called softly. 'On your feet, lads. Time we were off.' His section rose as one, dark shadows moving without sound. He led them away to the left, around the edge of the high ground, and they were shortly lost in the gloom.

Wingham hefted his Thompson machine-gun and pointed north. 'St Anne's awaits, gentlemen,' and he set off for his birthplace. For the first time the reality of his return struck him, an odd sensation that he couldn't quite shake. Nonetheless, with a mile to go until the outskirts, he pressed on. The raiders were relying on him to find the target; he had no intention of being found wanting.

CHAPTER TWELVE .. HOSTILE SEAS

When Wolfgang Herzog joined his First Officer on the *Puma's* bridge, the Cotentin Peninsula lay shrouded in darkness. Le Havre, he thought, had been a pleasant enough break while the *Puma* was refuelled, but now he must make a move. He waved a nonchalant hand to indicate it was time to cast off and sauntered to the bridge-chair. Making himself comfortable he extracted a pack of cigarettes from a breast pocket and made a selection. He placed the cigarette very deliberately between his lips, applied the flame from a match and drew a satisfying lungful of smoke. A thin smile distorted his face and he let the smoke dribble from the corner of his mouth. He reminded himself of how fortunate he was to be joining the flotilla at Cherbourg. Unlike the Bremerhaven-Wilhelmshaven command tucked away to the north, Cherbourg was frontline operational and as yet not involved with any convoy duties.

'Herr Kapitän! We are ready to proceed.'

Herzog looked round at his First Officer, a young, very enthusiastic Oberleutnant Rolf Leitner.

'Good . . . ,' he said, 'very good. Now, let us see if we can find our way along to Cherbourg. The Kommodore recommends we use the night to hide our departure. There are too many Frenchmen willing to chance spying on us. They risk their lives, but still they spy for the English.'

Leitner clicked his heels, ramrod straight. 'Jawohl, Herr Kapitän. The men cannot wait.'

'So be it,' Herzog grinned, 'take us out.'

Again Leitner clicked his heels, turned smartly away and issued his orders. From inner to outer harbour, slowly to start with but with ever increasing speed, *Puma* cleared the bomb damaged breakwaters and set course for the port of Cherbourg.

Twelve miles east-north-east of Telegraph Bay, *Brackendale* wallowed in the rolling waves, bows pointing east and making just enough headway to hold station. Three miles south of the destroyer's current position, the Cape de la Hague, the most northerly tip of Normandy's Cotentin Peninsula, remained hidden in the darkness. The darkness of the night gave the ship an eerie quality and Thorburn sat in the bridge chair feeling every slight rise and fall. The monotonous electronic 'ping' of the Asdic formed an intrusive backdrop to the otherwise silent bridge, reminding them all of an unseen enemy.

'Time?' Thorburn asked.

Martin answered. 'One-thirty, sir.'

'Thank you, Pilot. Are we holding station in relationship to Braye Harbour?'

'We are ten miles to the east, sir.'

'Very well,' Thorburn said, and tucked his chin down in his old roll neck jumper. If called on, he thought, *Brackendale* could create quite a diversion if he took her a few miles closer. He let the thought linger but knew he wouldn't. Churchill had prohibited the Royal Navy from taking offensive action against any one of the Channel Islands. They were British and the Prime Minister, on behalf of the King, had sworn not to fire on Sovereign territory. A small raiding party was within the bounds of acceptability along with the Oerlikon's heavy machine-gun fire for defensive purposes. Lobbing 4-inch shells at somewhere like St Anne's was a step too far.

'Number One.'

'Sir?'

'I think all watchkeepers would appreciate a hot drink. I wonder if we might arrange for the galley to conjure something up?'

'I'll see to it now, sir,' Armstrong said, and moved to the starboard ladder.

Thorburn heard him descend and smiled. His First Officer was never one to shy away from what others might consider a menial task. He could have called for the bridge messenger or had the request relayed down to the galley. But no, he took it upon himself to see that the crewmen on watch got a hot drink inside them, as per his Captain's suggestion. In Armstrong's eyes, if a job was worth doing it was worth doing himself.

Thorburn rubbed his eyes and settled his cap. The ship lifted to a roller and executed a slow corkscrew as the wave ran along the length of the hull. He felt it through the seat of the wooden chair and automatically recorded every subtle movement of the ship's behaviour. Strangely, it suddenly reminded him of his father. Retiring as a Major from the army, but unable to sit still for longer than five minutes, he'd found a second career as the shopkeeper of a general store. His mother was a long serving midwife, and even now might be answering a call to deliver another baby in the dead of night.

And it was often on lazy Sunday afternoons that he and his old man would leave the thatched cottage on the banks of the River Wye and head down to the wooden jetty and the small dinghy tied alongside. It was from there that his father had first taught an enthusiastic young Richard the intricate art of sailing and forever instilled in his son a lifelong love of the water. He smiled at the memory.

Footsteps sounded on the ladder and hot drinks began to be handed out. When Armstrong had seen to it that all the bridge personnel had got theirs he came up to Thorburn's shoulder and handed him a hot mug of sweet tea.

'I added a tot of rum,' he said quietly, and moved to the bridge screen.

Thorburn sipped it and let the potent drink

warm his insides. He smiled. 'Thank you, Number One.'

'Guns-Bridge!' came an urgent call from a voice-pipe.

Thorburn leaned forward. 'Bridge,' he answered.

'Enemy minesweeper, bearing One-seven-five degrees, course two-six-five. Range three-thousand.'

Thorburn sucked air, and then breathed out slowly. 'Hold fire, Guns.'

Carling acknowledged. 'Sir.'

Thorburn stepped over to the starboard wing and lifted his glasses towards the Cape. Nearby breaking waves met his gaze. He ignored them and looked further afield, without success. He swore beneath his breath and began again, traversing from left to right.

There! He had something, a hint of pale against the blackness. And there it was again, but gone just as quickly, a will-o-the-wisp. He let the binoculars rest and ran a hand over his eyes. Guns had done well to make that sighting, that ship was no more than a fleeting suggestion. But right now Thorburn wanted to avoid any form of contact. If it were at all possible he didn't want to alert the Germans to *Brackendale's* proximity.

'Number One.'

'Sir?'

'We've not been spotted and I'd prefer to keep it that way. If we get into a gun battle the sound might carry. We don't want to get the Germans excited on Alderney.'

'Should we follow? Keep it in sight?'

'No,' Thorburn said, thinking it through. 'We've been lucky. We saw Jerry, but he didn't see us. We start hanging on to his coat tails and we might come unstuck.' He licked his lips and frowned. 'No, what I intend to do is relocate and station *Brackendale* closer to Alderney, midway down the east coast. I don't think that the German is heading that way but if he is we'll be more able to lend assistance if needed.'

Armstrong shook his head, hesitant. 'But that makes a nonsense of Captain (D)'s orders. Those last instructions were pretty specific.'

'That's as maybe, Number One, but I'm convinced we're wasting time up here. If Wingham's lot run into trouble we'll be right there on hand.'

'I can't argue with that, sir.'

Thorburn smiled in the darkness. 'Good, then let's turn her round. Next stop Alderney.'

Armstrong acknowledged. 'Very well, sir,' he said, and bent to the pipe.

'Port twenty. Half ahead, make revolutions for sixteen knots.'

Confirmation echoed up the pipe. 'Port twenty, half ahead, speed sixteen knots. Aye aye, sir.'

Brackendale swung away from the headland and continued to turn until she'd come far enough round to steady up on the opposite bearing. Thorburn stood at the screen and hunched into his duffle coat. The destroyer's increased speed quickly translated into a cold wind, enough to feel raw on the skin. But it all made him feel more alive. *Brackendale* was purposefully on the move, rising and falling to the waves, no longer an idle spectator waiting in the wings.

He glanced round for Martin. 'Pilot, we'll take station midway down the east coast, a couple of miles off shore.'

'That'll put us in the grip of 'The Race', sir.' There was a disapproving edge to his voice.

'Yes, Pilot, and all the less likely that we'll be spotted.' Thorburn's intuition had come into play. To the untrained eye the power of the Race, a tidal flow of water squeezed between the Peninsula and the Island, would prevent a warship from holding station in such waters. A soldier wouldn't spend much time watching that particular stretch of the sea.

'Then we could try four-thousand yards, sir?'

'I can live with that.'

Martin leaned on the compass binnacle and checked the bearing. 'Port ten,' he ordered, and waited for the compass to respond. 'Midships . . . , steady. Steer two-five-oh degrees.'

'Two-five-oh degrees, aye aye, sir,' was heard faintly from below, and the ship steadied onto her new course.

Korvettenkapitän Wolfgang Herzog came to his feet and stepped forward to the *Puma's* bridge screen. A persistent drizzle obscured his view, not helped by the water continually streaming down the screen. He grunted his annoyance and moved to his left, out onto the unprotected wing. It made little difference; the fine rain forced him to blink repeatedly, the cold wind quickly numbing exposed skin. With a shake of his head, Herzog headed back to the master bridge and shrugged deeper into his leather coat.

'Coffee!' he demanded loudly. 'I am in need of a hot coffee.'

From the back of the bridge a voice snapped an answer. 'Jawohl, Herr Kapitän,' and footsteps receded down a ladder.

Herzog looked about for his Second-in-Command and found him braced at the forebridge talking to a young trainee officer.

'Oberleutnant Leitner, is the ship holding course?'

Rolf Leitner dismissed the younger man and turned to face his Commanding Officer.

'Ja, Herr Kapitän, the ship holds course west, north-west. In twelve minutes we will clear the Gatteville Lighthouse on our port side.'

'Good . . . , very good. Then you would agree we will be on schedule to arrive at Cherbourg as planned?'

'You are correct, Herr Kapitän. And then we

are to wait outside the harbour. May I ask why?'

Footsteps approached from behind. 'Herr Kapitän.' A tray was offered, on which a steaming pot of Brazilian coffee awaited his acknowledgement, and a large mug filled to the brim. Herzog inhaled the aroma, sipped, and nodded his satisfaction. The coffee came from his own supply, a judicious piece of forethought prior to the start of hostilities. Word of mouth had it that already the Ersatzkaffee substitute was beginning to circulate amongst the German population. Herzog had tasted it in Belgium and he would not willingly partake of it in future.

'Leave the tray,' he said, and continued to nurse the mug. 'Where were we?' he asked.

'I was wondering why we must wait outside Cherbourg, Herr Kapitän?'

'Well . . . , to 'wait' is probably not the right word, Leitner. A small reduction in speed would be nearer the mark. The facilities are not yet fully operational and an escort is required to guide us. And we will be newcomers to a flotilla, they must allocate a berth. But think of it, Leitner. A full Kriegsmarine flotilla ready for battle and we will be at the forefront.' He gave a self indulgent smirk that remained hidden behind his raised mug of coffee.

Oberleutnant Rolf Leitner clicked his heels. 'Thank you, Herr Kapitän,' he said, to show gratitude for being taken into his commander's confidence. 'If you will excuse me, I have my duties.'

Herzog waved a dismissive hand. All was as it should be and he thought how well executed was this move down the French coast. Now all that he needed was to complete an uninterrupted journey through Kriegsmarine waters before joining a Flotilla that made regular offensive incursions into British territory.

Behind a thin veil of persistent drizzle, the *Puma* continued on its passage west in compliance with Admiral Blomberg's orders.

CHAPTER THIRTEEN . .
ON THE QUIET

Paul Wingham reached the southern outskirts of St Anne's and motioned for the others to follow him round to the right. Now was the time for caution, no telling how many patrols there were around the town. He stopped at the deserted home of old Tom and Eva Parsons, some of the first to be evacuated. As far as he could tell in the dark, the tiny front garden looked a bit overgrown. He crept down the side and out the back. As he waited for the last man to catch up he noted the hen coop was empty. His own home, four-hundred yards further on but on the west side of the street, lay hidden in the darkness. And there was no reason to go near it. As much as his curiosity egged him on, there was nothing to be gained and everything to lose in taking unnecessary time to divert from the correct course of action.

They paused, the section down on one knee while he peered into the gloom and tried to spot any roving Germans. There were none that he could see and he moved to the little picket fence and eased open the rear gate. They filed through, and gently, very quietly, he closed the gate behind them.

Ratcliffe touched his arm. 'How much

further?' he whispered.

Wingham bent to his ear. 'About the same again.'

Ratcliffe nodded. 'Right.'

'Problem?' Wingham asked

'No, just curious.'

Wingham grunted and straightened up, eyes scanning the ground ahead. His intention was to take the coastal path along the cliff tops. Across the centuries the path had been formed by countless feet choosing the easiest route and right now that suited him well. On this side of the island the path would take them directly to Essex Castle with its familiar 'pepper pot' of a watch tower, easy to pick out even in poor light. From there he could cut left across to Fort Albert and find the German station.

'Come on, this way,' he whispered, and led them off towards the coast. He half smiled to himself. One thing about his proposed route; the waves crashing on the rocks at the base of the cliffs tended to give a man enough warning of his whereabouts. With weapons at the ready, they found the path and headed for the castle's ancient walls.

Paul Wingham urged them on. Time was critical.

H.M.S. *Cheriton* was almost at the end of her patrol line south-east towards Jersey, and Rutherford reminded his Navigating Officer it was time to reverse course and commence the next leg for Guernsey.

'Three more minutes, sir,' his Pilot said, and Rutherford acknowledged the warning.

'Very well,' he said, and turned his face away from the persistent drizzle. The weather had been fairly benign on the run down, but now they were on station the cold rain had become a menace, a distraction that the watchkeepers could well do without.

'Port twenty,' he heard being ordered down the pipe. That would take the ship in a swing to the north before heading back on a reciprocal course to that of the first leg. He waited, feeling the deck heeling over, adjusting his stance to compensate.

'Midships.'

Cheriton swayed upright, the wheel centred, rudders returning to line up with the keel.

'Steer three-oh-five.'

Faintly from the wheelhouse the Cox'n acknowledged. 'Steer three-oh-five degrees, aye, sir.'

Charles Rutherford moved to the starboard wing and peered into the drizzle. Hidden in the rain Guernsey sat approximately sixteen miles north-west of *Cheriton's* current position. In forty minutes the small destroyer would again make a turn to port in order to backtrack along this chosen route.

Hopefully, he thought, it wouldn't be too long before the raiding party were done and the wireless room got a signal telling *Cheriton* to go home. Patrolling an area of some eighty square miles with the idea of fending off a random enemy patrol boat was not exactly to Rutherford's liking and the sooner he was despatched on to something more meaningful, so much the better. No doubt, Lieutenant Wingham was enjoying himself reliving his childhood years amongst the dwellings of what was now Nazi held territory.

Water dripped off his nose and he hunched deeper inside his heavy duty coat. Watch and wait was the maxim, watch and wait.

Paul Wingham came to a halt and dropped to one knee. He gestured for the remainder of his section to take a breather. Here at the northern end of Essex Castle the walls of the 'pepper pot' were within fifty feet and he'd paused only to get his bearings. He squinted out towards Longis beach and the wide bay where he'd learnt to sail. It reminded him of family days out. Thankfully, he thought, his parents had evacuated in good time and were now both living in a small cottage north of Teignmouth. They were safe and that was a lot more than could be said for many.

He raised his binoculars and studied a line of trees. The trees formed the edge of a dark wood, but immediately to his front a large area of open ground gave cause for concern. Other fields spread out both left and right, but for Wingham time was at a premium, and it left him with no option but to cross that area of open ground. The one saving grace was a hedgerow that formed a partial barrier running down the right. If nothing else it offered some background cover to the movement of his section. It all went against his better judgement, but finding a safer route now was out of the question. Wingham took one last look before lowering the glasses to his chest, and then turned his head.

He looked over towards where Fort Albert should be, to the northeast of Braye harbour. It was probably a good thousand yards away but immediately to his front that line of trees blocked his view, on top of which and in these conditions there was nothing to see from here. But he well knew the ground between the two fortifications and he turned to the waiting men.

'Ready?' he called in a fierce whisper. Nods greeted the query.

'Right, stay close,' he said, and set off to thread his way through the clump of trees. Wingham led them on, forcing his way through low scrub grass. It was thick and wet, clinging to the boots, making each step an effort. He took a look behind. They advanced in good order, weapons up. For an instant he smiled. In the weeks leading up to this mission, training had been hard, very competitive. Looking at them now, the end result of a harsh regime, these tough, rugged, soldiers were all he could wish for. It had been worth all the pain, all the mutterings and all the swearing and cursing. He entered the line of trees, picked his way through and emerged into the open. He cleared the last of them and began crossing the gentle slopes. The Hill Road lay to his right and acted as a marker for his line of travel. Having covered two-hundred yards he found he was grinning like an idiot. The lay of the land was so familiar he felt he could have traversed it blindfold. They pressed on and long minutes passed before the end of the first slope was reached, without incident. At the end of it Wingham tensed as he cleared a dividing embankment and led them into the next field. He immediately felt more exposed. This was flat grassland, short and stunted with the winter's cold. Nothing grew taller than a man's boot sole, and only five-hundred yards ahead those dark forbidding walls remained ominously quiet. Deathly quiet. He peered intently at the battlements, hard to see in the dark. The stillness became unnerving and his heart quickened. At the main crossroads the old narrow gauge railway line came next and he waited while the section crossed over and spread out. Satisfied there was nobody behind them he too crossed the track and threaded his way to the front.

He looked round at the shadowy figures. 'Tony?' he called softly.

Ratcliffe was crouched and breathing hard but came nearer, staying low. 'Paul?'

Wingham pointed towards the castle walls. 'The reconnaissance reports indicated there were separate outbuildings beyond the walls on the eastern flank. Beyond the moat. You ready?'

'Right with you.'

'Good.' He peered at the rest. 'We're going up to the castle now. There's some cover, very bushy. If they've got guards try and keep it quiet. No shooting unless we have to. The longer Jerry are undisturbed the better.'

There were quiet grunts and nods of men acknowledging his advice. He checked the sub-machinegun, slipped the safety to 'off' and proceeded to head for the sprawling mass of gorse. Years ago he and young Billy had spent long summer days 'camping' in these bushes, even going so far as to light fires amongst tinder dry branches.

He encountered the first waist height thickets and forced his legs to push through the stiff fronds. It was hard to advance without noise and behind him the rest of the section fared no better. The walls of the castle overlooked his route and made for an unpleasant expectation of imminent discovery.

Wingham crested a slight rise and waved for them to pause. The vague outline of a small shack appeared ahead and at first sight there was a fair resemblance of what he'd seen in the aerial photos. He held his breath, listening. Silence. He estimated twenty-five yards and turned to signal their dispersal. They split up into three groups and he gave a thumbs up for the right flank to move. The left flank pair set off at a low crouch and with both teams committed he turned to Ratcliffe.

'You hang back until I call. Got it?'

Ratcliffe nodded.

Wingham glanced at his Royal Engineer, a Corporal Jeff Mason. They'd worked together in training and Mason was a short, tough Yorkshireman who, when push came to shove, was just plain bloody hard. His specialist skill revolved round explosives and his main purpose tonight was to lay the charges that would eliminate the target. He also had a few anti-personnel mines for when the Germans came to investigate. His sheer physical presence and dry sense of humour made him the perfect companion to have in tow.

Mason inclined his head and lifted the barrel of his Thompson. He was ready.

Wingham straightened and moved toward the shack or shed, or whatever it was.

He covered no more than twenty yards before he came to a halt at the edge of cleared ground. What at first sight had appeared to be some kind of wooden shack turned out to be anything but. Even in the darkness of a bleak winter night it was immediately obvious that the 'shack' was in fact two large flatbed trailers harnessed together. A separate 'pent' roof overhung both trailers and served to give the initial impression of a shed. The sides and ends were possibly fabricated from sheet steel and painted in overall camouflage grey. The immediate impression was one of rapid mobility if demanded. Ten yards further inland a tall, skeletal wireless mast stood easily a hundred-feet high. The clearance of the ground had to have been done very recently, it seemed freshly exposed under foot.

He tensed as a movement caught his eye by the base of the mast, then relaxed a little as he recognised the raiders swinging in from the right.. He motioned for them to advance and moved forward himself, wary. The left-flank party came into view closing in from a position at eleven o'clock.

Wingham got to within five yards and held up a hand. He went down on one knee and waited until everyone was ready. A closed door at the top of steps on the end of each trailer faced him and he stole silently over to the side of the nearest one. He looked at the left flank party, held up one finger and beckoned. Sergeant Steve Cochran rose to his feet, moved out in a wide semi-circle, and only then came round to the far door. Wingham pointed at Mason and urged him over, Cochran did the same to one of his own.

When both were positioned with fingers waiting on handles, Wingham let them try to open. Jeff grinned, it had moved under his hand. Wingham and Cochran slung their guns and drew fighting knives. This was to be as quiet as they could make it. Knowing Cochran had the same equipment, Wingham unclipped a red filtered hand torch from his webbing belt and prepared to enter. If nothing else, he thought, anyone inside will be startled by the light.

He looked across to Cochran and lifted his chin. Cochran nodded, and Wingham gave a hoarse command.

'Now!'

The door was snatched ajar and he thumbed the torch. He lunged in, low and left. A German lay in a bunk to his right, blinking in the red glow. Wingham didn't hesitate. The knife flashed in a sweeping arc and only the muted gurgle of a slashed throat disturbed the silence. He turned off the torch, struggling to regain his night vision. At the door he called for Ratcliffe.

The Lieutenant mounted the steps and with his own torch briefly surveyed the interior. 'I need five minutes,' he snapped. The once placid young signals officer had been transformed. Authoritative, efficient.

'All yours,' Wingham said, stepped outside and shut the door. He looked over at the silhouette of the castle walls, no lights, no movement, nothing to say the raiders had been discovered. The men were well spread out now, lying prone in a circle round the trailers. Cochran sat at the top of the other steps, content to wait.

'Jerry, inside?' Wingham asked

conversationally.

'Yep,' Cochran answered evenly. 'Long sleep now.'

Faint metallic noises came from inside Ratcliffe's trailer, and then some light tapping, followed by scraping.

Wingham took a walk round both trailers, killing time, willing Ratcliffe to hurry. As he came back round for the second time, Ratcliffe opened the door carrying a large holdall. It looked heavy.

'Got what you need?' Wingham asked.

'Yes, and more. Now I want to see the other one.'

'Feel free. I take it we can plant explosives?'

Ratcliffe grinned in the darkness, teeth glistening. 'Be my guest.' He placed the holdall at the bottom of the second set of steps and Cochran let him in.

'Mind the blood on the floor,' the Sergeant said quietly. 'Bit slippery.'

From behind his glasses Ratcliffe gave Cochran a sideways glance, moved inside and pulled the door closed behind him.

And while they waited, this time there was work to be done. In the first trailer, and round the base of the aerial mast, plastic explosive was lovingly squeezed into place, detonators inserted ready to be ignited and timers set. All that remained was for the Engineers to lay their mines as the raiders departed.

Sergeant Dave Cartwright had pushed north for almost a mile when he paused to take stock. Silhouetted against the night sky the walls of Fort Tourgis loomed out of the darkness. According to Wingham's map, Cartwright was now looking at the east side barrack block. It had been out here on the undulating grass slopes that the reconnaissance photographs had picked up the suspicious installation.

Faintly, from somewhere ahead, he thought he heard the sound of voices fluctuating with the strength of breeze. Of one thing he was certain, it wasn't English. He turned to the raiders.

'We're close,' he said, keeping his voice low, 'maybe two or three-hundred yards. Spread out line-abreast. When we know what we're dealing with we'll try and make it quiet. Right, let's move.'

He led them forward, cautious, stealthy, crouched from the waist, weapons ready. The voices grew louder, with no attempt at hiding their presence, supremely confident in their complete domination of the island.

A subdued but fierce hiss came from the right and the raiders dropped to one knee. Cartwright whispered.

'What is it?'

The man on the far right jabbed a pointed finger to his front, at the two o'clock position. 'Wagon and small light.'

Cartwright moved silently over to join him and found the light. 'I'll have a dekko. Wait.' He went down on elbows and knees and crawled closer. He slithered twenty yards and stopped. There it was, a large wagon with three wireless type boxes mounted on the platform. A soft green light emanated from some sort of screen. Two men sat on stools looking at the light, a third man wearing a fedora type hat watched on from behind. He noted a rifle and two sub-machineguns had been left leaning against a panel. Now and then the two men seated spoke to each other. It was enough, and Cartwright squirmed backwards. He rose to his knees and for a moment studied the shadowy figures. He pointed.

'You three circle round and watch the back door. We'll wait until you're in position.' He glanced at the remaining pair. 'We'll go in the front. Don't forget, we need prisoners.'

He waited until a movement beyond the trailer caught his attention. It was a signal, a hand waving slowly. He raised his fist and unclenched it, then closed it into a ball, then unclenched. The open hand disappeared, they were ready.

'Move,' he said, and closed in on the wagon, a fighting knife grasped in his fist. There was no hesitation, Cartwright went in hard. Springing onto the platform he punched the man wearing a hat, one hit, side of the temple. He collapsed, eyes bulging, and made not a sound.

The operators wore earphones, oblivious to what had taken place, intent on the screen. A knife appeared and touched a throat. The man froze. The other one reacted, reached for a gun. He died as a knife plunged into his heart.

Cartwright leaned down and pushed his face close to the German operator. He placed a finger on his lips. 'Shhh,' he mouthed. You didn't need to speak German with that one, he instantly became multi-lingual.

The German nodded, eyes wide, the point of a blade still pressing his throat.

'Tie his hands,' Cartwright ordered, and shoved him to the floor. He glanced at his watch. Might be another hour before Wingham appeared, hopefully with Ratcliffe in tow. If not then at least they had a prisoner for interrogation. And push comes to shove, he could grab what they could carry and take it back for the boffins to look at. In the meantime, they'd all seen an odd looking umbrella type contraption some yards away up on the low plateau. He would take a gander at this oversized "tennis racket".

'Joe,' he called quietly, and Corporal Underhill appeared at his side. 'Sarge?'

'We'll have a look at that thing over there,' Cartwright said. 'See if we can't dismantle it.'

'Right,' Underhill said, and took off.

What they found took them by surprise. The

"tennis racket" turned out to be a large concave dish, ten or twelve feet in diameter and affixed to a hand operated turntable. Nearby was an oblong box and from it ran a number of electrical wires.

'I think,' Cartwright said slowly, 'that Ratcliffe is going to be more than a little interested in all this.'

'Yeah,' Underhill grunted. 'Let's hope they get a shift on.'

Cartwright thought better of trying to dismantle it. Ratcliffe should make that sort of decision. And with that they ambled back to the wagon where one of the raiders was paying close attention to the man in the hat.

'Started groaning, Sarge. Thought we'd better shut him up.'

Cartwright grinned. The fedora hat had been rammed down over the man's eyes and he'd been well and truly gagged. 'Nice,' he said in approval. 'Very nice.'

And now they had two prisoners in the bag. They settled down to wait.

Major Hans Zeigler had not settled in his new surroundings. The room had a damp smell and with the exception of his calf length boots, he'd crawled under the blankets in full uniform. But the bed proved not to his liking, uncomfortable. And although he had been given what had been reserved as officers quarters, the heating was non existent. Eventually Zeigler clambered out of bed and stamped into his boots. He found his cigarettes and wandered over to the window. There were no curtains so he leaned against the frame and as he looked out at the old dark fortifications it occurred to him that he ought to test the guards. He had seen a duty roster and it identified three such areas. The east roof, the old western gun battery defences, and the southern coastal wall. Each area maintained a roving patrol rather than a static guard post and it amused him to think he might surprise an inattentive soldier.

He might also rouse the cook for coffee. It would help to inject a modicum of warmth into his body. The door creaked noisily as it opened and Zeigler stepped into the corridor with a grin. The cook would not thank him for being disturbed at this time of night but his duty was to the Wehrmacht and a man must realise there is a war on. He strode off down the passageway determined to bang on a few doors.

After all, if Zeigler couldn't sleep, why should they?

At 02.30 hours, in accordance with standing orders, a young Kriegsmarine Leutnant in Braye harbour ordered his Schnellboat to be fired up. Casting off from the inner jetty he took the boat serenely out beyond the end of the long breakwater and turned left to circumnavigate the island on an anti-clockwise patrol. It would make a change to the nightly clockwise deployments that had been the accepted method currently employed.

With his crew stood to at the guns, the young captain increased revolutions to a low cruising speed and began a detailed search of the craggy coastline. Infrequently he had the boat's small searchlight probe an inlet or a suspicious rock strewn outcrop. But as on so many previous nights, the inshore patrol proved fruitless.

Undeterred, the young officer pressed on towards Fort Tourgis and the southwest headland.

CHAPTER FOURTEEN .. STEALTH

Lieutenant Ratcliffe stuck his head out of the trailer door and peered into the darkness.

'Paul?' he called quietly.

'Here,' Wingham said, and crossed to the bottom of the steps.

'I need you to see this,' Ratcliffe said and gestured for Wingham to follow. Inside they shut the door and Ratcliffe turned on his torch. The subdued beam picked out a small screen and a large amount of ancillary equipment.

'What is it?' Wingham asked.

'I believe,' Ratcliffe said, 'we're looking at Freya, the German equivalent of our radar. If I'm right then this little box of tricks can track aircraft and give early warning of our bomber raids.'

Wingham nodded. 'All right, so what now?'

'I'm going to strip out one of these metal cases to take back,' Ratcliffe said and then indicated a file of technical looking papers. 'Those too. I think that explains how to manipulate the signal.'

'How long?'

Ratcliffe scratched his nose. 'Five minutes at the outside.'

Wingham patted him on the shoulder. 'All yours. We'll be waiting.' And he stepped out and closed the door. He stood at the top of the steps and looked around. All quiet. He managed to pick out Cochran and moved towards him, crouched down at his side. 'Explosives set?'

'Yep, all except Ratcliffe's trailer and timers. How long a delay do you want?'

Wingham grimaced, trying to work out timings. Forty minutes, say, to get down to Fort Tourgis and find the others. Thirty minutes for Ratcliffe to do his stuff and another thirty to get back to Telegraph Bay. He trimmed it slightly.

'Ninety-minutes should do.'

'Sure?'

'Sure as I can be.'

Cochran's teeth glistened in the darkness, a grin coming and going.

'Okay, we'll see to that.'

Wingham nodded, moved back to the steps and went down on one knee. A hollow tapping sound came from inside the trailer, then he flinched to a metallic bang. He lunged up the steps and opened the door.

'For Christ's sake keep the noise down.'

Ratcliffe peered round. 'Was it very noisy?'

'Any louder and we might as well go and call out the guard ourselves.'

'Sorry . . . , but I'm done now.' He lifted the metal casing and tucked it inside a second haversack, the paperwork stuffed down with it. The red glow of the torch was extinguished and they joined the others outside.

Cochran went in and laid plastic explosive, shaped it and inserted a detonator. He wired it to a timer, set the clock face for ninety-minutes and quietly closed the door.

Wingham called softly and led them away towards the aerial array. The other way, towards the Fort, is where a miniature minefield now existed. Nine small anti-personnel mines had been strategically placed where unsuspecting troops were most likely to appear. The first to explode would be the most important. A screaming wounded man with a missing foot served to achieve much more than the sum of such an insignificant detonation. The other soldiers would freeze, stopped in their tracks, fearful for their own safety. And the wounded man would have to be rescued, dangerous. That would take at least two men to carry him off to be looked after.

And if the remainder wished to continue the advance, the minefield would have to be cleared. Time consuming.

Melting into the darkness, Wingham and his Raiders stole away, a lethal trap carefully installed to catch the unwary.

Major Zeigler sat with one booted foot resting on an upturned packing case and sipped the hot coffee. Smoke from his cigarette coiled to the ceiling and he blew a gentle cloud towards the stove. The overweight cook, obviously annoyed by the Major's insistence that he be roused just to make coffee, stood by the stove and glowered. It pleased Zeigler that the man's sleep had been so rudely disturbed and he did nothing to indicate that the cook was dismissed. In fact, Zeigler felt the lone kerosene lamp was unnecessarily bright and ordered him to reduce the flame. The heavy drapes over the windows might well block the light but there was no need to assume it was impenetrable.

He finished the coffee, stubbed out his cigarette and stood to check his uniform. Satisfied, he extracted his Luger, checked the box magazine, reinserted it and slid the gun back beneath the flap. He also patted his jacket pocket to check for the spare magazine. He felt its outline, and reassured he could cope with any contingency that might present itself on this night, he made for the exit to begin his tour.

Wingham forced the pace. Dark as it was he closed them up and moved back inland before swinging right to skirt the town and make a bee line for Tourgis. He remembered a shallow ditch that ran east to west at the edge of a field and led them straight in.

When he judged they were about a hundred yards from the Fort's east facing wall he stopped and let them catch their breath.

'Sergeant Cochran!' he called in a loud whisper.
'Sir.'

'I can't see much from here, need to do a recce. I think I know where they'll be. If I'm not back in ten minutes you'll have to take over. Ratcliffe might be an officer but he'll follow your advice. Okay?

'Right. Ten minutes?'

Wingham nodded. 'Yep. Ten minutes.' He turned away and crouched, bent at the waist. Ten yards ahead he clambered from the ditch and bellied across an area of wasteland. And fifty yards on he stopped. The faint outline of a large solid looking bowl standing on edge made him steady his breathing and listen. Silence. He squirmed forward, another ten yards.

'That's far enough, sunshine.'

He froze. 'Wingham,' he said.

'Thought as much. We've been waiting.

'Any trouble?'

'Nothing to talk about.'

'Right, I'm going back to collect my lot. Won't be long.' He turned away, came to his feet and half running, half walking, he made it back to the ditch.

'Found them,' he said. 'This way.'

Cochran ushered the others from the ditch and Wingham took them across to be reunited with Cartwright's section.

It was then that Wingham realised Ratcliffe was missing. He hissed his concern.

'Where's Ratcliffe?'

They searched, no sign.

'I'll check our route in, see if he's out there somewhere.'

Sergeant Cartwright grunted. 'Right, quick as you can, sir. Time's moving on.'

But then, surprising them all, Lieutenant Ratcliffe calmly walked in and dropped his haversack to the ground. 'Christ that's heavy,' he said quietly.

Wingham closed on him, annoyed. 'Where've you been?'

'Me?' Ratcliffe queried, and he pointed out towards where they'd come from. 'I was inspecting that odd looking contraption out there.'

Wingham took a breath, annoyance dissipating. 'And?

'I do believe it's part of what the German's call a Wurtzberg, an improvement on the Freya. We thought it was still in the early stages of development. Looking at that, we might be proved right.' He removed his glasses, gave them a quick polish and returned them to his eyes.

'Let's have a look,' he said, and swung a leg onto the platform. He passed a hand over the buttons and switches, caressed the screen and leaned forward for a closer look at some hand-drawn diagrams. A file of paperwork, partly typed and half handwritten drew his attention and he hastily thumbed through.

'We need that,' he said, and passed it over. He then stood back, hands on hips and shook his head. 'I'm not going to try and dismantle any of that, it's too well put together. I just need to make a sketch.' He reached for a blank sheet of foolscap, chose a pencil from a pot, and with a flurry of movement rapidly reproduced a remarkably accurate drawing of the machine. Satisfied with the result he folded it once and tucked it inside his trouser map pocket.

'That's it,' he said. 'You can set your charges.'

Wingham didn't hesitate and nodded to the Engineers who immediately began producing plastic explosive from their haversacks. Collecting the bags containing the components belonging to the Freya site, the rest of the Raiders spread out into a watchful circle and waited for the word to go.

On the roof of Fort Tourgis, Major Hans Zeigler stopped making his rounds of the guards and cocked an ear in the direction of the experimental trailer. He crouched near the parapet of the east wing and edged nearer to the low wall. Peering at the trailer he frowned at the number of soldiers now visible. There had only been four personnel involved, including the 'hat'. From where, he wondered, had all these men come from?

And then he heard voices, briefly, an order issued in what sounded like English. He studied some of the shadowy figures and the realisation came that the troops were not Wehrmacht or Luftwaffe, but British. They were a British raiding group. He eased back from the low parapet and made for the door leading to the ground floor. He ran the length of a passageway that took him to a guard house where a soldier issued a challenge. It took Zeigler two minutes to rouse the guard and another five to assemble them all by the south facing main gate.

Corporal Roeder checked their weapons, made sure there was enough ammunition and reported all was ready.

Zeigler unsheathed his Luger and exited the gate. He led them round to the east, single file, weapons to the fore. Two-hundred metres from the trailer he ordered the men to spread out and form a wide circle around the intruders. If the Englanders made to leave, shoot to kill. The sound of gunfire would both alert and give direction to the others.

'Go!' he urged in a harsh whisper. 'Go!'

There were twenty Germans in total and all had fought in savage hand to hand combat as they battled their way through the towns and cities of Europe. They may well have had the recent easy life of conquerors but the obedience and duty deeply ingrained in such soldiers of the Reich saw to it that in moments they had melted threateningly into the night.

Zeigler found a convenient grassy mound from which to survey the area and dropped into the prone position. He was content to await developments.

Wingham peered at his watch. Another ten minutes and the Freya site would blow. Time to get a shift on.

'Are we done?' he asked quietly.

'Last timer being set now,' was the answer.

'Lieutenant Ratcliffe? Got everything?'

'Between us, yes.'

'Right then, form up on me and we'll get out of it. Prisoners?'

'We've got 'em, sir.' That came from Sergeant Dave Cartwright.

Wingham smiled to himself. 'Don't lose 'em,' he said and turned away for the march back to Telegraph Bay. Thirteen Raiders and two German prisoners began to find their way south in the darkness.

CHAPTER FIFTEEN .. FURY

A single shot broke the silence.

And the path behind exploded into a fury of stabbing flame and smoke. Men hit the dirt, returning fire.

A Raider screamed, his agony lost in the crash of gunfire. Sergeant Steve Cochran crashed to the ground on the cliff edge. Blood pumped. A bullet had smashed his right knee cap, deflected and buried itself in the bone of his femur. Tracer fizzed past his head and a stream of bullets kicked dirt. Through a mind-wrenching pain he dragged his gun to his shoulder, levered another round into the breech and squinted to find a target. Then a second bullet hammered his rib cage, smashed bone and penetrated a lung. His next breath was ragged, rattling, and he slumped, head down. Strangely, he thought, the savage agony of pain began to subside, the noise of battle fading. Blood bubbled from his lips. He managed a gasping intake of air. A shudder rippled through his upper torso and at that moment twenty-six year old Steve Cochran, husband, lover, and father to an eighteen month old baby boy, died in the midst of a minor skirmish that not many knew of and those that did had no time to dwell on.

A Bren gun hammered a short burst, aimed

at the seat of enemy tracer. Sub-machineguns added to the battle, and put down volley after volley, firing at will. The rain of bullets thrashed the ground at the cliff's edge and back along the path. A minute after the enemy's opening burst, the constant stream of return fire by the Raiders began to take effect. The enemy tracer slackened, faltered.

Wingham took advantage, shouted. 'One-section, up!'

Men sprang to their feet and sprinted forward. They were yards beyond Wingham when they went to ground, quickly laying down more covering fire.

'Two-section, up!' yelled Wingham, and they stormed into action, the sub-machine gunners firing from the hip. They forged past One-section before they too threw themselves down into firing positions.

Wingham gathered himself, came up to one knee.

'One-section! With me!'

And with that he was on his feet surging forward. The whiplash hiss of a bullet ripped past his ear, and another tugged his collar. He fired the Thompson from his waist, aiming low, running hard.

Cartwright's strident shout cut through the din.

'Down!'

Wingham threw himself onto the short grass

and caught his breath. He repositioned the Thompson, changed magazines, and looked for a target. Bullets threw up dust and he flinched.

The distinctive rasp of a Spandau hammered tracer over their heads. A man grunted and cursed. The noise increased, rising in ferocity. All the Raiders were now engaged in pouring suppressing fire along the top of the cliff. He raised his head, enough to gauge the distance. No more than twenty yards. He needed to act and made a decision.

'One-section flank right! Two-section with me!'

Wingham gave them a final glance and nodded to Cartwright. The Sergeant gave a tight lipped grimace and raised his Thompson.

'Up the Raiders!'

They plunged into the smoke, running hard . . . , right and centre. Wingham clamped his teeth, burst through the remnants of an exploding grenade and found a German lifting his rifle, aiming. He blasted three rounds at him. With five yards between them the bullets hit hard, slamming him backwards. Off to the right a second grenade exploded and the Spandau stopped, its gunners torn by shrapnel. Another German came at him with a bayonet. A big man, stocky, no neck. Wingham dodged the thrust, parried it with his Thompson, head height, and hit the trigger. Blood sprayed. The man's face disintegrated.

Tracer lit the path and he saw Cartwright stumble and fall into a German. The collision caused both to lose their weapons. Cartwright went down, dragging the man with him, and in that instant the German soldier screamed. The Sergeant pushed him away, wiped the stiletto dagger, and retrieved his Thompson.

All along the cliff top men fought and cursed, screaming and shouting. A Bren gunner fired from the waist and cut a gap in the enemy ranks. Five went down, but two attempted to bring up their weapons. The Bren gunner caught them with a short burst, then closed in and fired again. He stepped over them. There was more killing to be done.

A stick grenade tumbled through the air and Wingham yelled a warning.

'Grenade!' he shouted, diving clear. The explosion caught a Raider before he could react, blew him off his feet. When Wingham looked again the man's torso had turned blood red. Corporal Barry Atkinson convulsed once, lay still and died before Wingham could help.

A German rose up from behind rocks and fired at men to Wingham's right. It was a long burst from the German's sub-machinegun. It bracketed two of the Raiders.

'You bastard!' Wingham shouted, and levelled the Thompson. The bullets tore into the man's body; chest, arm and hip. He staggered, staring in shock, and dark as it was, their eyes met. He sagged but somehow managed to stay upright. He snarled something and brought the gun round.

Wingham's Thompson juddered in his hands, and in a moment of uncontrolled fury, he emptied the magazine. The soldier crashed to the ground, a dozen bullets embedded in his body.

Corporal Sven Roeder blinked blood from his eyes and wiped his forehead. A bullet had struck a glancing blow above his nose and he felt sick with the pain. Wiping his forehead didn't help, only serving to smear the blood. He cursed under his breath, eyes screwed up at the throbbing ache. He guessed the battle was almost run, there were too many against him. And he reluctantly accepted they were not the inexperienced soldiers he'd first imagined. As for Major Zeigler, there was no sign. He'd seen his officer running towards the cliff top but then he'd disappeared from sight.

Roeder shook his head. No good worrying about that now. Ruefully, he reached for a stick grenade, unscrewed the base cap and let the detonator cord fall free. He repeated the procedure three times and with the last one he tested the resistance when the cord was taut. A more pronounced steady downward pull would drag the roughened steel rod through the igniter, and from that instance the grenade would explode in five to seven seconds. He'd done it on so many occasions during the Blitzkrieg it barely registered on his subconscious.

The Corporal forced himself to stand, using the rocks as partial protection against enemy bullets. He thought there was an Englander hiding by an ancient stone sheep trough and he made that his target. A sharp pull of the cord and with his right hand he lobbed it at the shadows. A machine-gun hammered and he gasped as a round struck him in the side, waist high. He almost fell. The stick grenade exploded, loud in the night air. He primed another and hurled it in a flat trajectory. But it snagged in a bush and fell short, erupting in a vivid flash. Flames sprang up from the scrub heather. The Bren gun thumped into action, a stream of bullets seeking him out, and a Tommy gun added to the chaos.

Roeder dropped to one knee, blood soaking through his uniform. And then he heard a movement behind him, a footstep scraping stones. He spun round, grabbed at his gun and reached for the trigger, too late. A tall Englander stood close by, no more than ten paces. Roeder was hit by a half-dozen .45 bullets, chest and abdomen. He went backwards, arms flailing, shocked by the multiple impacts. He landed hard, gun torn from his hands. Trying to draw breath, he shuddered, unable to move. Above him the soldier stood with his gun pointed down.

Corporal Sven Roeder, with explosions and

tracer lighting the darkness, met the soldier's dark eyes. He saw no anger, no fanatical hatred, just an unemotional acceptance that he, the Englander, was still alive, while an almost dead man lay at his feet.

Roeder felt no pain, only an overwhelming urge to draw breath. His chest heaved to a rasping intake of air, but finally the Austrian born soldier of Hitler's Third Reich succumbed to a bullet wracked body and an enormous loss of blood.

A sudden movement to his left alerted Wingham to danger and he turned to face it. A German rising to his feet, rifle and bayonet thrusting. With an empty magazine, Wingham didn't hesitate. He unsheathed his fighting knife, stepped sideways, then twisted in close and lunged with the blade. He felt the jolt of resistance as the steel went through the ribcage. The German bared his teeth, hissing in pain, then turned his rifle, bayonet high, and jabbed at Wingham's head. Wingham saw it coming and jerked his head clear. But the bayonet caught the side of his neck and a warm rush of blood soaked his collar. He pushed harder with his knife, felt it grind its way in and then gave it a violent twist. The soldier grunted, eyes wide, as if in disbelief. Wingham tugged backwards, pulling the knife clear. Blood swelled and the German slowly dropped to his knees, rifle discarded, hands trying to quench the flow. Wingham changed mags, moved closer and finished it, a bullet to the brain. Satisfied, he stepped away and glanced along the line.

Then a man in German officer's uniform caught his eye. The man was retreating from behind a raised bank, walking backwards and keeping the battle under observation. Wingham moved towards him. If he could take the man prisoner then the need for more prisoners was unnecessary. A fresh batch of tracer lit the skirmish and he used the distraction to run forward. A pair of granite rocks acted as temporary cover and he took advantage. But the officer had spotted him and fired a pistol in Wingham's direction.

He retaliated with a short burst but not wanting to kill. He wanted the man alive. A grenade burst along the track and Wingham charged forward behind the explosion. As he came through the last of the smoke the German officer had fallen to the ground clutching his side.

Wingham bent over him and placed the muzzle of his gun against the man's cheek. He groaned and tried to sit up. Wingham let him. With the gun barrel an inch from the man's face, he pushed away the hand holding the wound. There was little in the way of blood and it appeared to be a grenade fragment. The man groaned again.

'You'll be okay,' Wingham said brusquely. 'On your feet,' and he jabbed him with the Thompson. Another groan but the man pushed himself upright, stood swaying. The sounds of battle were diminishing. Fighting at such close quarters seldom lasted long and it broke up into a few running skirmishes. Pain ran through the side of his neck and he winced, narrowing his eyes to the ache. He lifted a hand to the open wound, felt the blood and dismissed it as a scratch.

Three of the enemy had retreated back along the path, but one by one the Raiders hunted them down. The Germans fought hard, fought to the last, but it was a vain effort. The Raiders were in no mood for playing games. The Germans died under a hail of bullets.

Wingham wiped blood from his fingers and found Cartwright checking casualties.

'Three dead, four wounded,' Cartwright said in a hushed voice. About to elaborate he hesitated and peered closely at Wingham.

'You're wounded.' He said, and raised a hand to the bloodied collar.

Wingham shrugged his hand away. 'Leave it, I'm alright.' He snatched a glance round in the darkness.

'Is Ratcliffe in one piece?'

'A minute ago he was on the slope down to the Bay. The Gunboat's back.'

'Thank Christ for that. Get everyone aboard,

quick as you can. And I mean everyone, dead and wounded.'

'Yes, sir, I'll see to it,' Cartwright said and hurried off.

Wingham took a last quick glance around the cliff top and returned his attention to the officer.

'You speak English?' he asked, the muzzle of his gun still only an inch from the man's face. There was no response.

'English,' he said again. 'You speak English?'

There was a firm shake of the head, a shrug of the shoulders.

Wingham gave up and pointed along the path. 'Move!' he said.

The German inclined his head and limped off after the Raiders. Now and then he groaned, holding his side. Wingham prodded him with the gun, not inclined to sympathy.

From the north came the rolling thunder of a dozen explosions. The Royal Engineers had done well.

The moon chose that moment to make an appearance and cast a pale colourless light across the path and the gulley leading down to the bay. The Raiders made their way down, singly or in pairs, or carrying dead and injured. They slithered and stumbled and cursed and swore, slowly working their way to the beach. The sandy shingle had almost disappeared, the tide swamping the small inlet. But it gave the Gunboat greater access and enabled her to get that much closer to where the men assembled.

Two of the sailors began helping the wounded while the Raiders lifted up their dead and placed the bodies against the front of the cabin. Three lifeless soldiers.

Wingham saw it, saddened, and then angered. He prodded the officer in the back, a needlessly savage jab. The man grunted but reached out for helping hands, and was hauled unceremoniously onto the foredeck. Wingham clambered aboard and caught his breath.

'One of you keep an eye on him,' he ordered, and looked at the flying bridge for Kendal. 'That's all of us,' he said and Kendal touched his cap in acknowledgement.

The engines rumbled, increased in volume and the Gunboat reversed smartly away from the Bay. Clear of the rocks, Kendal put the boat in forward drive, turned to starboard and throttled up. He leaned into the cockpit and shouted down to the wireless room.

'Make to *Brackendale*, "Buttercup is yellow," and send it now.'

He hung there with his head inside until he heard it had been sent. He straightened and settled for the run north.

!CHAPTER SIXTEEN .. OPEN FIRE

Richard Thorburn had his binoculars clamped to his eyes and was searching the island for the source of faintly heard gunfire. The crackle of small arms had faded in the last few minutes, but as the moon broke through a bank of cloud he continued the search.

'Captain, sir?'

He lowered the glasses and turned to a messenger from the wireless room. 'Yes?'

'Signal from the Gunboat, sir. "Buttercup is yellow." That's all, sir.'

'Very well, acknowledge.' He thought for a second. 'And send them our position. Pilot will give you the coordinates. And copy all to *Cheriton*.'

'Aye aye, sir,' the man said, and stepped across to Martin at the chart table.

Thorburn rubbed his jaw. Alderney's shore line was easily discernible now and the darkness of the foreshore gave way to the strength of moonlight. Whatever had happened ashore that part of Buttercup was over. But the gunfire and explosions indicated a battle of sorts, and the Gunboat might be in serious trouble.

Brackendale's bow pointed south, the propellers turning just enough to hold her steady against the strength of the 'Race'.

He moved over to the compass binnacle and the wheelhouse pipe. 'Half ahead both. Make revolutions for eight knots.'

'Half ahead together. Speed eight knots, aye aye, sir.'

'Steer two-oh-five degrees.'

'Course, two-oh-five degrees, aye, sir.'

'Number One.'

'Sir?'

'Let's have everyone on their toes. We don't want to lose our Gunboat.'

'Sir,' Armstrong said, and began a check of the lookouts.

Thorburn reached for a bulkhead handset. 'Guns?'

'Guns, sir,' Carling said.

'Our people are on their way. Should be with us any time now.'

'Very well, sir. We're ready.'

Thorburn thoughtfully replaced the handset and gripped the rail with both hands. *Brackendale* pushed slowly ahead, making in the region of four knots against the power of the Race. If Kendal's Gunboat was undamaged she would approach at high speed, at which time he could reverse course and head back for Weymouth. *Cheriton* would probably steer via Alderney's west coast and they might not regain contact until they were in sight of Portland.

He squeezed the handrail and willed Kendal to make haste.

Kendal lifted his cap and smoothed his hair. His part of "Buttercup" had gone without a hitch and it was time to increase power and get Wingham's Raiders back home.

'E-boat! Dead astern! Thousand yards!'

Kendal spun round, raised his glasses and swore. The bastard had come out of nowhere, caught him totally unawares. And he could never outrun an E-boat, not with all the added weight. He wondered why they hadn't opened fire, there could be no doubting the Gunboat had been seen and the E-boat was closing fast.

'Emergency full ahead !' he snapped. 'Man your guns!' If he could just get far enough round the rugged coastline to where *Brackendale* waited he had a chance. The 'Hunt's' firepower had to make the German skipper think twice. Overloaded as she was the Gunboat nonetheless made a valiant effort to reach her top speed, the bows rising to skim the waves. He estimated she was ten knots shy.

Tracer flashed from astern, zipping low over the bridge.

'Open fire!' he yelled, and the gunners hit triggers. The quarterdeck 20-mm Oerlikons hammered. Multicoloured tracer whipped in from across the water. The bridge took a dozen hits and a machine gunner grunted in pain.

Enemy shells from a flak gun found the stern, punched holes in the stern rails. A sailor fell, rolled and went overboard, and an Oerlikon gunner took a hit in the shoulder, sagged.

Kendal gritted his teeth. So much for his part going without a hitch. Pray God *Brackendale* was near.

Richard Thorburn narrowed his eyes at the sudden eruption of tracer lighting the sea.

'E-boat! Dead ahead!' The alarm came from Jones.

Thorburn jammed the binoculars to his eyes. Who was friend, who was foe? And the answer was instantly obvious. Kendal's Gunboat was taking hits while firing at something just appearing from beyond the headland. The crew certainly seemed to be giving as good as they got. The Gunboat weaved, at speed, throwing off the enemy tracer.

And powering out into full view came the E-boat. A stream of tracer poured from its deck guns, and Thorburn pursed his lips. The boat was moving very fast. It was difficult to hold it within view through the lens. He let the glasses hang and snatched up a handset.

'Guns!'

'Sir?'

'You have the E-boat?'

'Yes, sir.'

'Then open fire.' With the handset still glued to his ear he heard the shouted command.

'Shoot!

The fo'c'sle guns bellowed, hurling shells across the water. They missed long. They fired again with a correction, and hit the water ahead of the target.

Either side of the bridge the Oerlikons thumped into action, their tracer curving away to smother the E-boat. The four-inch guns crashed off another salvo, water spouts lifting alongside the enemy. A moment later *Brackendale's* Bowchaser joined in. The distinctive staccato bark of the lone Pompom pumped 2-pound shells at the fast moving target. And the young man who'd run forward to bring it into action had a wealth of experience, a natural aptitude for hitting a moving target.

But for all the firepower directed at the enemy boat, Thorburn could see it still advanced at speed. And then his worst fears were realised.

Kendal's gunboat took an accurate burst of canon shells. Orange flashes rippled around the stern and the gunboat slewed to starboard, weaving erratically, slowing.

Thorburn clenched his fists. He only had one option. Turn *Brackendale* to port and give the E-boat a full broadside.

'Hard-a-port!' he yelled at the pipe. The guns crashed again, deafening, drowning out the Cox'n's acknowledgement. But confirmation came by way of *Brackendale* herself. She heeled smartly into the turn, the sudden change of direction pushing the starboard rail under water. Thorburn eyed the enemy boat, the way it was quickly closing the distance to Kendal. *Brackendale* had powered through almost sixty-degrees. It was enough.

'Midships!' he shouted.

'Wheel's amidships, sir!'

Brackendale lurched upright, and beyond, before settling.

'Steady,' Thorburn said, mouth close to the tube.

'Steady, steering one-one-oh, sir.'

In the Range-Finder, Carling didn't wait for an invitation. The 'ready' lights from the turrets indicated all were loaded and following his direction.

'Shoot!'

The main armament thundered, smoke billowing. The multi-barrelled Pompom hammered into action, the starboard Oerlikon chattering. And with the range having come down to a little under fifteen-hundred yards the renewed weight of firepower took effect.

Immediately ahead of the E-boat a four-inch shell exploded on impact with the water. The shock wave threw the boat wildly off course before it regained some form of steering control. And for a vital few seconds the enemy boat lay parallel with *Brackendale's* starboard beam. A stream of tracer converged on the hull, reinforced by another four gun salvo. A wave hit *Brackendale's* starboard beam and she heeled, then settled. The secondary armament never ceased firing, bracketing the E-boat from end to end. Kendal's boat still dished it out but with less intensity.

The end came suddenly. Whether it was the result of a four-inch shell or the unrelenting combination of small arms fire, there was no way of telling. The E-boat might have been setting up for a torpedo attack on *Brackendale*, holding course directly towards the small destroyer's starboard beam. Whatever it was the boat held a straight unwavering course and that was too long. Incendiary rounds enveloped the cabin and a fire sprang up, a ball of flame engulfing the occupants. Then a four-inch shell exploded close, showering the boat with shrapnel.

The E-boat blew up. It disintegrated in a brilliant flash, the explosion hurling debris in all directions.

Thorburn gave a tight smile. 'Bloody marvellous,' he said, and then leaned to the pipe. 'Half ahead. Make revolutions for ten knots. Steer one-seven-oh.'

'Speed ten, course one-seven-oh. Aye aye, sir.'

Thorburn had raised his binoculars in an attempt to asses Kendal's damage. The Gunboat lay at an odd angle, her speed almost negligible, and it looked like some of the Raiders were coming up on deck.

'Number one, prepare the quarterdeck with a

rescue party, port side. I think the Gunboat's in serious trouble.'

'On my way,' Armstrong said and clattered down the ladder in search of crewmen.

Thorburn changed position to stand on the compass platform and watch the distance to the Gunboat diminish.

'Slow ahead.'

'Slow ahead, aye, sir.'

'Starboard twenty,' he said. *Brackendale* turned, slowly, easing up to the Gunboat and presenting her port quarterdeck as the place to get them aboard. It also gave him the advantage of holding a bearing of due south, just in case anything else came round the headland.

He took a pace across to the port side and looked aft. A wave slapped the Gunboat and it thumped the side. Armstrong waved a hand at the bridge.

'Stop engines,' Thorburn said, and *Brackendale* sighed to a halt.

A line was passed from Gunboat to destroyer, the boat gathered in and secured, and the wounded began to be transferred. Willing hands lifted and helped support the injured and Doc Waverly took charge. The bodies came next and were reverently laid between galley and searchlight housing.

The Gunboat was then hit by a breaking wave, lurched up, banged the side and settled. But she settled much lower, and all involved realised the need to hurry. So then came those who were still in one piece. Amongst them Ratcliffe and Wingham, both careful to pass over a weighty haversack apiece.

'Mind that,' Wingham called up to the quarterdeck. He saw Armstrong. 'Get those somewhere safe. I think it's what we came for.' He gave Ratcliffe a leg up and then turned back for his prisoner. Two of the Raiders held him tightly and Wingham grinned.

'I'll climb up, you hand him to me.'

They nodded, but one said, 'Need to hurry, sir. This old tub won't last much longer.'

Wingham glanced at the deck, the water washing across the bows. He reached out for the ship's side and hauled himself up. The prisoner accepted the need to save himself and reluctantly climbed up into Wingham's custody.

Armstrong grabbed the German and passed him along to the Bosun. 'See he's secured below.'

'Aye aye, sir.'

A Leading-Hand called a warning. 'Better untie the boat, sir. She's going.'

The First-Lieutenant nodded but hesitated. 'Where's Lieutenant Kendal?'

From the gunboat's flying bridge a face appeared. 'Right here, old chap,' Kendal said. 'And no, I'm not going down with the ship. Just making sure everyone is off.'

He lifted himself onto the quarterdeck and pointed to the line.

'Let her loose.'

The Leading-Hand deftly unravelled the rope and dropped it onto the foredeck. The gunboat wallowed and again thumped the side.

Armstrong turned to the bridge and waved a hand.

Thorburn acknowledged and turned to the pipe. 'Slow ahead both.'

Brackendale trembled to the turn of the props and began to move, and on the quarterdeck the crew of the Motor Gunboat stood and watched her final moments. She sank stern first, finally succumbing to the inrush of water.

Kendal gave her a fond salute, a casual touch to the peak of his cap. As the small destroyer moved away, all that remained on the surface were a few scraps of damaged wood and a lifebelt riding the waves.

Thorburn moved to the bank of pipes. 'Port twenty.'

The Cox'n gave the repeat and *Brackendale* turned out from the island and swung north.

'Half ahead. Make revolutions for twenty-five knots. Steer Oh-four-five degrees.'

'Speed twenty-five knots, steer oh-four-five degrees, aye aye, sir.'

Brackendale vibrated to the extra power and surged ahead. Thorburn cast a glance back over the stern expecting to see another E-boat following up. But the waves remained empty of enemy activity and he turned to face the bridge-screen.

'I need everyone on their toes,' he said loudly. 'The Germans are not done with us yet.'

Brackendale powered on, bow wave billowing back from her sharp stem. Spray curled over the screen and the cold wind blew colder.

Armstrong clambered up onto the bridge and reported.

'Lieutenants Wingham and Ratcliffe okay, sir. They lost three Raiders dead and have seven wounded. The Doc's treating two in the sick bay. We have two prisoners being looked after by the Bosun.'

The ship lifted and leaned, dipped and straightened. Hand holds were at a premium, knees bending to absorb the movement.

'And they managed to hit their targets?'

'I think so, yes.'

Thorburn nibbled at his bottom lip and then grinned. 'Be so good as to ask Lieutenant Wingham to join me on the bridge.'

'Sir,' Armstrong said and made for the ladder.

Down in the Petty Officer's Mess, the Bosun, accompanied by Able-Seaman Jack Mills, who'd been temporarily diverted from his duties at the depth charge rails, were keeping an armed vigil over the two prisoners. Under the Bosun's orders, the armoury had issued one Webley revolver and a handful of bullets.

The Bosun had not chosen Mills on a whim. He knew that Jack Mills had a reasonable understanding of German. Ordering him not to reveal his bilingual abilities to the German's but to listen and report anything useful, the Bosun plied them with hot drinks and cigarettes. It was a deliberate ploy to induce a relaxed atmosphere and see what transpired. It didn't take long for the Major to strike up an animated conversation with his subordinate, and Able Seaman Jack Mills listened with interest. For the rest of the trip home to Portland the Major, totally unaware of being eavesdropped in his own language, foolishly revealed much that was of vital importance to the Admiralty.

Jack leaned back against the bulkhead and busied himself by pretending to examine the pistol, feigning a total lack of interest in the Major's rambling's.

Armstrong made an announcement from the back of the bridge. 'Lieutenant Wingham, sir.'

Thorburn turned and offered his hand. 'Paul . . . , glad you made it.' In the same moment he spotted the dark patch on Wingham's collar. 'Is that blood? You okay?'

Wingham chuckled. 'Just a scratch. Your Doctor cleaned it up.'

'Good. Now . . . , how did it go?'

The ex Sherwood Forester smiled. 'I think one could say, mission accomplished. Ratcliffe is more than happy. What was originally thought to be wireless equipment turned out to be radar stuff. The second one was very new, in the experimental stage.'

'Ship! Bearing Red-one-twenty, sir.'

Thorburn and Armstrong grabbed binoculars and scanned the darkness.

'Guns-Bridge!'

Thorburn answered. 'Bridge.'

'It's *Cheriton*, sir.'

Armstrong lowered his glasses and smiled sheepishly. 'Better safe than sorry.'

'Very true,' Thorburn said, pleased that *Cheriton* had rejoined. At the very least they would enter harbour in good order. He turned back to Wingham.

'Thank you, Paul,' he said. 'I'll get a signal off to Captain (D). Let him know the outcome. Anything you wish to add?'

'No, not yet. There'll be a debrief soon enough.'

Thorburn nodded. 'Without a doubt. Right, I'll let you grab a bite to eat. I think the galley prepared some bully beef sandwiches.'

'Just the job,' Wingham said, gave a quick salute and made for the starboard ladder. Thorburn turned back to the screen and grasped the rail. Three hours from now and they'd all be safe inside the harbour.

CHAPTER SEVENTEEN .. CAST OFF

Manoeuvring *Brackendale* into Portland's harbour at night proved to be a lot more complex than when they'd arrived in daylight and Thorburn gave his full attention to negotiating the numerous moorings looming up out of the darkness. Easing cautiously through the breakwater he noted *Cheriton* clinging tightly to his stern rails and made a mental note to have a quiet word. Wouldn't take much to cause a collision.

'Port twenty!' he snapped as a moored armed trawler appeared directly in his path. At low revs, *Brackendale's* bows came slowly left.

Armstrong, who'd taken station up for'ard by the single Pompom called to the bridge. 'Midships!'

Thorburn passed the order to Falconer and *Brackendale* stopped her swing. He watched warily as the destroyer's stern, no longer pushing out to starboard on the turn, straightened and missed the trawler by a couple of yards. Bit close for comfort, he thought, and strained to see ahead for the quayside and the berth that had been nominated for *Brackendale's* arrival.

Armstrong called again. 'Starboard thirty!'

'Starboard thirty,' Thorburn repeated to the

wheelhouse.

Falconer acknowledged. 'Starboard thirty, aye, sir.'

Thorburn gripped the rail, apprehensive. The ship veered right and only then was he able to pick out the subdued shape of a harbour tug swinging gently to her mooring.

He shook his head. According to everything he'd heard, and everything he'd seen with his own eyes, Royal Navy losses were steadily mounting. In the Channel alone the numbers had exceeded forty for just the May and June of 1940. God knows what it had reached by now. But the shake of his head indicated conflicting thoughts. If Portland harbour was anything to go by there appeared to be not the slightest shortage of operational warships.

'Midships,' Armstrong called. And then after a short pause. 'Our berth is three points off the port bow.'

Thorburn looked that way and thought he could detect a vacancy along the granite wall.

'Very well,' he said. 'I have the ship.' To the voice-pipe he said,' Port twenty, slow ahead together.'

'Port twenty, slow ahead both. Aye aye, sir.'

'Steady . . . , steer one-two-five.'

'One-two-five, aye aye, sir.'

Brackendale eased towards the quay and down the ship's side an array of fenders were slung to protect against bumps and scratches.

He gauged the space between wall and ship. It would not do to have spent half the night overcoming enemy opposition only to end up denting *Brackendale's* side plates through bad seamanship.

'Stop starboard.'

The destroyer's bow closed on the wall, slowly. Fenders were shuffled along below the guardrail, judgements made as to the possible point of impact.

'Stop port.'

Brackendale drifted in and lines were thrown to be caught by those ashore and the eye of the cables were looped to the bollards, secured.

Thorburn pushed back his cap and rubbed his forehead. The worst was over.

'Captain, sir?' There was an urgency in the query.

He turned to find Able-Seaman Jack Mills standing rigidly to attention. He returned the man's smart salute.

'What is it, Mills?'

'The Bosun told me to report to you, sir.'

Completely in the dark, but assuming the Bosun thought it important, Thorburn went along with it. 'Go on.'

'I've been guarding the German prisoners, sir. After a while the officer started talking to the soldier. We didn't let on I could speak German, sir, and that officer talked pretty freely. When I told the Bosun he said I was to tell you straight away, sir.'

Thorburn inhaled slowly. 'Tell me what, exactly?'

Mills glanced around the still crowded bridge. 'Not sure I should say, sir.'

Thorburn quickly grasped the situation. What Mills had to say was important and he thought it confidential enough that he didn't want to blurt it out in front of everybody.

'Mister Martin,' he said, 'I'll be in my cabin. Ask the First Lieutenant to disembark the Raiders, wounded first. And leave the prisoners until I give the word.'

'Aye aye, sir.'

Thorburn looked at Mills. 'Right, young man, with me,' he said, and with that he made for the Captain's cabin.

As the feeble winter sun of a new day spread its pale light across Portland harbour, H.M.S. *Vibrant*, the five-thousand ton light cruiser moored out near the northern breakwater, stirred into life. The ship's commander, Captain Gerald Fitzpatrick R.N., O.B.E., had risen early, as was his custom and now sat at his desk reading yesterdays newspaper headlines. Cigarette smoke spiralled towards an open scuttle and he absentmindedly stirred his tea. His steward had gathered the discarded newspapers from the wardroom before the break of day, then tidied them together before stacking them neatly on his desk.

Fitzpatrick grunted as he read an article and sipped tea. He appeared somewhat older than his years and the thinning grey hair had long since receded from his temples. The deep set eyes and prominent nose gave his weathered features a hawk like appearance, enhanced by the permanently deep set wrinkles across his forehead. The rows of colourful medal ribbons displayed on his left breast bore witness to a distinguished career in the service of King and country. He turned another page, smiling as he did so. It amused Fitzpatrick to compare the previous day's headlines with what actually transpired during the following hours.

A loud knock on the door broke his concentration.

'Come in!' he said, and folded the paper to one side.

A wireless room messenger stepped in holding a pink slip. 'Signal, sir.'

'Give,' said the Captain holding out a hand. He straightened out the fold and read through, frowning, the lines in his forehead becoming ever more pronounced. As he finished reading he took a deep breath.

'Very well. Tell them to acknowledge.'

'Aye aye, sir,' the man answered and backed out of the cabin.

Fitzpatrick rubbed his jaw and stubbed out the cigarette. The frown changed to a smile and the deep set eyes found a scuttle and the view it gave across the harbour. If he'd read that signal correctly *Vibrant* might soon be putting to sea. Action imminent.

Richard Thorburn came awake to an insistent call from his Steward. As he opened his eyes sunlight flooded the cabin and he squinted against the brightness.

'Ten o'clock, sir. Tea's ready.'

'Alright, thank you Sinclair, I'm awake.' He swung his legs out of the bunk and sat up, blinking. His eyes felt raw, heavy, but he forced himself to his feet, shrugged into a dressing gown and padded out into the day cabin. His pack of Senior Service sat next to a steaming mug of tea. He selected a cigarette, lit it and drew a lungful of smoke, held it, and then slowly exhaled. A hazy cloud of blue drifted and he slumped into a chair.

Sinclair diplomatically cleared his throat. 'Excuse me, sir, but the First Lieutenant asked if he could see you? He said it was important.'

Thorburn managed a tired grin. 'Well,' he said, 'being as you've let me sleep for half the day, I expect it is urgent.'

'But, sir, I only followed your orders. You said to call you at ten . . . .'

'Yes, yes . . . , I know. My fault entirely.' He gave him a sideways glance accompanied with a wide grin. 'Just don't do it again. Now, the First

Lieutenant, you'd better tell him I'm awake.'

Sinclair bobbed up and down. 'Of course, sir, yes, sir, immediately, sir.' And he scurried off to find Armstrong.

Thorburn felt the stubble on his jaw and his thoughts returned to the previous night's events. And, more pertinently, the talk with Able Seaman Mills. When Mills had passed on all that he'd heard spoken between the German Major and the other prisoner, Thorburn thanked him and suggested he get some sleep. In the meantime he got Doc Waverley to code up an urgent message and had it sent through to Portland's Officer-in-Command, detailing the main points of that conversation. Only when the message had been properly acknowledged did he retire to his bunk.

The bang on his door was followed by Armstrong almost jumping into the cabin. 'Sir,' he began, out of breath. 'You are requested to attend a meeting with a Captain Fitzpatrick aboard *Vibrant* at 13.00 hours.'

'Right,' Thorburn said, amused at seeing his First Lieutenant so flustered. 'Plenty of time. It's only just gone ten.'

'Yes, sir, but there's an Admiral Tennant giving the briefing.'

Thorburn came to his feet. 'Is there indeed. In that case it'll be best bib and tucker.'

'And there's a Fleet destroyer, *Kingfisher* I think. She's been summoned. *Cheriton* too.'

Thorburn eyed Armstrong and nodded thoughtfully. 'That makes four all told. Cruiser, destroyer and two Hunts. Something's in the wind, that's for sure.'

At ten minutes to one o'clock, Thorburn stepped off *Brackendale's* motor boat and onto *Vibrant's* companionway. A minute later he was greeted by the cruiser's First Lieutenant and escorted along to the Captain's cabin. Ushered inside he found *Cheriton's* Charles Rutherford already seated and took the chair next to him. A minute to 13.00 hours, *Kingfisher's* Captain entered and sat, and they waited.

At precisely one o'clock an officer wearing the insignia of a Vice-Admiral, closely followed by a Royal Navy Captain, both entered and took their places either end of the large desk.

Vice-Admiral Sir John Tennant, R.N., K.C.B., C.B.E., moved to stand with his hands thrust deep inside his jacket pockets and cast a thoughtful eye over the small group of assembled officers. Normally a resident of Devonport, a long phone call to the War Office had brought him here to the Captain's cabin aboard H.M.S. *Vibrant*.

'Gentlemen,' he began. 'What I am about to say is classified. May I remind you that any further discussions should only take place with those cleared to the appropriate level.' He hesitated before continuing, his keen eyes exploring each face in turn.

'Over a month ago our embassy in Montevideo reported that an old freighter called the *Castillo de Maria* had sailed from the port of Buenos Aries, destination unknown. Although extensive enquiries were made at the time, the ship's cargo remained a mystery. That in itself piqued our curiosity. Any ship's manifesto departing Buenos Aries was normally discovered prior to sailing.' He tapped his fingers on the desk. 'Nothing more had been heard of her until last night.' He straightened in the chair and then leaned forward on his elbows.

'Last night, gentlemen, as some of you are well aware, a raiding party landed on Alderney and information was obtained identifying that same merchantman as having called in at the Spanish port of Cadiz. She has since departed for the Bay of Biscay en route to Cherbourg. According to that information we now understand that the freighter's cargo includes a large payment in gold and an industrial shipment of tungsten.'

Sir John broke off and waved an expansive hand in the general direction of London. 'Churchill has agreed that an attempt must be made to intercept the *Maria* and confiscate her cargo. Accordingly in approximately six hours His Majesty's light cruiser *Vibrant* will depart Weymouth and take passage for the waters west of Guernsey. Her close escort will be the Fleet destroyer *Kingfisher* accompanied by *Brackendale* and *Cheriton*. The 'Hunts' will assist in screening *Vibrant*. That'll give all parties enough time to reach the designated area and hopefully make a timely interception.'

'Bearing in mind the importance of the *Maria's* cargo, it has to be assumed the Germans will make every effort to escort her into a safe anchorage. Above all our objective is to prevent that ship from breaking the blockade.' He paused to take a breath and turned to Fitzpatrick.

'You wish to add anything, Gerald?'

Fitzpatrick rubbed his jaw, head tilted in thought. 'Only this,' he said. 'We have been selected at short notice and given little time to familiarise ourselves with the organisation of such a newly formed flotilla. Nonetheless, gentlemen, I expect us all to perform our duties as befits every captain that commands one of His Majesty's warships. Needless to say, although we may be at somewhat of a disadvantage in not knowing exactly where the *Castillo de Maria* will be, I am sure that when the opportunity arises, we will execute our orders with both integrity and honour.'

Thorburn grimaced and thought what a pompous bastard Captain Fitzpatrick was. He stole a glance at Rutherford but found no sign of derision on the man's face and suspected it might be only his personal take on the Captain's idea of a pep talk.

The Admiral continued. 'That, gentlemen, is

the current picture. I leave it with you to organise the relevant signals and ensure all parties are aware of their duties.' Sir John eyed each of them in turn. 'You can take it as read that I will personally discuss the pros and cons of this mission with Captain Fitzpatrick and hopefully, by the time we're done, we'll have covered most situations that might crop up.' He looked at his watch. 'Any questions?' He paused. 'No, . . . , then I'll let you get back to your ships. I'm sure you have much to do.'

It was late afternoon when *Brackendale* cast off and turned out from the quayside to head for the Breakwater Fort. A keen east wind tugged the halyards, cold, and men shrugged deeper inside their waterproofs. Thorburn stood in his customary spot at the bridge-screen, chin tucked into the roll neck jumper and his sea going cap pulled hard down over his eyes. Other than the sighing of the wind, only Lieutenant Martin's terse orders to the wheelhouse disturbed the quiet.

Standing at Thorburn's shoulder, Armstrong concentrated on watching the harbour's assorted shipping swing by and turned to look aft beyond the taff rail. *Cheriton* held station two cables length astern, a trace of smoke from her funnel. He swung back to peer ahead and just managed to catch *Kingfisher* commencing a turn round the end of the breakwater.

And so the three destroyers slipped silently out into the open waters of the English Channel, and well astern, faintly seen against the outline of Weymouth town, H.M.S. *Vibrant* rang up 'slow ahead' and ventured out in the wake of her escorts. Once level with the lighthouse at Portland Bill, *Kingfisher* made a slight alteration of course and headed southwest for the waters north of Cherbourg. Destination, a pencilled point of longitude and latitude on a chart covering the sea west of Guernsey.

On the high, wide bridge of the *Castillo de Maria,* Capitán Carlos Menéndez moved to the chart table and for the third time in an hour swivelled his dividers along the length of plot. He frowned at the ship's estimated position and shook his head in annoyance. Leaning both hands on the table, he puffed out his cheeks in exasperation. The *Maria* was capable of ten knots but from the outset the weather had been against them and by his reckoning they'd achieved no more than seven. Now with daylight fading he walked to the front of the bridge and looked up at the looming clouds. Heavy, dull, a permanent canopy of grey that gave his navigator no chance of fixing their position. And whatever distance they'd covered, there was a marked chill in the air. It smelt of the north, fresh. It was a damp smell that was different to that of Spain, or even in his home port of San Pedro back in Argentina.

Menéndez smiled at the thought. His family lived in a ranch-style house with a roof of orange tiles, and gently arched adobe walls that overlooked a garden full of exotic flowers. It sat on the banks of the Paraná River, a broad, gently flowing body of water that meandered lazily south to Buenos Aries and the mouth of the River Plate. It would probably be hot now, hot enough for siestas at midday, and the children always argued that they wanted to play.

And his beautiful wife Sofia would wag her finger and gently admonish them before frowning and pointing to their rooms. Yes, he thought, the sun would be shining from a blue sky, flowers in full bloom, fish rising in the river, and none of it would smell anything like this damp, cold, miserable air of the north. Carlos Menéndez moved back to the chart and rubbed his chin. He would hold this course for another six hours. If after that time the weather had not cleared enough for a sighting of the stars he could always turn east and look for land. Dangerous, but if necessary . . . .

He ambled over to the starboard wing and peered out through the rain streaked glass. Somewhere over there was France. After a long moment he turned and walked the length of his wide bridge. Beyond the port side plating he stared out an empty expanse of Atlantic Ocean and sighed. Those that had chartered his ship had paid well, a small fortune, and rightly so for the risks he was taking. And the nine members of his crew were also being well rewarded, although they were not aware of the contents of the many packing cases.

He thought again of Sofia. She knew where the money was kept. In the event he did not make it back to San Pedro then she was at liberty to use the money as she saw fit. With care it would last a lifetime, and the beautiful Sofia had a good brain when it came to money. And Sofia had a sister, the lovely Ingrid, who had married a German officer, an attaché at the Embassy. He was well thought of by Hitler's hierarchy and had been promised a promotion. Sofia and the children would always be welcome in Ingrid's home. He smiled again. He had seen to it that his family were well provided for. Now all that mattered was his ability to return from this journey and help them enjoy the proceeds.

A faint pale yellow glow brightened a cloud above the horizon and he studied it with care. His navigating officer might well take advantage if the clouds cleared and the moon appeared overhead. He moved back to the bridge-chair, nodded to the man on the wheel, and called for his First Officer.

Ricardo Francella came hurrying on to the bridge, a velvet lined box in his hands. He smiled at Menéndez, placed the box on the chart table, and after carefully undoing the clasp, reverently removed the brass sextant.

'I guessed, my *Capitán,* that you hoped for a sighting, that I might manage to fix our position. Is that not so, *Capitán?*'

Menéndez nodded slowly. He and Francella had been together for six years and he had high regard for the little man's skill as "Pilot" for the *Castillo de Maria.*

'That is correct, my friend. You might soon see the moon and stars. Maybe, it will be enough.'

Ricardo Francella bobbed his head and stepped forward to the screen. A glance at the scudding clouds and he made for the starboard wing. Outside in the cold he turned up the collar of his leather jacket and waited.

Menéndez contented himself in the knowledge that his First Officer was an expert in all things navigational and that patience would always be rewarded.

As the old freighter pushed ever onwards, he took a deep breath and, like Francella, he chose to wait.

Unbeknown to either Menéndez or his navigator, four-thousand metres off the ship's starboard quarter a U-boat tracked their every move. It had been their constant companion since leaving Cadiz and once again the U-boat's commander ordered the periscope raised for a precautionary check on progress.

Satisfied that they were holding station as required, and nothing untoward had happened to their charge, the periscope was withdrawn and the U-boat descended to a precautionary depth of twenty metres. In thirty minutes the ritual would be repeated and then with night time firmly established, and with no more risk of aerial observation, he could surface the boat, recharge the batteries and continue monitoring the old rust bucket at his leisure.

There was little glory to be had in escorting one old merchantman, but the U-boat's commander understood that it was the Fuhrer himself who had ordered this mission. The ship's safe arrival was of paramount importance and as such the commander required all hands to be extra attentive to their duties until a surface escort arrived to take over.

Only then could the boat return to the far Atlantic in search of unsuspecting convoys. Much glory was to be had in increasing tonnage sunk while on offensive patrol. U-boats were for hunting and killing, thinning out the sheep, starving Great Britain into submission. Reluctantly he returned to his cabin and sank onto his bunk. For now he must rein in his eagerness to take on the convoys. In the meantime the hourly routine would continue until U-113 reached the required zone for release or received fresh orders.

CHAPTER EIGHTEEN . .
THE ROAR OF GUNS

Thorburn stood at the fore-bridge and raised his old Barr and Stroud binoculars. The sun had long gone, only the faint residual of grey remaining on the western horizon. It was a moment that every watchkeeper on board a ship recognises. He smiled. Most landlubbers would never understand what true significance it held. That first, faint alteration from daytime light to the slow withdrawal of the horizon marks the instant a lookout curses the coming night and prays for the beginning of another day.

'Time?' he asked.

Armstrong was Officer-of-the-Watch. 'Six-twenty, sir.'

Glasses firmly locked to his eyes, Thorburn mumbled. 'Thank you, Number One.' Seeing nothing silhouetted against that darkening sky he lowered the glasses and glanced to starboard. Two miles away and vaguely seen in the all encompassing gloom, *Vibrant* pushed on, her bow wave glinting white as it broke to swirl alongside. A mile ahead, *Cheriton* zig-zagged her way south, only visible because he knew she was there and he expected to see the evidence. As for *Kingfisher*, she held station well to starboard of the cruiser, her outline sharply drawn against the dim light of the western horizon.

He let the binoculars hang and jammed his hands into the pockets of his duffle coat. The wind had picked up from the north, strong enough to blow waves into flying foam. *Brackendale*, as per Captain Horton's last order, was making fifteen-knots and zig-zagging off the cruiser's port beam. *Vibrant* herself was going through a number of random course alterations as her own answer to submarine avoidance.

Thorburn again turned his gaze to the east and even in that short space of time, the horizon had disappeared, black sky melting into the dark sea. He leaned forward to look down on the forward gun mount, the twin four-inch barrels now barely visible. The guns' crew were stood to at Action Stations as were the rest of the ship's company, a necessary precaution as night descended.

'Starboard five,' Martin said to the pipe, and *Brackendale* altered towards *Vibrant*, commencing the next leg of the zigzag.

'Midships . . . , steer two-two-oh degrees.'

The repeat sounded faintly from below. 'Steer two-two-oh degrees, aye aye, sir.'

Thorburn suppressed a smile. It all sounded like a routine exercise. The helm order given, the repeated acknowledgement echoing up the pipe, the faint ring of the telegraph, all so familiar. But turning *Brackendale* onto what was effectively a collision course with a Royal Navy cruiser, was not an ideal situation. Particularly during the hunt for a blockade runner.

'*Kingfisher* signalling, sir.' The report was followed by the clatter of an Aldis lamp acknowledging.

Thorburn raised his glasses beyond the cruiser's bow and found *Kingfisher's* lamp blinking.

'What's she saying, Yeoman?'

'Message reads, "take station for anti-submarine screen." Message ends, sir.'

'Very well,' Thorburn said. 'You heard that, Pilot?'

'Yes, sir,' Martin said, and leaned to the wheelhouse pipe. 'Half ahead, make revolutions for twelve knots.'

Brackendale slowed.

'Port five, steer one-nine-five degrees.'

The Cox'n confirmed. 'Port five, one-nine-five degrees, aye aye, sir.'

Thorburn caught Armstrong's eye. 'Let's have Asdic on the bridge repeater, Number One.'

Armstrong nodded and moved to the speaker. A moment later the solid 'ping' of the underwater transponder echoed round the bridge, the rhythmic electronic pulse hunting beneath the waves.

Thorburn moved to his bridge-chair and jammed his boot against the pipe bracket. 'So, Number One, from where do we think the *Maria* will appear,?'

'Near the coast I shouldn't wonder. Makes more sense to me. What I don't understand is if the Germans occupy all the French ports , why on earth risk the longer trip to Cherbourg?'

'Agreed,' Thorburn said. 'I was wondering that myself. Might be the railways are damaged, but not from Cherbourg.'

'Or the gold,' Armstrong added. 'Extra security.'

'Port five!' Martin ordered sharply, an edge to his voice.

Thorburn looked round in response and saw that the cruiser had altered course towards *Brackendale,* and erring on the side of caution Martin reacted by turning away.

Thorburn rose from the chair and took a pace closer to the screen. Fists planted on his hips he studied the relationship between the cruiser, *Kingfisher's* position off the cruiser's starboard bow, and *Cheriton* pushing on ahead of them all. He thought *Vibrant* had probably made her turn unnecessarily more severe than need be and therefore put *Brackendale* into an awkward situation. At the same time he recognised the cruiser's right to manoeuvre as she saw fit. A capitol ship always took precedence.

'Give us another five degrees, if you will Pilot. 'Let's keep well out of the way.'

Martin nodded. 'Aye aye, sir,' and he leaned to the pipe. *Brackendale* answered Falconer's input to the helm and eased further out to port.

Thorburn eyed the distance achieved and nodded his satisfaction. 'Steady on that, Pilot. Should keep us out of trouble.'

In the last of the fast fading light he spotted a few grins from around the bridge before the watch settled back into its routine, the singular, persistent 'ping' of the Asdic a constant reminder as to the reason why.

The officer in charge of the escorting U-boat had satisfied himself that the *Castillo de Maria*, now almost under the cloak of darkness, could be left to continue her solitary passage until met by the escorting flotilla. The same night time conditions allowed U-113 to surface, increase speed to sixteen-knots and allow himself and his crew that exhilarating feeling of totally unhindered movement. Not yet twenty-two, Kapitänleutnant Konrad Drexler was the epitome of Nazi perfection. He was handsome, fair haired and viewed the world through a striking pair of vivid blue eyes. He was also the youngest son of the much heralded, now retired, Admiral Heinrich Alexander Drexler.

It had been during what became known as the Battle of Jutland, on the 31st of May 1916, that Konrad's then youthful father, Korvettenkapitän Heinrich Drexler led by example in taking his outgunned destroyer to head off a Royal Navy Flotilla of destroyers. His almost suicidal attack was later acknowledged to be a major influence on how the German fleet of Battlecruisers executed a tactical manoeuvre that initially forced the Royal Navy to retreat.

For the young Konrad that weight of expectation was a lot to live up to but he felt certain a career of equal measure awaited him. Admiral Karl Dönitz had personally introduced him to the Fuhrer at a Nazi Party rally and the great man had shaken his hand while congratulating him on being given command of U-113.

And in the meantime, as dusk settled over the Bay of Biscay, his boat had executed its latest mission with complete success. The least he could expect from such an important mission was a favourable report and another rung on the ladder towards promotion. It was surely only a matter of time. He stretched, yawned, and turned up the collar of his jacket. The chill air made a man appreciate the warmth of the control room.

The first hint of rain spattered the bridge and Drexler took a final glance round the platform.

'Stay sharp, my friends. Stay sharp,' and with that he lowered himself through the hatch in search of the warmth below.

Beyond the horizon towards Cherbourg, five German warships were at that very moment pushing south at high speed. A signal from the *Castillo de Maria's* U-boat escort had informed

Kriegsmarine headquarters that the "special cargo" was now two-hundred kilometres from port.

Leading the flotilla, Korvettenkapitän Wolfgang Herzog, tasked with bringing the ship to the sanctuary of German waters, stood at the back of the *Puma's* bridge and as darkness came, watched the other four ships powering ahead in line astern. With flags snapping tautly at mast heads, bow waves flying high, he felt an overwhelming pride in commanding such an important mission. It was rumoured the Fuhrer was personally involved, awaiting the outcome. It would not do to fail. He lifted his glasses and focussed on the last in line, a Narvik. And the next nearest, also a Narvik. Both vessels were well armed and fast. Then there were the two Type 23's. They were named after 'Birds of Prey', and each carried six torpedoes in two triple-mounts. At over 900 tons and both armed with three 105 mm guns, *Hawk* and *Buzzard* could be relied on for aggressive action if required.

Herzog turned and moved back to the bridge screen. The last light of the western horizon faded and darkness prevailed. Then a crescent moon made an appearance between scudding clouds, with enough light to give his lookouts fair warning of any unusual sightings. In a few short hours he would rendezvous with the *Castillo de Maria,* and under express orders to stay well clear of the French coast, he would swing north for Cherbourg. It had been emphasised on numerous briefings that there must be no possibility of a French coastal watcher reporting the passage of a well escorted cargo ship.

Korvettenkapitän Wolfgang Herzog nodded his approval. With the U-boat's last reported position as their guide, a well armed German flotilla pushed on towards an old tramp steamer and a very important cargo.

Richard Thorburn sat at the desk and made an entry into the Captain's log. It was routine, and similar to whatever the Officer-of-the-Watch had written. He closed the book, stretched, and glanced at the time. Two hours since sunset. He considered going back up to the bridge but then the lookouts would only feel the extra burden of their skipper's eyes watching their every move. And the reality of course is that the Captain should be conserving his strength for when most needed, not unnecessarily interfering with the watchkeepers.

There was a knock on the door.

'Come,' he called.

Armstrong stuck his head in. 'Got a minute, sir?'

'Of course, Bob. What's up?'

The First Officer closed the door with a quiet click and turned to hover, shifting his weight.

'Sit,' Thorburn urged, waving his hand at a

chair.

Armstrong hoisted the chair out and folded his long frame onto the seat. He looked down and twisted his cap between his fingers before meeting Thorburn's eyes.

'It's Doc Waverly, sir,' he began, sounding almost apologetic.

'Go on.'

'Well you suggested early on that the wireless room make use of him for decoding the signals.'

Thorburn grinned. 'And I gather he's very good at it.'

Armstrong smiled and nodded. 'Yes, by all accounts, he's quick and accurate. Petty Officer Langsdale is suitably impressed.'

Thorburn frowned. 'So what's the problem?'

The eyes went down, another twist of the cap, and Armstrong cleared his throat.

'It's just that he's taken to spending more and more time in the W/T office. The Telegraphists have rightly complained that it's a distraction. There isn't much spare room in there and they feel awkward with him sat behind.'

'I see,' Thorburn said slowly. 'So you want me to have a word?'

'It'd be better coming from you, sir. I know if I mentioned it, he'd be his usual affable self but in this particular case I thought it should be you.'

Thorburn chuckled. 'You mean, because I suggested it in the first place it's down to me to rectify the matter.'

'Something like that, yes sir.'

'All right, Number One. Get me the Signal and W/T Logs . . . , and I'd better have a gander at the Cypher Logs while I'm at it. Then you can leave it with me. Anything else?'

Armstrong straightened in the chair, a look of relief on his face. 'No, sir, nothing else. That's all.'

Thorburn stood. 'Good . . . . Now if you'd like to ask the Doctor to attend me in my cabin in say,' he glanced at his watch, 'fifteen minutes, that would be splendid.'

Armstrong came to his feet and lost the look of relief. 'Now, sir? You want me to ask him now?'

A slow smile returned to Thorburn's face. 'I think that would be wise considering the current situation. No time like the present, eh?'

Armstrong tilted his head slightly, narrowed his eyes, and gave his Captain a broad grin of understanding. 'So, I might not be the one to give him the bad news but . . . ,' and the grin faded. It dawned on him that he could not fully escape the blame. 'Right, sir. I'll send him in.' And with that he turned away, stepped out and pulled the door shut.

Thorburn reached for a cigarette, applied the flame of a matchstick and blew smoke. He thought it would be interesting to see Doc Waverly's reaction and smiled at the prospect.

There was a clatter of feet overhead and a short barked command, and quiet returned. *Brackendale* rolled to a long swell and he felt the ship slide over a crest before regaining her equilibrium. He took another lungful of smoke and waited. The good doctor would be along soon enough.

The thunderous roar of heavy gunfire rolled across the sea and at that exact moment the alarm shrilled for Action Stations. Running boots and muffled shouts sounded along the decks and watertight doors slammed into place. Thorburn grabbed for his duffle coat, banged his cap on and slipped the old Barr and Stroud binoculars round his neck. In seconds he was at the foot of the starboard ladder and headed for the bridge. Stepping on to the back of the platform he shrugged into the duffle coat and moved toward the compass platform. From the wheelhouse pipe he heard Falconer report.

'Cox'n at the wheel, sir. Course one-seven-oh.'

And a bulkhead pipe, 'Depth charge crew closed up, sir.'

Armstrong reported. 'It's *Vibrant*, sir. Opened fire without warning.'

Thorburn lifted a handset. 'Guns?'

'Sir?'

'What have we got?'

'Faint red glow to the south beyond the horizon. Off the port bow, sir.'

'Captain, sir! Signal from *Kingfisher*.'

Thorburn turned to a wireless operator, a slip being offered. The darkness made it difficult.

'What does it say?'

'German flotilla at one-seven-five degrees, range twelve miles. Prepare to engage. That's it, sir.'

'Very well,' Thorburn said, stepped onto the compass platform and levelled his glasses at the horizon. He found a fluctuating pulse of red, nothing more.

Again the roar from the cruiser's six inch guns reverberated across the water, her 'A' and 'B' turrets hurling shells out beyond *Brackendale's* horizon.

'Guns-Bridge!'

Thorburn leaned to the pipe. 'Bridge.'

'German destroyers. Two, possibly more.'

Armstrong grabbed his arm. 'Sir! *Vibrant!*' He jabbed a finger at the cruiser.

Thorburn peered through the darkness and found the warship powering ahead, her bow wave rising in drifts. She was heading directly for the red tinge on the horizon.

'*Kingfisher* signalling, sir!' The call came from the Yeoman on the starboard lamp.

'Read it!' Thorburn snapped.

The small hand lamp glittered, and Thorburn caught the minimal flicker of a shaded lamp shining from *Kingfisher's* bridge.

'Message reads, "Support *Vibrant*. . . . Attacking." Message ends, sir.'

'Very well, acknowledge.'

Armstrong moved closer. 'What about the

Maria? With all this commotion she'll be looking to scarper.'

'Unless she's already with that flotilla,' Thorburn offered, wondering whether he believed what he was saying.

'*Vibrant* is leaving us in her wake,' Armstrong warned.

Thorburn frowned and bent to the wheelhouse pipe. If he was to follow *Kingfisher's* orders he needed to hold station. 'Make revolutions for twenty-five knots!' he snapped.

Falconer acknowledged, loud up the pipe.

'Speed twenty-five! Aye aye, sir!'

The telegraph rang faintly and within a minute *Brackendale* lifted her prow. Thorburn felt the power of the engines through his feet, relishing the small destroyer's turn of speed.

The bridge repeater for the Asdic became a garbled mess, no longer able to transmit clearly, the noise of *Brackendale's* speed churning the water disrupting the signal.

'Turn that damned thing off,' Thorburn said, pointing to the speaker.

Brackendale twisted to a wave, thumping long rollers. Men braced against the motion, struggling for purchase where none existed, toes locked inside their sea boots. For the most part, those on the bridge faced the elements as they always did, silent and wary, always on the alert for the next unexpected wave. On the gun mounts, those on the fo'c'sle fared better than many of the other crews, sheltered to some extent by the curvature of the shield. The midship Pompom crew, standing on the exposed position above the galley housing, fared the worst. What little protection was afforded by the shrapnel casement left them wet, cold and hunched away from the windswept spray.

For the quarterdeck gunners the galley housing offered some protection from the wind, but with the guns facing astern, the weather none the less funnelled inside the turret.

At the bridge-screen, Thorburn watched *Vibrant* with a frown. She appeared to be moving at top speed, drawing away from *Brackendale*, the gap between ships increasing. He leaned to the wheelhouse pipe.

'What's our speed, Cox'n?'

'Twenty-six knots, sir.'

'Very well,' Thorburn said, the frown deepening. If *Vibrant* continued on at that rate then with that sort of speed differential between them *Brackendale* would be left floundering in her wake.

'We'll be hard pushed to hang on to her coat tails, Number One.'

'Yes, sir,' Armstrong agreed.

Thorburn rubbed his jaw. 'Did you see *Cheriton*?'

'Once possibly. Thought I saw her outlined against the red glow.'

Brackendale buried her bows into the flank of

a wave and staggered, the sheer weight of water enough to impede her progress. She came up slowly, gallons of seawater sluicing down her gunwales.

Thorburn made up his mind. 'Right, Number One, we've no option but to join the attack.' He raised his voice. 'You lookouts watch out for torpedoes. Those buggers have a nasty habit of firing off all they've got before disappearing into the distance.' He bent to a bulkhead pipe.

'Guns?'

'Guns here.'

'Keep me informed. Can't see much from down here.'

'Aye aye, sir.'

Thorburn took a deep breath and raised his glasses at *Vibrant*. She was two miles distant now, a shadow with a milky bow-wave. He saw her begin to veer off to starboard and vaguely caught the swing of her six-inch guns coming round to port. Her four-inch followed, lifting to a forty-five degree angle.

A movement well beyond her bows caught his attention. It was *Kingfisher* and there could be no doubting her intentions. His binoculars showed a rampant destroyer making all of forty-knots and throwing up a magnificent plume of spray. Her guns were ranged at maximum elevation and she was riding the waves with great determination.

He brought the Bar and Stroud glasses round

to search beyond *Brackendale's* bow but the small destroyer's winding pitch defeated him. He let them hang on his chest, squinting into the cold.

'Guns-Bridge!'

'Captain.'

'Difficult to be sure but it appears to be three German destroyers and a couple of Narviks. Best estimate is a southerly heading at about forty knots, sir. One of the Narviks is on fire amidships but they seem to be getting it under control.'

'Thank you, Guns. Keep me posted.'

'Aye aye, sir.'

'Number One!'

'Sir?'

'All stations manned?'

'They are.'

'Good.' He pointed at the bows. 'Who's that on the bow-chaser?'

'Leading Seaman Kennedy, sir. A volunteer off the midships crew. "Guns" rates him very highly.'

'Does he indeed? Let's hope he's right. Takes a lot of guts to stand up there under fire.'

Vibrant let rip from her forward turrets, the flash robbing Thorburn of what little night vision he'd acquired. The roar of the six-inch guns followed, deafening. He leaned to a pipe. 'What's the firing range, Guns?'

'More than we've got, sir. Twelve miles.'

'Right.' He thought for a moment. 'Any sign of that freighter?'

'No, and we've been looking.'

Thorburn grinned. There was a hint of disgruntlement in Carling's voice, as if to say there wasn't any need to ask.

'Very well,' he said. 'If you get a chance at the destroyers open fire when ready.'

'Open fire when ready. Aye aye, sir.'

And then *Kingfisher*, moving at an angle to port, let go with a full broadside; all of her 4.7-inch guns.

Thorburn lifted the glasses and this time he found the enemy and a number of splashes as shells rained down amongst them.

'Guns-Bridge!'

'Go ahead,' Thorburn answered.

'I think I can reach them now,' Carling said.

A large wave slapped *Brackendale* on the port plates. She slewed to starboard before answering the helm, and then clawed her way back on course.

'All yours Guns.'

There was a moment of hesitation and then the fo'c'sle guns thundered out a first salvo. A pair of four-inch shells arced high across the intervening gap . . . , and plunged, to miss short. Thorburn worried his bottom lip. At least they were having a go. Maybe *Brackendale* was on the down roll when the fire button was pressed. Four seconds later the guns barked again, another pair of shells on their way. The acrid whiff of cordite enveloped the bridge, stinging the eyes and throat. He coughed, choking on the evil taste. But now, along with *Vibrant*, *Kingfisher* and *Cheriton*, *Brackendale* too was dishing it out.

'Bloody marvellous,' Thorburn managed between coughs, and gripped the wooden chair back. 'Bloody marvellous.' They were committed to a course of action and it suited him well. What he had not seen, try as he might, was any evidence of the *Castillo De Maria* in company with the German destroyers. And the speed with which they now turned tail and fled certainly showed him no signs of them escorting a freighter.

A mile or so beyond the starboard bow, *Kingfisher* powered on, her guns permanently engaged in trying to bring the enemy to heel. To *Brackendale's* port side, Rutherford's *Cheriton* was doing her level best to even the odds. Her main armament had found the range but Thorburn could see no hits.

Armstrong shouted, pointing over the starboard side. 'That destroyer! Where's it going?'

Thorburn jammed the binoculars to his eyes and managed to briefly hold the German in focus. It was almost on the horizon, definitely moving at high speed and quickly fading into the darkness. *Kingfisher* swept through his field of vision, crossing *Brackendale's* path from right to left, chasing hard after the main flotilla. A ripple of gunfire sparkled from the stern of the German ships. *Cheriton* and *Kingfisher* replied, unleashing salvoes in reply.

Brackendale's guns also crashed out a salvo, but Thorburn was more concerned with that destroyer heading south. He looked at *Kingfisher*, debating whether to inform her of his intentions. Her Captain was busy, might not appreciate the significance of one German warship detaching itself from the battle. No, he would act on his own initiative.

'Starboard twenty!' he called to the wheelhouse.

'Starboard twenty, aye sir.'

Brackendale canted on the turn, the port rail partially submerged.

'Midships . . . , steady . . . . Steer one-seven-five degrees.'

'One-seven-five degrees, aye aye, sir.'

The small destroyer swayed upright and settled to her new course. Well astern a fresh starshell burst beneath the scudding clouds, and more gunfire echoed across the water. But for *Brackendale* darkness enveloped the ship and Thorburn paced the forebridge. He knew that in reality he was actually at a major disadvantage. The German destroyer had a much greater turn of speed than his own. It might be capable of forty-knots whereas *Brackendale* might manage twenty-seven, and he allowed himself a faint grin . . . , if it was downhill and with a good following wind.

What he was banking on was that the German

was making for the freighter. Once the destroyer became her close escort its speed would be more or less governed by the old steamer. And if the *Castillo de Maria* truly carried such an important cargo then her escort would be compelled to stay close. Defend to the bitter end.

Thorburn turned to the shadowy presence of Armstrong in the bridge-wing. 'Number One.'

'Sir?' Armstrong said, stepping closer.

Thorburn peered out beyond the fo'c'sle. 'I'm working on the assumption that this German will lead us to the freighter. Quite what happens when we all meet up I'm not sure. That's if we don't lose him in the meantime. Probably play it by ear, just let the pieces fall where they will.'

Armstrong didn't reply and Thorburn shot him a sideways glance. The darkness revealed little, only the glint of an eye.

'There is another possibility, sir.'

'Go on.'

'The freighter might already have an escort and we're on a wild goose chase.'

Thorburn breathed in, exasperated. As always Armstrong was correct and it was something he hadn't considered.

'In that case, Number One, I'll endeavour to slow their passage.'

'What about *Vibrant*, sir?'

Thorburn cleared his throat. 'When we find the *Maria* we'll signal her position. Wait for *Vibrant*.'

Armstrong raised his binoculars. 'I hope 'Guns' has that Jerry in sight. I've lost him.'

Thorburn leaned to the pipe. 'Guns . . . , are we still in contact with that destroyer?'

'Yes, sir. Fine on the starboard bow, five-thousand yards. But not for much longer. We're at least ten knots slower.'

'Very well,' Thorburn said. 'What's our heading, Pilot?'

'One-eight-five, sir.'

'The same as our target?'

'Yes, sir, the last I saw.'

Thorburn rubbed his forehead in frustration. Give or take, they were heading south and all he could do was plough on in the hope of discovering a rendezvous.

'What's our speed?'

'Twenty-seven knots, sir.'

Thorburn grimaced in the darkness. The Chief would be frothing at the mouth. If *Brackendale* had any chance of keeping up with her quarry it might well warrant bursting the boilers, but the reality said otherwise. He sighed and succumbed to the inevitable.

'Half ahead together. Make revolutions for twenty-five knots.' *Brackendale* slowed, a little. And for Thorburn it was time to take his seat in the bridge chair. He jammed a frustrated boot against the pipe bracket and forced himself to be patient.

CHAPTER NINETEEN . .
BATTLE JOINED

Korvettenkapitän Wolfgang Herzog demanded more from the *Puma's* engine room and vented his feelings on the members of his bridge watch.

'For God's sake,' he ranted. 'Can we not lose this destroyer? We cannot rest until this merchant ship is in Cherbourg and I do not want to hear anyone tell me this Englander is still on our heels.' He paced the bridge, angered by the sudden appearance of the Royal Navy. It was only by luck that the flotilla had survived the cruiser's initial attack, and then the British destroyers came head on. He shook his head. Why must the Royal Navy attack in such a way? Did they not see we defend and flee, fight again when the stars align more favourably. Always our speed keeps us away from trouble, and this time, he thought, the *Puma* lets the rest of the flotilla act as bait, drawing them further and further away from *Maria*.

'Kapitän!'

Herzog turned. 'What?' he snapped.

'The enemy destroyer, Herr Kapitän, it no longer follows.'

Moving to the far corner of the bridge, Herzog raised his binoculars to the north, across the stern rails. Dark sky, a darker sea. A slow pan from left to right. Nothing. He lowered the glasses and took a deep breath. Why he wondered, did he still get the feeling he was not clear of danger. A shake of the head dispelled any further doubts and he strode back to his chair. No matter, the Englander is not quick. He will soon lose track of the *Puma*. He settled in his chair and checked on *de Maria's* last reported position. At this speed he would be up with the old steamer in less than forty-five minutes, and the honour of escorting her into Cherbourg's harbour would belong to one man. Korvettenkapitän Wolfgang Herzog.

Menéndez had been alarmed by what he'd seen on the northern horizon. There could be no mistaking the flashes for anything less than gunfire, the lurid orange glow of flames a faint backdrop to the explosions. He lifted the glasses and settled the sockets to his eyes. A starshell blossomed, white bright in the sky, swaying beneath its parachute. Warships. Indistinguishable through his binoculars, the range too great for precise focus. But he'd seen enough to convince himself to alter course away. Go east . . . , make for the nearest French coast. He traced an imaginary line across the chart and found the chain of Channel Islands might well provide some sort of refuge. The island of Jersey lay directly to the east and he was sure the

Germans occupied all the islands. And it would certainly be under the protection of a coastal gun battery. Had to be a better alternative than being sunk at sea.

'Come right!' he snapped at the wheel. 'We go east.'

'East,' the man confirmed, and Menéndez grunted, glasses taking in the glowing horizon. He lowered them, crossed to the port wing and stepped out into the cold air. With the ship swinging right the port wing gave him a panoramic view to the north and he again steadied the binoculars. The starshell fizzled out, gun flashes faded, and other than the merest hint of a red glow all became quiet. He pushed his way back into the bridge and moved to the compass housing. It indicated nine-one degrees, almost due east and he breathed a sigh of relief. Good enough, but he reminded the helmsman of his duties.

'Watch your heading,' he warned abruptly, and took a pace toward the screen. Somewhere out there beyond the bows was landfall, if only the engine could be coaxed into giving him the last remaining effort. He crossed to the bulkhead telephone and called the engine room. When the answer came he pictured the thirty-eight year old Miguel Cabrera sweating in his grubby vest, the soggy half chewed cigar between his teeth.

'You want more from the engine, Capitán, no? Always you ask me for more. One day the boiler will burst . . . , then what will we do? But you ask so I try. I do my best, no?'

Menéndez nodded at the handset. 'Of course, Miguel, you do more than I ask, always. But this time it is different, there are warships, many warships. And maybe some are not so friendly. You understand me?'

There was a moment of hesitation, and then, 'I hear you, my Capitán. I give you everything. Do not worry.' The call was disconnected and Menéndez replaced the handset. Miguel Cabrera was an honest, hard working engineer who loved the mechanical intricacies of his trade and Carlos Menéndez knew his trust would not be misplaced in one such as Cabrera the engineer. And sure enough, within a few moments, he felt convinced that the *de Maria* had managed to gain another couple of precious knots. He grasped the mahogany rail and prayed for salvation.

Brackendale rode a wave and thumped the flank of the next. She twisted to starboard, and again buried her bows. Frothing seas sluiced down the fo'c'sle, swept down ladders and creamed aft along the gunwales of the main deck. Sea boots were tugged and footholds became precarious, and on the quarterdeck men hung on to every available handhold.

Thorburn balanced with grim determination against the incessant rolling, drifts of spray drenching the bridge. The cold, salt laden water found its way into every exposed area of skin and regardless of what a man had chosen to wear, the weather found the slightest chink in the armour. *Brackendale* was making twenty-five knots and more than twenty minutes had elapsed since 'Guns' had lost sight of the German destroyer. The wheelhouse had kept them on the last reported course and Thorburn was beginning to wonder how long he should keep pursuing an unseen enemy.

'Number One,' he called, and Armstrong stepped adroitly across from the starboard wing. He braced himself against the bridge screen.

'Sir?'

'Penny for your thoughts?'

Armstrong swivelled to lean his back against the screen, face turned away from the spray.

'I think at this rate we'll be bloody lucky to regain contact. That destroyer could be anywhere within a hundred and eighty degrees of our bearing. It's a bit of a long shot, sir.'

Thorburn nodded his agreement. 'Dead right,' he said, hunching away from the wind. 'I can't argue with that. I just feel we're onto something. He was in too much of a hurry to be playing games. We might be losing ground but my instinct is to follow this through. Stay on the bearing.'

Armstrong gave him a sideways look. 'For how long?'

Despite the situation, Thorburn grinned.

'Good question.' He chuckled. 'I don't think Brest is on the itinerary.' A bigger wave rolled beneath the ship and forced them to find a hand hold. A splash of ice cold water slapped Thorburn's face and he made up his mind.

'We'll hold this bearing for another thirty minutes and if we've not found our little friend by then, we'll call it quits.'

'Very well, sir,' Armstrong nodded, and waited. But with nothing else forthcoming he edged his way back to the starboard wing. A lookout stiffened at his approach, alert behind the binoculars. Armstrong eased away to leave him alone, let him be to carry out his duty. The sailor didn't need anyone in authority breathing down his neck.

Armstrong looked back at the screen and the dark figure of Richard Thorburn, the man their Lordships had chosen for command of His Majesty's destroyer. He didn't envy him wearing that extra half stripe. It was at moments like these that you certainly earned the privilege. Not in the much heralded heat of battle, not during the cut and thrust of close quarters fighting. No . . . , it was when you made a decision that personally affected the lives of an entire crew. And right, wrong or otherwise, you then had to live with the consequences. He pursed his lips and not for the first time Armstrong felt he had much to be thankful for. When push came to shove he was more than happy to remain as understudy to a man he considered to be a fine example of leadership.

The ship twisted to another roller and he braced for the next trough.

On *Cheriton's* navigating platform, Charles Rutherford was in his element. The destroyer was at peak power, knifing the waves aside, bow wave flying high. She was making twenty-seven knots, maximum speed, and he could feel the vibrations through his sea boots.

The guns thumped again, blasting off another salvo, the smoke whipping away in the icy wind. Enemy shells struck the sea off the port bow, exploding on impact, sending up columns of seething water. From the enemy stern, twin streaks of tracer curved towards *Cheriton*, and the rattle of machine-gun bullets danced along the bridge housing.

Rutherford steadied himself against the bridge-screen and lifted the binoculars. The German ship veered to port, away from the last fall of *Cheriton's* shells. A ruddy glow came from amidships, a small fire below decks. The German's afterdeck main armament fired again and Rutherford gritted his teeth in expectation. He lowered the glasses, waiting. With a shriek two shells passed overhead, to explode well astern. Rutherford shuddered. Close.

He leaned to the pipe. 'Port ten!'

'Port ten, aye aye, sir. Port ten of the wheel on.'

'Midships!'

'Midships, aye, sir.'

'Steady . . . , steer oh-eight-two degrees.'

'Oh-eight-two degrees. Aye aye, sir.'

Cheriton sheered left, away to port, beginning to cut the arc of the German. At the same time the move allowed all of *Cheriton's* guns to train on the target, lifting and traversing until the gunnery officer was satisfied.

'Shoot!'

Six guns bellowed, wreathed in smoke and flame. They recoiled, ejected the casings, were loaded, breeches closed, ready. Four seconds.

'Shoot!'

The guns blasted, hurling shells across the sea. *Cheriton* shuddered to the detonations, and Rutherford lifted the glasses to watch for hits.

He saw the moment a gun on the enemy's quarterdeck fired. The shell scythed in and exploded on *Cheriton's* port side boat deck. The cutter was obliterated, decking pierced and left smouldering. Another shell hit the waves off the port bow and shrapnel rattled the side.

Rutherford managed a mirthless grin. *Cheriton's* guns were making inroads. Two hits on the afterdeck housing. The German twisted in an attempt to throw off the Royal Navy's gunnery, to no avail. And the next salvo brought strikes along the fo'c'sle deck. A fire sprang up, flames threatening the bridge structure, licking round the forward gun housing.

But then *Cheriton* took a direct hit. The shell detonated on the Pompom platform and the explosion blasted the gunners from inside to out. Men died. Instantly. Others crawled with agonising wounds, bleeding, shocked. The gun captain lay slumped, staring at his severed arm, blood pumping. The call went out for stretcher bearers.

'Starboard ten!' Rutherford snapped, knowing he *must* alter course. A second German destroyer had bracketed *Cheriton* and he changed tack, if only for a moment.

He caught a glimpse of *Kingfisher* heeling to starboard, hard over, gleaming in the light of a starshell. Her guns flamed, fully engaged

'Port twenty!' he shouted over the gunfire.

'Port twenty, aye, sir!' *Cheriton* swept upright, heeled to starboard, the sea swirling along her length.

'Midships!'

The Cox'n spun the wheel, the rudder centred.

'Steer three-five-oh!'

'Three-five-oh degrees. Aye aye, sir!'

And Rutherford grimaced. He'd closed the gap, although he wasn't sure how. Maybe the German had internal damage, holed below the waterline? He turned to the bulkhead telephone.

'Engine room?'

'Yes, sir.'

'Crack it on, Chief. Everything you can give me.'

'Aye aye, sir. Full ahead both.'

Rutherford returned the handset, snatched up his binoculars, levelling them over the screen. *Cheriton* was hurting, casualty list growing, but it looked like perseverance was paying off.

The chase was on.

H.M.S. *Kingfisher* powered in towards the enemy. Her guns raked a destroyer ranged at five-thousand yards, shells tearing at the steel plating. Violent explosions ripped apart the interior, inflicting casualties, and Germans died. *Kingfisher* closed in, holding the target stern on, avoiding any possible repeat of a torpedo attack. Not that *Kingfisher* herself was limited. Her armament included two banks of 21-inch torpedoes, five to each bank, and Captain T. Horwood had recent experience of their use. His Torpedo Officer had made a successful attack on a German destroyer at Narvik.

Then from starboard the flash of gunfire preceded several near-misses. Columns of water shot skywards. The gunnery officer split his firepower, the afterdeck main armament taking on the new threat. One bank of tubes was immediately prepared and deployed over the starboard side in case the opportunity arose. The ideal range would be somewhere in the region of three-thousand yards. Amidst a cacophony of gunfire and flying spray the Torpedo Officer watched and waited.

CHAPTER TWENTY . .
HIDE AND SEEK

South of the battle and twenty nautical miles east of her last reported position, the *Castillo de Maria* ploughed on towards the island of Jersey. On the bridge, Capitán Carlos Menéndez paced and worried over exactly from where the enemy ships might emerge. The important thing he concluded was distance gained from when he'd decided to make the turn away. Depending on conditions, any lookout searching for one old tramp steamer in the vast spaces of these waters would be lucky indeed to make a sighting. The *Maria* might even be beyond a warship's horizon, a perfect way of escaping the Royal Navy's attention.

He turned to his chair. All this, of course, was pure conjecture. He had no way of knowing what was taking place to the north, only instinct guided his actions. The thought of making it home to his family came to mind and he stuck out his jaw. There was a grim determination to push on regardless, gain as many miles as he could squeeze in.

The *Castillo de Maria* shouldered the next wave to one side and ploughed on. Another mile chalked off.

On the *Puma's* bridge, Korvettenkapitän

Wolfgang Herzog checked the time, let out an exasperated grunt and cursed. He grabbed the phone to the gunnery tower.

'Herr Kapitän?' came the instant response.

'Do you see the *Maria*, Leutnant?'

'There is no sign, Herr Kapitän.'

Herzog sighed and rubbed his forehead. If his calculations were correct and the U-boat's report had not been in error, then by now they should have rendezvoused with the *Maria*.

'Look again!' he snapped, and slammed down the phone. He turned on his Second-in-Command.

'Leitner,' he said, the bitter ring of anger in his tone. 'Reduce our speed and commence a search pattern. That freighter cannot be far, even with poor navigation.' He thought for a moment. 'I suggest we head east. Even an idiot will know there is safety near the French coast. He may have turned that way.'

'Jawohl, Herr Kapitän,' Leitner answered and passed the bearing to the wheel.

The *Puma* leaned into the turn and Herzog compressed his lips. It could surely be only a matter of time before the *Castillo de Maria* was sighted.

The phone from Gun Control buzzed loudly.

'Ja?' he demanded.

'We have searched to every compass point, Herr Kapitän. Empty sea is all we have.'

Herzog relented, a little. 'So be it,' he said.

'Concentrate your search to the east. I feel the freighter may be seeking refuge elsewhere.'

'Jawohl, Herr Kapitän, we search ahead, beyond the bows.'

Herzog slipped the phone back on its bracket and momentarily shut his eyes. For once he felt convinced he'd taken the right course of action. He straightened his shoulders and strode to the chair. The *Maria* would soon be under his protection.

The dull sheen of *Brackendale's* fo'c'sle emerged from a bank of rain and Thorburn shook water from his cap. The rain had been easing for the last five minutes, a Godsend for the watchkeepers. Thick weather when trying to scour the seas for danger was not a lookout's favourite pastime and there was a palpable sense of relief as the rain front passed through. Glancing at the sky, Thorburn thought he glimpsed one or two stars through gaps in the cloud cover.

'Guns-bridge!' It was urgent.

Thorburn snapped an answer. 'Bridge!'

'Enemy destroyer! Bearing one-four-five, range seven-thousand, speed fourteen, course oh-nine-five.'

'Very well,' Thorburn said. 'Number One!'

'Sir?'

'Action Stations.'

'Aye aye, sir!' Armstrong said, and leaned

to the bulkhead. The clamour of the alarm resounded through the ship and the crew not on watch hurried to their stations.

Thorburn gazed down at his sea boots, brain moving into overdrive. Enemy about four miles away and heading east, for the French coast. Fourteen knots was very slow, it might be searching. Either way *Brackendale* was moving far too quickly; a stealthy approach would be far more appropriate.

'Make our speed ten knots, Pilot,' he ordered. He needed the breathing space, concerned by the sudden contact. Not entirely unexpected, just a little disconcerting. *Brackendale* eased, the bow wave softening.

Armstrong acknowledged a string of voice-pipe and telephone calls, until every station had reported in. And at that point he was able to report to the Captain.

'The ship is at Action Stations, sir.'

'Very well, Number One,' Thorburn said, binoculars raised over the port wing. He found only an empty darkness. He reached for the bulkhead phone.

'Guns?'

'Sir?'

'Report your target.'

'Enemy is bearing red one-six-five, range seven-thousand, speed fourteen, course oh-nine-two.'

'Very well. Regular reports please, Mr Carling.

There's nothing to see down here.'

'Aye aye, sir.'

Thorburn edged closer to Armstrong. 'We seem to have found our little friend, Number One.'

'Yes, sir. The question is, has he found *his* little friend?'

Thorburn grinned in the gloom. 'If not,' he said, 'we'll soon find out.'

'Guns-Bridge. Target bearing oh-nine-oh, range seven-thousand.'

'Very well,' Thorburn acknowledged and realised *Brackendale* was still pushing south across the German's stern. He needed to order a change of course. And now they were at Action Stations he may as well officially take command. He stepped onto the compass platform and glanced round at the crowded platform.

'I have the bridge.' He leaned to the wheelhouse pipe. 'Cox'n?'

'Wheelhouse, sir.'

'Port thirty.'

'Port thirty, aye aye, sir.'

The ship canted to starboard, bows swinging, and Thorburn kept one eye on the compass rose. She was nearing the mark.

'Midships.'

'Midships, aye, sir.' The angle of lean changed as *Brackendale* came upright.

'Steady . . . , steer Oh-nine-oh.'

'Steer Oh-nine-Oh degrees. Aye aye, sir.

'Guns-bridge!'

He cocked an ear to the pipe. 'Captain.'

'Target bearing oh-nine-five, speed eight knots, range seven-thousand, five-hundred, sir.'

Thorburn narrowed his eyes and nodded in the darkness. 'Thank you, Guns. We'll hold station for now. If I'm right that destroyer is about to rendezvous with the *Castillo de Maria*.'

'Sir, our Range Finder has the German in sight. But if he looks our way we might well be seen.'

Thorburn hesitated, it was a timely intervention, and not to be ignored. 'If he opens fire, feel free to engage. But not until.'

'Aye aye, sir,' Carling confirmed, and Thorburn stared at the compass. The enemy was headed towards friendly territory, and if he maintained his current course he'd make initial landfall on Jersey. Thorburn looked up into the cold wind and peered beyond the bows. And then a slow smile of understanding spread across his face. The chosen course wasn't of the destroyer's making, it was more likely the *Castillo de Maria* missing her rendezvous. Something had possibly spooked *Maria's* captain and he was seeking sanctuary in the only way he knew how. The nearest Nazi held port.

And he guessed that the German Kapitän, having come to the same conclusion as Thorburn, had embarked on a search pattern in an attempt to find her.

'Number One,' he called to the port wing.

Armstrong turned and stepped closer. 'Sir?'

'I think we're about to find our prey.'

Armstrong didn't reply immediately and Thorburn glanced round at his dark profile. 'What is it?'

The ship met a roller and twisted, the hull heaving over the crest. Thorburn tried again. 'Number One?'

'I don't have a good feeling about this,' Armstrong said, just loud enough for Thorburn's ear but no others. 'We might have over extended, sir. If there's more than one . . . .?' He left the rest to the imagination.

Thorburn chuckled, surprised at Armstrong's reticence. He'd never been backward in coming forward, it was one of the things that Thorburn admired about him, forthright in his criticism if he felt circumstances warranted it. But this had the ring of genuine uncertainty.

He let the laugh fade. 'What's the trouble?'

'I just wonder whether that destroyer has radar. If it does, they might be drawing us in to an ambush.'

Thorburn wiped his mouth and frowned. The First Lieutenant had a point, there could be more enemy ships in the offing. But if the enemy had radar then surely they would have found the freighter already. And for Thorburn the *de Maria* was a priority. Tungsten was a crucial component in the manufacture of armour-piercing shells and 'Guns' had mentioned that he'd seen how effective they were during trials with the Royal Artillery. Thorburn felt it was his duty to take the risk. If *Brackendale* came up against serious opposition then the least that could be done was to slow the enemy's escape. *Vibrant* and *Kingfisher* were nearby.

'Point taken, but I really don't have much choice. That freighter can't be allowed to disappear. If there's the slightest chance of stopping her I have to take it. Understood?'

Armstrong turned and a twisted smile teased his lips. 'Damned if we do, damned if we don't, sir.'

Thorburn nodded in answer. 'Something like that, yes. But we're the ones who've ended up in the stew. We'll have to live with it.' He saw Armstrong straighten up and stick his chin out.

'In that case, sir,' he said, the usual grin returning, 'permission to hoist the Battle Ensign?'

For a moment Thorburn hesitated. The flag's white background would show up like a sore thumb making it more likely *Brackendale* would be spotted. He compromised.

'Have the signalman bend it to the halyard. We'll raise it on contact.'

Armstrong's grin broadened in the darkness. 'Aye aye, sir,' he said, his enthusiasm restored, and he moved to the back of the bridge. A call to the flag deck and the White Ensign was pulled from a locker in readiness.

In the Rangefinder abaft the bridge, 'Guns' Carling noted a change in the behaviour of a lone German destroyer. It looked to be increasing speed, the wake a little more pronounced. He would study the ship a while longer before making his report. Clarity of information was important.

CHAPTER TWENTY-ONE . . SIGNALS

On board the *Puma's* bridge Herzog heard a shout. 'Ship! Off the starboard bow, Herr Kapitän!'

Herzog snatched up his binoculars and focussed on the given position. A blurred image swam across the lens and he adjusted the knurled wheel to sharpen the view. Persistent drizzle made it difficult to be certain but he felt sure he was looking at the *Castillo de Maria*.

'Increase to half speed and come five-degrees left,' he ordered. He heard the repeat and felt the renewed tremble from the engines. He gave the turn another minute and then settled on a fresh bearing.

'Steer zero-eight-five.'

He took another look through the glasses. The *Puma* was now stationed neatly off the *Maria's* port quarter and approaching at twice the speed.

Herzog moved over to the starboard wing and waited as they closed on the old freighter's port beam. He wondered if the ship's captain spoke German. It would make things considerably easier if that were the case.

'Enemy destroyer! Dead astern!'

Herzog spun round and jammed the glasses to his eyes. And there it was. He cursed and lowered the binoculars. The Englander looked to be well in range and he cursed again. No time to dwell on it, he must give the *Puma* fighting seaway, get clear of the old steamer.

'Open fire!' he shouted.

The stern gun mounts thundered, a pair of shells winging towards the enemy.

'Engines full ahead! Come left thirty degrees!'

The *Puma* heeled hard to starboard, increased speed and clawed away from the freighter. And as the ship came round with the port beam facing Herzog's tormentor, his Gunnery Officer brought all guns to bear and gave the Englander a heavy broadside.

Thorburn recognised that moment of extreme danger and reacted.

'Hard-a-starboard!' Full ahead both!'

The pair of fo'c'sle guns crashed out an instant reply, Carling obeying his Captain's last order.

And then *Brackendale* leaned into the turn as enemy shells splashed down where she would have been. Both Thorburn and Carling had acted instinctively, acutely aware of the need to counter the threat.

Braced against the angle of lean, Thorburn eyed the stern transom of the freighter. *Brackendale* was crossing her wake and would shortly emerge on her starboard side moving south. He raised his binoculars at the German destroyer and caught the moment its guns fired again. But *Brackendale* was coming up to maximum speed and easily avoided the salvo.

'Midships!' he called to the wheelhouse pipe.

'Midships, aye, sir!' Falconer acknowledged, and the small warship lurched upright as he corrected the wheel.

Thorburn eyed the freighter, less than a thousand yards distant, and made the decision to move parallel to her bearing. It would give the German commander a moment of hesitation. He wouldn't want to risk shooting if there was any chance of a stray shell hitting the *Maria*.

He bent to the pipe. 'Port twenty.'

'Port twenty, aye aye, sir.'

And again the nimble destroyer swept into a fast turn, the bow wave leaping high. And she quickly reached a point where she was running alongside.

'Midships . . . , steady . . . . Steer oh-nine-oh degrees.'

'Oh-nine-oh degrees, aye aye, sir.

'Make revolutions for twelve knots.'

'Speed twelve knots, aye, sir.'

Thorburn heard the ring of the telegraph and waited for the bow wave to slacken.

Down in the engine room Bryn Dawkins caught the movement of the telegraph and reached for the throttles, bringing the revolutions down until *Brackendale's* forward momentum corresponded to the skipper's requirements. It was hot and noisy, and with the ship in action it called for high levels of concentration. The stokers kept one eye on him and the other on their own responsibilities. Sign language became the only reliable way of communicating, and like all stokers everywhere they were adept at making themselves understood. Beads of sweat ran in rivulets down straining muscles, blinked away from stinging eyes, and all the while men flinched to the hammer of the quarterdeck guns overhead.

Bryn Dawkins wiped his hands on a piece of waste cotton and glanced at a pressure gauge. It was holding. His eye returned to the telegraph. There'd be many more alterations to come before this night was through.

On the *Maria*, Carlos Menendez was in turmoil. One moment it seemed his prayers had been answered by the appearance of a German destroyer. The next, all hope dashed when a British destroyer came barrelling out of the darkness. And now the two warships were joined in battle with no telling who might come out the victor. All he could do was hold course and put his trust in the Gods. Surely he had not come all this way only to be sunk within touching distance of salvation.

The crash of gunfire resounded through the rain and Menendez winced in expectation of a shell detonating somewhere on his ship. How helpless he felt in the face of such overwhelming force.

He was an unarmed merchantman with no means of mounting any form of retaliation. If the British chose to sink him there was little he could do to argue. He paced the bridge, his fate in the hands of God. It might, he thought, be a little late to start praying.

Vibrant had found the range. The light cruiser's six-inch guns crashed off another salvo, the shells arcing across the void. At twelve-thousand yards the weight of her artillery found the target. A pair of high explosive shells from the forward mounting plunged into the *Hawk* and detonated on the stern superstructure. One of the *Hawk's* 105mm guns took the full force of the explosion, wiped out the gun crew and unseated the barrel from its mounting. A fire sprang up in the ammunition hoist, the flames tracking toward the magazine.

A third shell struck amidships, tore through the deck plating and buried itself in an engineering compartment. It failed to detonate on impact but remained as a lethal threat below decks.

The *Hawk's* Kapitän listened to the damage reports and made the decision to disengage. He had lost a third of his speed and would never be able to take up a position to launch his torpedoes. No one could blame him for pulling out of the battle.

'Make smoke!' he ordered, and as the thick fog boiled astern to cover its movements, the 'Bird of Prey' slipped away to the north.

On *Vibrant's* bridge, Captain Gerald Fitzpatrick R.N., O.B.E., congratulated his gunnery officer on an excellent 'shoot'.

'Well done, Freddy! My God you've done us proud! Sent him packing, tail between his legs, what?' He rubbed his hands in anticipation of the next move. 'Any sign of that old freighter?' The question was a generalization with no real expectation of a meaningful answer.

But Lieutenant-Commander Ray Phillips, Fitzpatrick's Second-in-Command, had noted an enemy destroyer breaking off from the engagement. And then he'd seen *Brackendale* taking up the chase.

'Might be to the south, sir. A German headed that way at speed.'

Fitzpatrick stuck out his chin. 'Did he, indeed?' He raised his binoculars and picked out *Kingfisher*. She looked to be shelling a fleeing destroyer. The *Cheriton* had got herself into a nasty looking fight, swapping high explosive with a fast moving Jerry. Multi-coloured tracer flashed between ships. But where, he wondered, had the fifth warship got to?

'That makes four accounted for, where's the other one?'

Binoculars scoured the surrounding seas and

a lookout shouted a warning. 'Enemy destroyer! Red one-forty. Nine-thousand yards, sir.'

A bridge full of binoculars swung round to check out beyond *Vibrant's* port quarter.

Fitzpatrick found the target and immediately understood the danger. His escorts were engaged elsewhere and this ship could be setting up for a torpedo strike. A full flowing bow wave indicated a fast approach and showed the German commander didn't lack courage. But Gerald Fitzpatrick, for all his apparent good natured bonhomie wasn't lacking in a bit of grit and determination himself, and decided to show the enemy two could play that game.

'Hard-a-port!' he snapped.

Phillips repeated. 'Hard-a-port!'

And Pilot passed the command to the wheelhouse. 'Hard-a-port!'

Tentatively at first, then gathering momentum, H.M.S. *Vibrant* responded, and five-thousand tons of Royal Navy cruiser leaned majestically into the turn.

The German ship chose that moment to alter course to launch torpedoes. In so doing it presented 'Guns' with all of its starboard side.

Beneath the bridge the forward fo'c'sle turrets followed the Rangefinder's direction and traversed onto target. The twin mountings of six-inch guns were loaded in readiness, and the Gunnery Officer waited for the ship to steady.

Fitzpatrick judged the moment. 'Midships,' he

ordered.

The warship came out of her turn, stabilising, reacquiring her centre of gravity. With four giant propellers pushing her on at twenty-eight knots the ship powered in towards her adversary. "Guns" gave the command.

'Shoot!'

The fire button was pressed and the 'ting-ting' of bells sounded in the turrets.

The guns roared.

Smoke and flame erupted into the night. Travelling at 2,760 feet per second, four 112 pound high explosive projectiles ripped across the waves. With a range of less than 10,000 yards the guns had been set on a low trajectory, and eight seconds after exiting the barrels the shells found their target.

The German destroyer sustained three direct hits, the fourth shell missing the bridge by a hair's breadth. But in this instance, three were enough. The thin side plating stood no chance against such a combined weight of firepower. No-1 boiler room burst open to a violent explosion and scalding steam vented in a whistling hiss. The sea flowed in. Where a bulkhead divided the engine room from the stern fuel oil tanks, a six-inch shell exploded on the waterline and a fireball ripped through the lower decks. The entire engine room personnel were incinerated and on the main deck three of the crew were killed outright. Lastly, a shell hit the steering gear flat, detonated and obliterated the machinery that turned the rudder.

The ship staggered under the explosions, the damage too great, and water rushed into jagged holes. The reduction in speed was plain for all to see, and the warship leaned, wallowing to a standstill, already low in the water.

Vibrant's main armament fired again and this time there could be no escape. The shells struck low beneath the fo'c'sle and blew a gaping hole in the side plates. Tons of seawater poured in and within minutes the ship was down by the head. The German guns fell silent. Nine minutes after first making contact the ship capsized to starboard. It hung there, precariously half submerged, the main deck perpendicular to the sea. Men and rafts slipped and slithered into the waves

Fitzpatrick had seen enough and turned *Vibrant* to port. In other circumstances he would have ordered the rescue of men in the water. But not in this case, not now. The threat to *Vibrant* was too great. Cold hearted? So it might seem, but the rationale for saving lives could not be justified when enemy forces might reappear at any moment.

In compliance with his orders H.M.S. *Vibrant* steadied, settled to a bearing of one-oh-five degrees and hurried off in search of the *Cheriton* and *Kingfisher*.

Receding in her wake and hidden by a sudden

squall the lingering death of a German warship passed unnoticed. Inundated by the colossal influx of water the ship slowly slid under and descended towards the sea floor. Creaking and groaning under immense pressure the tortured hulk of twisted steel finally came to rest on a protruding ridge above a deeper trench at a depth of 1,800 metres.

On the rain swept surface all that remained were a few desperately overloaded rafts and drifting wreckage. Bodies of the dead tangled with floating debris, rising and falling to the tumbling waves. Few if any of the remaining swimmers lasted long in the freezing temperatures. Covered in oil, burnt, wounded and with lungs gasping for clean air, they splashed helplessly towards one of the wallowing rafts. In time, the forlorn splashes ceased, and only an ever spreading patch of flotsam bore witness to a battle lost.

And southeast of the devastation, a five-thousand ton Royal Navy light cruiser re-established contact with *Kingfisher* and prepared to lend the weight of her firepower to the Fleet destroyer's main armament. For Captain Fitzpatrick his biggest concern remained the whereabouts of the *Castillo de Maria*.

Brackendale rode a long roller and corkscrewed through the following trough. Blinding sleet swept in from the north and in seconds what little of the dark seascape that had been visible was gone.

Thorburn cursed. The weather had intervened and placed him in a difficult situation. Most battles he could handle, ship to ship, even ship against two ships. That was an accepted risk, one captain's skill against another, gun against gun. But when the weather closed in and left a man unsighted then all bets were off. Warships manoeuvring to avoid gunfire were suddenly vulnerable to accidental collision as a vessel loomed large from within a white wall.

No, he thought, it was time to put some distance between himself and the enemy.

'Hard-a-starboard!' he snapped at the wheelhouse pipe.

'Hard-a-starboard, aye, sir,' Falconer called up the pipe, and firm hands grasped the wheel, hauling the small warship round to the south.

'Midships!'

'Midships, aye aye, sir!'

Thorburn eyed the compass. 'Steady!'

'Wheel's amidships. Steering one-eight-four degrees, sir.'

Almost due south Thorburn gauged. It would do for now.

'Very well,' he said, and turned to peer astern over the port quarter. Only a curtain of white greeted him. He turned back to the bridge-screen, the sleet beginning to stick in tight crevices, building inch on inch. Armstrong stood to his left, hands tucked deep inside the pockets of his duffle coat.

'Number One,' he called quietly.

'Sir?'

'I think it's time for a sighting report. Warn the W/T office.' He lowered his head to look at the deck gratings, gathering his thoughts.

Petty Officer Langsdale appeared with his notepad and turned to stand with his back to the sleet.

'Take this down . . . "Admiralty, repeated to *Vibrant*. Target located fifteen miles southeast of enemy flotilla. Course 092, speed ten knots. Type 24 destroyer in close company. Have engaged." Get that off quick as you can.'

Langsdale finished jotting. 'Aye aye, sir,' he said, and made for the wireless room.

Thorburn rubbed his face, wracking his brain as to his next move. It was all right to take avoiding action but what next?

'Number One.'

'Sir?'

'We're blind in this, but hopefully it'll clear. It strikes me if I take *Brackendale* east at speed I could get well ahead and intercept their line of travel. Might even find clear weather.'

'Mmm,' Armstrong mouthed, 'not forgetting the *Maria's* final destination was Cherbourg. Now the destroyer has found her, she might resume her true course.'

Thorburn gave a small nod. Armstrong was

right. He lifted his face to the sleet and let the cold penetrate. The icy flakes were bracing, reviving, giving him a fresh perspective. And it was then that he realised Fitzpatrick would also recognise the true picture. *Vibrant's* chart room would have the entire plot laid out clear as day. One glance at the respective positions and Fitzpatrick could make an educated guess as to the next moves, including the likelihood of the freighter resuming her original course.

'Captain, sir?'

He turned to the Chief Yeoman, and Langsdale reported, '*Vibrant* acknowledges, sir.'

'Very well,' Thorburn said, 'carry on,' and he turned back to Armstrong.

'Right, Number One, that'll do for me. We'll head east, get ourselves in position and see what transpires. Better than swanning about blind with no inkling of the enemy's whereabouts.'

It was so dark now, the sleet impenetrable, that his First Officer's reply was heard rather than seen.

'Change course then, sir?'

'Yes, Number One. Due east if you will.'

'Aye aye, sir. Due east it is.' Armstrong leaned to the pipe. 'Port thirty. Steer oh-nine-oh, Cox'n.'

'Oh-nine-oh, aye aye, sir.'

Brackendale answered the helm, sweeping round to the east, a fleeting outline cloaked in a shroud of white.

Thorburn leaned to the pipe. 'Make

revolutions for twenty-five knots.'

'Speed twenty-five. Aye aye, sir.'

The volume of sleet steadily increased until trying to look over the bridge-screen was a waste of time. Thorburn left it to the lookouts and stepped over to his chair. Wiping off the build up of icy residue, he sat and rammed a booted foot against the bracket. He thought back to Portland and the briefing, and shook his head. The best laid plans of mice and men . . . .

Wolfgang Herzog gave up any chance of finding the Englander, the sleet was too much, and he must not lose the *Castillo de Maria*. With visibility down to a few metres it would be too easy for a freighter to disappear and it seemed the *Maria's* Capitán might be so inclined. And with every passing minute the freighter moved closer to the French coast. That was not so good an idea; the Capitán must be persuaded to follow the *Puma* to Cherbourg. Herzog would have to manoeuvre the *Puma* alongside and converse with the man on the bridge.

In these conditions that would be no easy thing to do. And he felt he would have to do it himself. No-one else amongst his executive officers had the required experience.

In *Vibrant's* W/T office a Telegraphist listened to a fresh signal coming in through his headset. Jotting the Morse Code message on a signal pad he keyed a temporary acknowledgement and tore the slip from his pad. He waved it in the air and a messenger snatched it from his hand. A Sub-Lieutenant took it, read it through and decided it was important enough for him to be personally involved. In less than a minute he was stood by Fitzpatrick's shoulder.

'Captain, sir.'

Fitzpatrick turned his head. 'Mister Cleverly,' he beamed. 'What have we got?'

The Sub-Lieutenant offered his Captain the slip, who took it and leaned to the quiet light of the chart table. He read it thoroughly and straightened to glance round the bridge.

'Pilot,' he called. 'Get those coordinates plotted.' He handed him the signal slip. 'It looks like *Brackendale* has found our blockade runner.

The chart was duly annotated and Fitzpatrick took a look to establish the position. He nodded.

'Mister Cleverly, you may acknowledge.'

'Sir,' said the Sub-Lieutenant and turned smartly for the back of the bridge.

Fitzpatrick raised his glasses and traversed them across the bows. He found *Cheriton* heeling into a starboard turn. The enemy had accelerated away at high speed and *Cheriton's* captain had obviously decided to assist *Kingfisher*. Which placed *Vibrant* in the somewhat awkward position of being isolated from her escorts. Never the best of situations. And although the German flotilla had been well and truly routed, Fitzpatrick knew of only one confirmed sinking and that had been by his own guns.

Now he had *Brackendale* requiring assistance and his priority was the *Castillo de Maria*. Time to join forces.

'Number One. Get a signal off to *Kingfisher* and *Cheriton* and have them close on *Vibrant*. I'm going after *Brackendale*.'

'Aye aye, sir.'

Fitzpatrick frowned in the darkness. It was all well and good deploying the Royal Navy to find a lone freighter in the Bay of Biscay, but utilising the night to cloak their movements made for difficult navigation. It was to be hoped that Lieutenant-Commander Thorburn knew his stuff.

'Pilot, do we have a plot for the *Maria*?'

'We do, sir. I suggest we steer oh-six-five degrees. That would place us three miles north and west of her current position. I've also assumed her destination as Cherbourg. We've had no other information, sir.'

Fitzpatrick accepted the logic. 'Quite so,' he said. 'In that case, Pilot, feel free to alter course. Fifteen knots, if you will . . . , until *Kingfisher* and *Cheriton* have joined.'

'Aye aye, sir.'

Orders to the wheelhouse were passed, repeated and acknowledged. *Vibrant* began a wide turn and with *Kingfisher* and *Cheriton* finally breaking off the engagement, she steadied on a bearing of oh-six-five degrees. The two destroyers took station on either flank and together the three warships increased to a speed of twenty-five knots. Once again the search for the *Castillo de Maria* was in full swing. This time thought Fitzpatrick, it was no longer a needle in a haystack. They had a confirmed set of coordinates to go by and *Vibrant*, as was her duty, had answered the call.

In Whitehall's communications centre at the Admiralty's below ground Operational Headquarters, a hurried meeting had been set up with the Director of Operations. The wireless section had received a number of specific signals relating to recent events in the waters west of Guernsey and the duty officer alerted the Commodore. Knowing the priority given to *Vibrant's* deployment the information was passed up to Senior level whereupon the Admiral liaising with Churchill's staff took a personal interest.

The decision was taken to wait for further clarification before waking the Prime Minister.

At Plymouth, in Devonport's Royal Navy W/T office the same signals had been observed, noted, and passed to Vice-Admiral Sir John Tennant's staff. The decision was taken to inform Sir John who read through the signals before thanking them for their vigilance and returning to bed.

Likewise, in the W/T office at Chatham Dockyard, the signals were intercepted and logged, the Chief Petty officer on duty well aware Captain Pendleton would need to be informed of anything untoward. He lit another cigarette and reached for his steaming mug of tea. It was turning out to be a long night.

Richard Thorburn stamped his feet on the iron gratings and brushed an accumulation of sleet from the arms of his duffle coat. Much to everyone's relief the sleet had finally cleared away to the west and the heavy clouds had parted to reveal a sky full of stars. Sub-Lieutenant Martin immediately reached for his sextant and began taking readings. The lookouts cleaned off their binoculars, gave the optics another polish and settled into the rubber sockets. At last they could make out the subtle difference between sea and sky, the horizon dimly revealed.

For Thorburn the empty seas proved to be both a blessing and a concern. A blessing because no shouted alarm called for instant action. A concern for *Brackendale's* Captain because he'd banked on getting ahead of the quarry. With no ships in sight he was forced to doubt the wisdom of his actions. Maybe Armstrong's musing was correct and the *Maria* had resumed the northerly heading. He realised that Martin had concluded taking a fix on the stars.

'Mister Martin,' he said, 'I have a conundrum for you.'

Martin crossed to the chart table in readiness. He'd played this game before. 'Sir?'

Thorburn also moved to the table and in the quiet light of the bulkhead lamp looked down and studied the chart.

'Can you show me the *Maria's* position when we were last in contact?'

Martin ran his dividers back along the plot and pointed to a cross. 'There.'

'And her course was?'

'Oh-eight-seven.'

'Right . . . , assuming she was persuaded by the German destroyer to turn north for Cherbourg at ten knots, what would be her current position?'

'Turn north at ten knots for twenty-five minutes . . .' He stepped his dividers along an imaginary line. He made a pinprick hole in the chart and emphasised it with a pencilled cross. 'Give or take, about there, sir.'

Thorburn nodded. 'Now . . . , given that she maintains that bearing at a speed of ten knots, I need you to give me a course and speed to intercept at the earliest opportunity.'

Martin scribbled a calculation down the edge of the chart, voicing unintelligible numbers to himself. He placed a parallel rule on the chart, flicked a faint line towards the port of Cherbourg and then swivelled his dividers along the length. Drawing a circle round the anticipated point of interception he finished off the triangle by drawing in the hypotenuse. Another scribbled calculation and he stood back, looking up.

'Our course would need to be three-five-six degrees at a speed of twenty-six knots. Estimated time to interception, thirty-two minutes from commencing the turn.'

Thorburn gave a slow nod and nibbled his lower lip. 'Very well, we'll try it.'

Armstrong cleared his throat. 'Bit of a long shot, sir.'

Thorburn half smiled. His First Officer had reverted to form.

'Yes, Number One, it is, but nothing ventured, nothing gained. And I do have your earlier advice to go by.'

'But I only meant . . . .'

'And it was a point well put,' Thorburn said. He moved to the bank of voice-pipes. 'Steer three-five-six degrees. Make revolutions for twenty-six knots.'

'Course three-five-six, speed twenty-six knots. Aye aye, sir.'

Thorburn pushed back his sleeve and peered at the time. It showed seventeen minutes past eight. Add another thirty-two minutes and it would be nigh on ten to nine. He moved to the bridge-screen and grasped the rail.

This time, he thought, if the weather holds, then there would be no backing off. No waiting for the cruiser, or *Kingfisher*. Attack on sight and devil take the hindmost. Go in hard on the German destroyer and *Maria* would be exposed to Fitzpatrick's guns. And that was really all that mattered.

Brackendale lifted to a wave, spray hitting the screen, and Thorburn smiled. She was straining at the leash, relishing the chase. He raised his face to the wind, a taut smile tugging his mouth.

CHAPTER TWENTY-TWO . .
TORPEDO RUN

On board the *Puma*, Herzog leaned his elbows on the starboard splinter shield and looked across at the old *Castillo de Maria*. A half moon glinted on the upperworks of the bridge and not for the first time he shook his head in amazement. There could be no denying she was a rust bucket. A battered, weather worn, paint-stripped tramp steamer, and at any other time he wouldn't have given her a second glance. But what she carried was no ordinary cargo and he was sure the Fuhrer had an interest in her safe arrival.

A scurrying cloud front dropped a dark veil across the moon and the freighter became a mere outline. He hoped her Capitán would continue to obey orders; he'd been very reluctant to follow Herzog's reminder to resume passage for Cherbourg. That uncertainty prompted Herzog to take nothing for granted and he'd posted one of his sailors on permanent watch in the shelter of the signal deck. He gave a last shake of his head and stepped back to where his Navigating Officer attended a temporary chart table.

'They are coming, Hans?'

'Jawohl, Herr Kapitän, but only three. We lost a Narvik, sunk.'

'Mmm . . . , that is bad. But with *Puma* also, three should be enough.'

'I think *Hawk* is damaged, Herr Kapitän. It is not yet clear what is the cause. Steering or power, but not so fast.'

Herzog sucked air through his teeth. Four destroyers, one of which was damaged. If his Flotilla had managed to throw off the hunters then it should suffice. But if the cruiser found them again . . .? And as far as he knew no real damage had been done to any of the Englanders.

He moved back to the starboard splinter shield and again peered at the *Castillo de Maria*. If only she could go faster, but no, she lumbered along as if it was still peacetime, as if being in the middle of a war was of no consequence. Once more Wolfgang Herzog shook his head. At this rate it would be hours before they found refuge in Cherbourg's inner harbour.

Cheriton found herself rapidly falling behind both *Vibrant* and *Kingfisher*. On the bridge Rutherford fretted at his small destroyer's inability to keep up with her consorts. And what, he wondered, had happened to *Brackendale*?

'Sir?'

Rutherford looked round at his Second-in-Command.

'What is it Barry?'

'Casualties, sir. Four dead, six wounded and one missing. The wounded are down with the

Doc. And the Pompom, sir . . . , gone. Direct hit.'

Rutherford winced. One missing, probably blown overboard. He stiffened, a formality.

'Very well, Number One. Carry on.'

'Aye aye, sir,' his First Officer said, and moved away for the starboard ladder.

Rutherford turned back to the bridge-screen. He squeezed the rail until his fingers ached. The fact he no longer had the multi-barrelled Pompom was bad but not critical. The number of dead and wounded . . . , not good. He'd never come to terms with members of his own Ship's Company becoming casualties. He looked upon such things as a Captain's responsibility and therefore something which he should rectify at the earliest opportunity.

Blast the bloody Germans, he thought, but at least he might soon have a second chance. *Cheriton* pushed on in vengeful pursuit.

Captain Fitzpatrick gave up on his attempt to search ahead beyond *Vibrant's* fo'c'sle and let the binoculars hang. Sleet turning to rain made for poor watch keeping conditions and he thought better of it. Leave it to the Range Finder Control Tower. Up there, 'Guns' had every advantage, particularly height and therefore distance.

'What's our speed, Number One?'

'Thirty knots, sir.'

'Very well,' Fitzpatrick said, and stepped over to the port wing. Raising the glasses he traversed them out across the port bow and then focussed in on the fast moving *Kingfisher*. As he looked the rain eased, clouds scudding by, and the moon's pale light shone briefly on her upperworks. Her bow wave cascaded over the fo'c'sle and she was stern down driving forward at what looked to be maximum speed.

Fitzpatrick snorted. 'My God,' he said aloud. 'See that, Number One. What a sight. Magnificent.'

The First Officer nodded from behind his binoculars. 'Yes, sir. Quite impressive,' he replied, sounding enthusiastic but privately thinking it all looked a bit too cavalier. He was quite content to be on the bridge of something a bit more substantial.

In the darkness of a night made that much darker by persistent sleet and rain, *U-113* cut through the waves, both diesels hammering. At the same time the batteries were harnessed and taking on a fresh life-giving charge.

Konrad Drexler rode the bridge of the conning tower and swayed with the U-boat's rolling twist. He wiped his jaw clear of spray and decided the control room might be more comfortable.

About to turn for the hatch and go below, a flash of gunfire lit the darkness and Drexler spun round, eyes narrowed at the unexpected encounter. He glued his eyes into the sockets of his Carl Zeiss binoculars and concentrated on the northwest. A dull sheen glistened through the sleet and he blinked, astonished, and looked again. It was a large warship, a cruiser, and he was in no doubt as to its origins. It belonged to the Royal Navy. He allowed himself a grim smile, almost unable to believe his luck. If ever a U-boat found itself in the right place at the right time then this was it. Moving from left to right, the cruiser was firing towards the north-east. He brought the binoculars round and searched beyond the U-boat's bows, and there, still some kilometres distant he found a German flotilla. One had caught fire, a red glow emanating from amidships.

'Lookouts below,' he ordered, and the men scrambled down the tower.

He called to the control room, urgency in his voice. 'Make ready with all bow tubes!'

The Executive Officer could be heard repeating the order. 'Prepare and load all bow tubes.'

'Clear the bridge!' he shouted, and the gunners dropped from sight.

Drexler concentrated on the British ship. There had to be destroyers close by, no cruiser would be this far south without destroyer escort. He searched in the direction of the German flotilla, ignoring the red glow and traversed the lens towards the darkness to his right. A deeper shadow crossed his vision and he backtracked until he had it. A Fleet destroyer, moving away at speed and leaving the cruiser completely exposed to the U-boat's attack.

He swapped from his standard pair of binoculars to a pair of strong night vision glasses. Attaching them to the top of the Target Bearing Transmitter he relocated the cruiser and began passing all relevant information down to the 'Attack Table'. The well practised transfer of 'readings' into calculations would result in a firing solution. Minutes passed, the cruiser firing regular salvos. And then a starshell detonated beyond the German warships leaving them clearly outlined against the brilliant flare.

Drexler instinctively tucked himself down behind the steel fore-bridge the bright light sure to reveal *U-113* closing for the kill. But nothing happened, no gunfire aimed in his direction and it dawned on him that he was actually outside the flare's swaying light.

'Torpedoes ready, Herr Kapitän!'

Drexler wiped his face and gripped the steel screen. The cruiser was making a good thirty knots almost directly across his bows. To have any chance of a hit he decided to aim off and fire all four torpedoes in a spread pattern in the hope that at least one found its target. At that speed and with a range of just under five-thousand metres nothing could be guaranteed. But the opportunity had come his way and it was better to make the shot then let the cruiser draw away without making the attempt.

He bit his lip, holding his nerve.

'Open bow tubes.' He ordered, voice raised. There was a short pause before his Executive Officer replied.

'Bow tubes one through four open,' came the call from below.

'Stand ready,' he warned.

U-113 powered on, maximum speed, riding the waves. Spray ballooned back across the deck plates, foam rushing over the saddle tanks. The boat dipped and swayed over peaks and troughs. It was an exhilarating ride and Konrad Drexler revelled in it. A final calculation, and he waited for another two-hundred metres, letting the range come down to a little over four-thousand. The torpedoes would be travelling at seventy kilometres an hour, with the cruiser at nearly half that but going away.

'Fire one!' He gave the warship three seconds.

'Fire two!'

A shell screamed overhead. The Royal Navy had woken up. But the 'eels' were on their way.

'Fire three!' A pause.

'Fire four!'

A shell plunged into the sea off the port side, another astern.

'Alaarrrm!' he shouted. 'Alaarrrm!'

He dived for the hatch. The U-boat began its slide under, chasing the depths, and Drexler threw himself into the tower. He slammed the hatch above his head and secured it.

'Thirty-metres,' he demanded from inside

the tower. 'Right rudder, hard round.' His feet touched the decking and he looked for the compass. They were moving through east on the turn.

'Make our heading south,' he said.

The helmsman adjusted the wheel. 'Jawohl, Herr Kapitän,' he acknowledged, and the compass steadied as the boat came round due south.

Drexler nodded and glanced inquiringly at his First Officer. He was stood by the Attack Table, stop watch in hand, counting off the seconds. 'Well?' he asked.

'All torpedoes running, Herr Kapitän,' he said. 'Fifty-seconds until the first strike.'

The crew of *U-113* stared at one another and waited.

On *Puma's* bridge, Wolfgang Herzog gave the signal for all ships to engage the enemy with a full broadside of torpedoes, a tactic that had proved to be successful in the past. No doubt the sharp-eyed Royal Navy lookouts would spot the tell tale signs of torpedo tracks but that was to be expected. The whole idea behind such a move was to disrupt their attack, and anything that caused them to slow was a positive outcome. Chaotic alterations of course to avoid being torpedoed might well lead to collisions and panic, and if by chance a torpedo struck home, all to the good. In the meantime his flotilla would then make best possible speed in the opposite direction.

What concerned Herzog most was the British cruiser. She had come very close to hitting the *Puma* and in the same salvo had struck the Narvik. It had started a fire just forward of the quarterdeck, obliterating the aft housing. The commander had reported six crew killed.

He raised his glasses, picked out the shape of the cruiser and warned his port signalman he was about to give the order to fire torpedoes.

'Now!' he snapped to the signalman, and a brief flicker of light sent the order to commence firing. From *Puma's* bank of tubes, six torpedoes thumped out from the starboard side and splashed into the waves. In line astern and within moments of each other, another twenty-four sleek torpedoes found the water, accelerated hard and homed in on the three designated targets.

As he swept his binoculars down the foreshortened length of the cruiser, an unexpected early explosion coincided with a great upheaval of water erupting from the cruiser's side beneath the forward funnel. The bow wave immediately fell away and she slewed hard round to starboard, exposing her port waist to Herzog's torpedoes.

Cheriton was four-thousand yards adrift of *Vibrant's* stern when the U-boat's torpedo struck the cruiser. Rutherford blinked as it exploded in a vivid flash of red and orange flame. Pushing on at best speed, Rutherford had eased his destroyer towards *Vibrant's* starboard quarter in an attempt to close the gap in what he perceived was a move by the cruiser to veer south. Rutherford therefore attempted to cut the corner. As a great column of water burst upwards along her starboard side *Vibrant* staggered and slewed hard round. In moments he could see her listing and it shocked him how quickly she lost forward momentum. But her guns had not been silenced and a full broadside crashed out towards the enemy destroyers. Of one thing he felt certain. That strike must have come from a submarine and the obvious area to search had to be south.

'Starboard twenty!' he ordered.

With the ship already at twenty-five knots she heeled hard to port and quickly turned onto what Rutherford presumed would be the reciprocal course to a torpedo's run.

'Midships . . . , steady . . . , steer one-seven-five.'

The wheelhouse acknowledged.

'Half ahead both, make revolutions for fourteen-knots.'

'Speed fourteen, aye aye, sir.'

'Let's have Asdic on the job, Number One.'

A minute later, with the underwater dome lowered from out of its storage compartment, the operator flicked a switch to begin the search.

Electronic pulses emanated from *Cheriton's* keel and with the ship's speed reduced to prevent disruption of the signal, they waited for a return echo to indicate the presence of a U-boat.

A second loud explosion erupted from astern and he turned to see *Vibrant* hit again, but this time over on the port side. For a moment he frowned and then realised it had to be the German flotilla taking advantage.

For Kapitänleutnant Konrad Drexler the possible sinking of a British cruiser would long live in his memory. Few submariners could ever know the thrill of such an attack. Admiral Dönitz must surely greet him with much ceremony at the quayside. The bands would strike up a martial tune and the women would throw flowers. Salutes and speeches would follow in praise of *U-113's* exploits and Drexler could imagine a personal introduction to the Admiral. And there would be one other officer with whom he could share his pleasure, his father Admiral Heinrich Alexander Drexler. He too would be proud.

Nine miles to the south and east, Richard Thorburn caught the flash of gunfire to the north. A sudden squall made the flashes waver, the rolling thunder of the cruiser's guns reverberating across the waves. Sleet came in sideways, a curtain across the sea.

'Guns-Bridge!'

'Bridge,' Thorburn answered.

'Enemy destroyers under fire from *Vibrant* and *Kingfisher*. I think the *Maria* was sailing north-east, difficult to say. No sign of *Cheriton*.'

Brackendale banged into the next roller and threw spray at the bridge. Thorburn wiped his face and clung to the rail.

'Very well,' he said. 'We'll hold course. Open fire when there's something to see, preferably not at the freighter.'

'Aye aye, sir.'

Thorburn ordered an increase in speed, squeezing the last revolutions from the engines. The gunfire increased in volume and even through the opaque sleet they could determine the orange-yellow flashes.

'Number One,' he said with a raised voice.

'Sir?'

'A quick tour of the ship would be useful. A quiet word where needed. You know the drill.'

'Of course, sir. On my way.'

Thorburn watched him go, wiped sleet from his face and turned back to the screen. Again he heard the deeper roar of *Vibrant's* six-inch guns. The battle grew louder.

Sub-Lieutenant George Labatt clung onto the port quarterdeck rail and leaned over to peer ahead through the sleet. The noise of the guns echoed from across the water and he thought he spotted a subdued glow. It was gone before he could be sure.

'See anything?' It was Armstrong coming down the port rail.

Labatt wiped spray from his face. 'Not really, just a flicker in the distance.'

He saw Armstrong look up at the Pompom crew. 'They ready?'

Labatt grinned. 'Itching to get started.'

Armstrong tilted his head. 'It'll come soon enough, less than five minutes now.'

Labatt straightened and moved to the bottom of the galley deck-house ladder. He reached up. 'I'll join them.' He clambered to the top and stepped onto the platform.

Positioned high on the housing, the four-barrelled Pompom trained round in its mounting. Leading Seaman Gunner 'Taff' Williams had settled comfortably to the back sight and nodded as Labatt came to stand close.

'All right, Williams?' he asked.

Taff nodded beneath his steel helmet. 'So far, sir.'

'Good. You might find something to shoot at soon. The Captain's doing his best to find a German destroyer. Okay with you?'

Williams grunted his approval and caressed the Pompom's trigger. He glanced at the ammunition feedrails ensuring there was a ready supply. His primary role was 'layer', the oft abused 'up and downer', and along with his eight man gun crew they'd notched up a formidable amount of confirmed 'kills'. It was a remarkable tally and Williams had a natural flair for dispatching enemy aircraft.

Labatt leaned back against the protective screen and took a slow intake of breath. He Looked towards the bridge and grinned. Up there his Captain would be making the necessary decisions that enabled him to fight the ship. From Labatt's perspective the man could do no wrong. Joining ship as a mere Midshipman straight out of Devonport's training establishment, the young Labatt had quickly found his Captain to be generous with his time, unstinting with his praise, and the one man who'd properly unravelled the mysteries of using a sextant. And then there was Thorburn's ability to put his faith in such a youngster and trust him with the most onerous of duties.

George Labatt's 'Mentioned-in-Despatches' was awarded after he'd helped to man the fo'c'sle guns during a harrowing battle with a large German destroyer. When push came to shove the Captain had recognised a devotion to duty that others might lack and had rewarded him for his bravery. The promotion to 'Sub-Lieutenant' followed shortly thereafter, a recognition of stout leadership.

The driving sleet faded and stopped, the heavy clouds clearing. Pale moonlight bathed the sea and in that moment Sub-Lieutenant George Labatt found the battle laid out before him.

He levered himself away from the screen and prepared to direct the gunners in their choice of target.

Thorburn wiped his mouth with the back of his hand, the extent of the battle plainly revealing itself from behind the clearing sleet. A German flotilla lay off the starboard bow, *Kingfisher* zigzagged towards them, guns blazing, and *Vibrant's* six-inch guns blasted regular salvoes at the German destroyers. She lay about eight-thousand yards off *Brackendale's* port bow.

Thorburn shouted at the Control Tower. 'Open fire!'

The guns reacted instantly and the forward pair belched smoke and flame, cordite whipping back across the bridge.

He snatched up his binoculars and scoured the sea beyond the Germans. There surely ought to be some sign of the freighter skulking in the background. Try as he might all he found were empty waves.

But then, as he traversed the glasses back towards *Vibrant* Thorburn realised that the cruiser had been badly hit, literately stopped in the water. She'd obviously suffered mortal wounds but still engaged the enemy. Thorburn peered ahead at the Germans. He lifted the glasses and scanned from port to starboard and found all four enemy ships had deployed torpedo tubes over their starboard sides. They were still holding in line astern, a classic Kriegsmarine tactic. *Kingfisher* surged back into view, heading straight for the enemy, her 'A' and 'B' guns hammering smoke and flame. Glowing tracer whipped between ships, red and green incendiary, blistering white. Sparks flew, ricocheting off armoured steel. Men died.

He let the glasses drop and looked again at the cruiser. She had settled evenly, the water almost up to her main deck. God knows what it must be like below decks. Boats had been swung out from their davits and yet there were no obvious signs of sailors preparing to abandon ship. And more importantly all her guns, six-inch and four-inch, continued to bombard the enemy. He looked again at the German ships. The neatly disciplined line had dissolved into 'every man for himself'. Shell splashes thumped the sea between the warships and as he looked the last in line took a direct hit on its quarterdeck.

'*Vibrant* signalling, sir.' A lamp clattered to acknowledge the call.

He swung round to glance at the cruiser's bridge. Then her signal lamp flickered.

'Read it,' he said.

An enemy shell screamed low over their heads and Thorburn flinched. *Brackendale's* guns roared in reply and the starboard Oerlikon burst into action.

'From *Vibrant*, sir!' The Yeoman shouted

to make himself heard. 'Message reads, "*Brackendale* will find *Maria*. Sink if . . , n. e. c. e . . ,s s a, necessary." Message ends, sir.'

'Very well, acknowledge.'

The shutter clattered and fell silent.

'Guns-bridge.'

'Bridge.'

'*Cheriton* bearing Red-ninety. Range eight thousand, course one-seven-five, speed fourteen-knots.'

Thorburn trained his glasses off to port, distant. And *Cheriton* swam into his lens with a quiet bow wave. Thorburn frowned, perplexed. Was she hunting a U-boat, Rutherford using his own intuition as to where a torpedo may have originated? Maybe the German flotilla had not hit the cruiser.

He let the binoculars rest and hang by the strap, and *Brackendale's* guns thumped more shells at the enemy. Tracer ripped in from ahead and smashed the screen, shards flying. A man grunted with pain, sank down. Someone bent to help him.

Thorburn frowned and narrowed his eyes in an attempt to blot out the battle. He had his orders, clear cut he thought, but where to start? If he'd been able to follow the original calculation by Martin, then the *Maria* should've been intercepted somewhere off to the right beyond the Germans. He peered over the damaged screen at *Kingfisher*. She was making a thorough nuisance of herself and attracting the attention of both the nearest Germans. He might be able to use her as a decoy and slip away before turning north again.

He snatched a last look at the cruiser and made up his mind. It was now or never.

'Hard-a-starboard!' he snapped at the voice-pipe.

And *Brackendale* heeled hard to port, guardrail awash, clawing her way to starboard, her bow wave thrashing the fo'c'sle. Thorburn took note of his ship board surroundings, knowing he must eliminate all chances of being detected. Muzzle flashes and tracer helped an enemy locate the ship, not ideal.

He bent to the Control Tower's voice-pipe. 'Cease fire, Guns!'

'Cease fire, aye aye, sir.' And Carling passed the order. 'Check! Check! Check!'

The four-inch main armament fell silent and after a couple more shouted commands the Oerlikon and lastly Labatt's Pompoms followed suit. *Brackendale* steadied towards the east and faded into the darkness, quickly leaving the battle astern.

CHAPTER TWENTY-THREE .. ATTACK

U-113 slid slowly south, every minute adding metres of distance between itself and the strike on the British cruiser. Suspended one-hundred metres beneath the waves, *U-113* pushed on. Konrad Drexler grinned at the members of his crew. According to the time elapsed on his Executive Officer's stop watch, it was the second torpedo that had detonated against the cruiser's hull. At that time a check through the periscope revealed the cruiser to be heeling hard to starboard, the rails under water. It was a moment to savour. By his estimate a five-thousand ton Royal Navy cruiser had fallen victim to his attack. He chuckled and slapped his thigh.

'This will please the Fuhrer, my friends. I tell you now, we will receive great honour for this night's work.'

Another explosion resounded against the hull and he looked sharply at his hydrophone operator. Easing the headphones from his ears the man nodded and tilted his head, eyes half closed.

'Torpedo I think. Not ammunition. I thought I heard many torpedoes in the water.'

Drexler blinked and pursed his lips. That

would be the Kriegsmarine tactic, more so with a crippled cruiser to aim at. But he wanted no confusion about his identity.

'Make our depth one-twenty.'

'One-twenty metres,' said the First Officer, and the boat dipped its nose to descended deeper into the dark waters.

Drexler corrected his stance against the sloping deck and nodded to his navigating officer. 'We have done enough damage. We go home, to Cherbourg. Let the men know.'

'Level. One-twenty metres, Herr Kapitän.'

'So be it,' Drexler acknowledged. 'And come left to nine-zero degrees.'

'Left to nine-zero degrees. Jawohl, Herr Kapitän.'

Slowly, quietly, U-113 began to turn and depart the scene, creeping away for the safety of coastal waters.

The turn for the French Peninsula had not been completed when the hydrophone operator barked a warning.

'Propellers, Herr Kapitän!'

Drexler met Engel's eyes and questioned with a jerk of his chin. The man listened intently and gave a harsh whisper.

'North-west,' came the answer, and he closed his eyes in concentration.

Drexler waited. The man was no novice, well able to evaluate the difference between the pitch of propellers.

He opened his eyes. 'High speed screws, Herr Kapitän.'

'Verdammt,' Drexler cursed. He had seen one Royal Navy Fleet destroyer engaging the Kriegsmarine on the surface, but there'd been no sign of one emerging from the west.

'Exec,' he said sharply, 'rig for silent running.'

The boat became a submerged ghost, only the electric motor and slow turning propellers giving any indication that humans interacted within the elongated iron drum.

Drexler watched Engel. His slightest movement gave meaning to the world above, an Englander's approach, or not. A partially raised eyebrow, a tilt of his head, eyes narrowed or closed as he listened. The easing of an earphone and then the fixed stare, a prelude to danger.

And then all inside the steel tube heard it, the hated sound of an underwater search. It announced itself as a high pitched chirruping, what the British called Asdic, an electronic pulse transmitted as sound waves. If the sound wave met something solid the pulse was reflected back to the destroyer, and every member of *U-113's* crew had experienced just such a situation.

Engel's eyes dilated. 'Asdic, Herr Kapitän.'

At that moment the entire crew heard the ringing pulse of the destroyer's search.

Drexler mouthed a question. 'From where?'

'Starboard astern.'

Drexler uttered a harsh whisper. 'Left rudder, half over.' It was the first move in a game of cat and mouse and a U-boat commander must always try and keep the surfaced warship trailing behind. That way the submarine presented the smallest surface area to their electronic surveillance, but also allowed *U-113* to hopefully slip farther away from the hunter.

Engel grimaced. 'Attacking.'

Drexler glanced at the depth gauge. One-hundred and twenty metres. It took time for a depth-charge canister to sink so deep, precious time in which he could manoeuvre the boat. Now the insistent noise of the destroyer's engine and propellers could be heard through the pressure hull. The sound echoed overhead.

'Splashes!' Engel spat. '. . . . Five.'

'Emergency full ahead! Come hard left!' Drexler raised his eyes imagining the destroyer passing over, screws churning the waves. For vital seconds the Englander would be deaf to U-113's movements.

'Steer two-seven-zero.'

'Two-seven-zero.'

Then came the detonations, mind wrenching, and Drexler grudgingly admitted they were well placed. The ear shattering explosions slammed against the hull and the boat twisted to the violent blows. The deck canted nose down, the ferocity of explosive lifting the stern and sending U-113 deeper. The main lighting flickered and died, pitch black before the emergency lighting cut in. It took the Engineer minutes to regain control, the boat levelling out at one-ninety metres. An oil gland on a vertical pipe sprang a leak, the black residue dribbling down the side.

'Slow ahead,' Drexler ordered and with the last explosion fading astern the boat reverted to silent running. He concentrated on Engel.

'The Englander turns to port.'

Drexler closed his eyes, imagining the destroyer returning to check the surface for oil or debris. With no proof of a 'kill' her captain would mount another search. He turned to his Executive Officer.

'Take us down, Jurgen. Two-hundred metres.'

Dive planes rotated, the boat edged deeper and levelled off at two-hundred metres below the hunter.

Drexler returned his gaze to Engel. The metallic 'ping' swept over and under and round the U-boat's cylindrical shadow but no resulting echo reflected off the hull.

Konrad Drexler gave a tight grin. He knew a thing or two about underwater hide and seek.

The *Castillo de Maria* ploughed on towards Cherbourg. Not that Menéndez favoured the port of Cherbourg over any other French port, it was just that the Kapitän of the *Puma* had confirmed their position and a bearing to Cherbourg had been plotted. And the man from South America had allowed himself to be persuaded that Cherbourg would be the best course of action.

So now, even though his German escort was fighting desperately to fend off the Royal Navy, Menéndez had used the driving sleet to hide his ship from British eyes. He crossed to the port bridge-wing, stepped outside into the bitter wind and levelled his binoculars at the receding battle. The sound of gunfire met his ears and muzzle flashes accompanied the rolling thunder. Here and there orange fireballs blossomed momentarily to light the darkness as a shell exploded on target. Tracer criss-crossed the sea.

Carlos Menéndez shivered from the cold wind and stepped back inside. He rubbed his hands to get the circulation going and moved over to where steel ducting brought warmth from the big coal fired boiler. He peered ahead through the sleet spattered screen and rubbed his jaw. For the first time in a long while, Carlos felt truly worried. He was a kind man in reality, not prone to bullying or engaging in slanging matches. He much preferred the quiet life and right now he wondered what had possessed him to get involved in such a risky enterprise.

Whether he actually felt frightened, well that was something else. He knew he was no coward. As a youth in an Argentinean dockyard he'd faced down more than one bunch of drunkards looking for trouble. When needed he'd been good with his fists and not shied away from confrontation.

He clapped his hands and straightened his back, stuck his chest out. Turning to the rear of the bridge he found First Officer Ricardo Francella had appeared and was bent over the chart table.

'Ricardo!' he called loudly, 'How much longer must we sail these waters? Or are we never to reach French shores?'

In the quiet light of the chart table his First Officer looked up in consternation. 'Not so long, my Capitán. We must be patient, *de Maria* is old, no? We cannot expect her to always be on time.' He spread his hands in supplication. 'Our engineer can only do his best, Capitán.'

A stray shell thumped the sea off the port quarter, a column of spray rising. Menéndez thrust a pointed finger at the falling foam.

'Not always on time, doing our best? At this rate, Ricardo, our best might never be enough. You hear me?'

His First Officer shrugged, a forlorn gesture. 'I am sorry, Capitán. I will have words, see what we can do.'

Menéndez showed his teeth in a broad grin. 'Good, my friend, very good. Well said. I am sure you can make things better. Kind words, mind? Encouragement, no sticks.'

The dull sound of a harsh explosion reached their ears. If ever anyone needed encouragement there it was. Ricardo Francella bobbed his head and was gone, and Menéndez turned back to the screen. As he squinted through the mottled glass the sleet increased in strength and he lost sight of the fo'c'sle. The *Castillo de Maria* might yet escape her tormentors.

Kingfisher plunged into the increased volume of sleet and Horwood immediately broke off the contact. It was all well and good taking it to the enemy when dealing with reasonable visibility, not so good when a veil was drawn.

'Cease fire,' he called. And to the wheelhouse pipe. 'Hard-a-port!' He glanced at the compass and watched the swing as she came round towards where *Vibrant* had last been seen. Whether she was still afloat, time would tell.

'Midships.' The compass settled. 'Steady . . . , steer two-eight-five.'

'Two-eight-five, aye, sir.'

'Revolutions for ten knots.'

Kingfisher eased down from her fighting speed. As long as the sleet fell so thickly, Horwood felt able to chance a U-boat still being in proximity. And he had to approach the cruiser with caution. The crew could be abandoning ship, men and boats in the water.

'You lookouts,' he called. 'We're approaching *Vibrant's* last seen position. There's likely to be men in the water. Keep a sharp watch.'

Clad in heavy oil-skins the watchkeepers

cleared icy flakes from their eyes and redoubled their efforts to spot the first sign of survivors. Binoculars, useless in the white haze, were left untouched.

Lieutenant-Commander Charles Rutherford brought *Cheriton* round under full helm and onto the U-boat's signal. The 'ping' of the Asdic on the bridge repeater was clear as a bell and in accordance with each small alteration of course Rutherford felt he was going 'right down the throat' of his quarry. And he thought how satisfying it was to have the chance to seek and destroy a single enemy vessel. He still remembered how helpless he'd been when the E-boats had attacked the convoy. In some small way this felt like vindication of an outstanding debt, not an E-boat granted, but another form of equally detested seaborne stealth. Along with that a Royal Navy light cruiser needed to be avenged. A lot of sailors had probably paid the price for this U-boat's deadly attack. *Cheriton* ran on, the depth-charge reload complete, the crew tense, those in the Asdic cabinet straining to hold the target. The time between 'pings' grew shorter and a judgement was made as to the U-boat's depth. Settings were applied to the detonators and a warning issued to the depth-charge crew.

Rutherford gripped the bridge-rail and stared into the sleet. A thought crossed his mind and he gave a taut smile. The surface engagement astern of *Cheriton* might well be constrained by the weather but not so for this hunter. From the beginning of anti-submarine warfare this had always been a game of hide and seek and even in the best of weather, except for electronic aids, both antagonists were blind to each other.

The last fifty-yards to the calculated point of release were covered in absolute silence and then the fire button was pressed. This time six canisters went down, two from each of the hand-operated rails, and a thrower hurled one depth-charge up and out from either side of the quarterdeck. The 'pattern' sank into the depths and at five-hundred feet below the surface, each 290 pound canister of TNT began to explode.

Inside the pressure hull of *U-113*, Engel had reported hearing splashes from the next series of 'water bombs'. Drexler immediately ordered, 'Hard right rudder! Depth one-fifty, full ahead both.'

The boat's motors transmitted power, sucking life from the batteries. The dive planes gave lift and the sleek hull twisted to starboard. They waited, eyes raised in expectation, trusting in the Kapitän's experience. The first detonation came before the turn was complete, hammering the hull. The next explosion stunned the mind, shockingly brutal, driving air from battered lungs. Lights went out again, flickered, and came back on. The stern lifted and *U-113* went into an unintended down angle. Wide eyed men looked to each other for reassurance - there was none to be had.

Another shattering blow left them deafened, panting for air. Periscope seals succumbed to the pressure waves, leaking at the glands. The fourth charge activated early, noisy but outside the killing zone. The fifth, launched from a thrower found the right depth, collided with the port side saddle tank, rolled off and slipped deeper before exploding beneath the stern hydroplanes. Valves jolted open and water trickled from a dozen lines, the bilges filling. Worse yet, the stern dive plane operator reported his wheel sticking.

Drexler reached for a hand hold and gave a confident smile.

'The Englanders are blind comrades. We have had worse in the Atlantic, no?'

It was all bravado and the crew knew it, but in the circumstances they were happy to go along with it. They were fortified by each other and the brave words of their commander.

The last depth charge failed . . . , initially.

It struck the conning tower, glanced off, clattered over the 20mm machine-guns, dropped onto the flak gun 'bandstand' and then lodged between the gun's pedestal mount and shield. Firmly wedged in place the canister was dragged deeper by the U-boat's uncontrolled dive.

Finally, at a depth far exceeding the

hydrostatic pistol's original setting, the mechanism suddenly activated and initiated the expected sequence of events. Two-hundred and ninety pounds of prime TNT combusted instantaneously in a violent explosion. The resulting shock wave led to a catastrophic breech of the U-boat's pressure hull.

Where the base of the conning tower met the curvature of the hull a crack appeared. Under the enormous forces imparted by 260 metres of external pressure, a jet of water cascaded into the control room. Lights went out. Pipes fractured and sheared, batteries became inundated, a motor jumped off its mounting and a torpedo came loose to fall from its rack. A man died, squashed beneath. As the emergency lighting again flicked on the carnage revealed was overwhelming and complete. Men lay sprawled in contorted heaps, screaming with the agony of broken limbs. Eardrums had burst, blood oozing, tongues bitten, teeth smashed. Bones subjected to extreme shock snapped and punctured the skin, arteries pumping blood. A furious violence had been visited on the boat and the fragility of the human body had been amply demonstrated.

Konrad Drexler clawed up the steeply sloping deck. Excruciating pain lanced through his chest and he grunted in disbelief. He made a desperate attempt to staunch the enormous inrush of water. But it meant more clambering up the almost vertical incline of a U-boat in free fall.

Then he caught sight of the depth-gauge. The needle passed below the 280 metre mark and trembled down towards 300. For the first time in his life, Drexler felt afraid. He turned his head and found Engel's eyes staring wildly, bulging in their sockets. The gaping fracture widened, the pressure hull failing, seawater becoming a torrent. The weight of water served only to hasten the U-boat's demise.

In the forward torpedo room, the outer and inner doors imploded and the men who'd so diligently tended their lethal cargo of 'eels', drowned in a welter of foaming seawater.

In the engine room, now the highest part of the boat, the electric motors ground to a halt. The propeller glands and packing failed, and the rudder, already damaged by earlier explosions, broke free. Another leak revealed. The pressure inside multiplied until breathing became unsustainable, ribs cracked.

The Chief had no illusions as to what was coming and prepared for the inevitable. He braced himself between a diesel engine and the curvature of the hull and waited for his lungs to cave in. It wasn't long in coming.

Konrad Drexler dragged his eyes across to the depth gauge. In the fading light of a single flickering bulb he saw the boat had plummeted to a depth of 310 metres. He had often wondered what the true crush depth of a Mark VII U-boat was and he knew he was about to find out. But the rising flood of water robbed him of the answer. Fear was replaced by acceptance. The water had settled chest high for a while, but now, moved by whatever forces were involved, the water rose swiftly to cover mouth and nose. The instinct to survive had forced him to hold his breath. Then unable to fight any longer his lungs filled with water and Konrad Dexter met his death in the exact same cruel way so many innocent, unsuspecting merchant seamen had perished at his command.

Minutes later the crushed remains of *U-113* came to rest in the darkest depths, the ancient silted floor momentarily disturbed before finally settling over the grave of one more iron coffin.

On the waves above *U-113's* last resting place, *Cheriton's* Asdic compartment reported strange sounds that the operator had never previously heard. They were the screeching of metallic surfaces grinding together, and lastly the dull boom of a collapsing bulkhead. Of one thing the operator could be certain, he'd lost contact with the U-boat.

Standing at the fore-bridge, Rutherford cursed. Why had they lost contact? Had the U-boat given them the slip? Had the two depth-charge patterns been enough to convince him to stay down and slink away? Going by the operator's report of unusual noises it could also be that *Cheriton* had registered her first 'kill'.

Unlikely with only two patterns dropped, but possible. In any event, an uncertain outcome dictated he commence 'lost contact' procedure and begin combing the area in an ever widening square search.

He cursed again, shaking his head. Or should he abandon this particular mission and go to the aid of *Vibrant*? He moved to the port bridge-wing and trained his binoculars aft beyond the quarterdeck. What little he could see through the sleet convinced him the cruiser appeared very low in the water. Surely his duty lay in going to the rescue of what must be many men in the water?

He checked with Asdic. 'Anything?'

'No contact,' came the reply.

Rutherford made up his mind and leaned to a voice-pipe.

'Port twenty.'

The helmsman acknowledged, the ship heeled gracefully to starboard and Rutherford steadied her onto a bearing that would take them close to the suffering cruiser.

He gripped the rail and allowed himself a small smile. He couldn't be certain but deep inside he felt quietly satisfied that he had gone some way to avenge the loss of so many sailors in the east bound convoy that the E-boats had attacked off the North Foreland.

CHAPTER TWENTY-FOUR ..
CAPTAIN LABATT

Thorburn's face was red raw, the wind driven stinging needles of sleet continually thrashing his unprotected skin. But visibility had improved, marginally, and he was determined to make every effort to find the *Castillo de Maria*. The weather was still thick enough that if he found the merchantman now there was a strong possibility that he could force her to accompany him out of the immediate vicinity. If the current rate of precipitation continued the Germans would be hard pressed to discover *Maria's* whereabouts. There were a few 'ifs' thrown in to that equation but at the moment he thought the outcome more likely to favour a small Royal Navy destroyer. And during the last few minutes it had occurred to him that with a bit of improvisation there might well be a way to maximise the chances of success.

Despite his numbed face he managed a smile. 'Mister Martin, do you feel we have the freighter within our grasp?'

'If she's maintained her course then we must be very close, sir.'

Thorburn grimaced. There it was again, another 'if'. He moved to the chart table. 'Show me.'

Martin flicked on the feeble bulkhead lamp, lifted the protective oilskin and pointed.

Thorburn looked hard at the circled dot and the line of bearing which they had originally followed. All a nice theory and Martin's plotting brought it to life, somehow making it real. And yet if he removed the pencilled workings the chart would reveal the bare truth; a very large expanse of water it was easy to get lost in.

'Guns - Bridge!'

Thorburn spun round and leaned to the pipe.

'Bridge!'

'Fine off the starboard bow. Might be the *Maria*. Two-thousand yards at a guess. Only caught a glimpse.'

'Very well,' Thorburn said and changed voice-pipes. 'Starboard five.'

'Starboard five. Aye aye, sir.'

'Midships . . . , steady. Steer oh-one-oh degrees.'

'Wheel's amidships, steering oh-one-oh, sir.'

Thorburn straightened and peered over the screen. He brushed a dusting of sleet from his arms and then raised his binoculars. Just as quickly he let them hang. God, he thought, how he hated this bloody weather. Sleet, sleet, and more sleet. It was a blizzard in all but name so it might as well snow and be done with it. He turned his back to the weather and hunched down slightly out of the wind. But then he reminded himself of how it was this very limited visibility that had helped him achieve his aim. If that *was* the *Castillo de Maria* out there, then just this once God could be forgiven.

'Guns - Bridge!'

'Captain here.'

'Ship dead ahead. It's the *Maria*. Range eighteen-hundred. She's seen us, altering course to starboard.'

Thorburn peered ahead and now, even without the doubtful aid of his binoculars he could see the outline of the old freighter.

'Well done, Guns. Stick a shot across her bows. Might bring 'em to their senses.'

The fo'c'sle mounting traversed over the starboard bow and the right barrel cracked off a single round. A plume of water rose and fell ahead of the rusting bows and moments later a man appeared on the starboard bridge-wing waving a white cloth.

Thorburn leaned back to the Range Finder's voice-pipe. 'I intend to close on her port side, try and speak with her captain. Keep the guns trained on her bridge. Might make him think twice.'

'Aye aye, sir.'

'Pilot,' he said. 'Bring us up along her port side, close as you can. Bridge to bridge would help.'

'Bridge to bridge,' Martin said sounding a little apprehensive, but followed with a firm, 'Aye aye, sir.'

The manoeuvre took a nerve wracking six or so minutes as Martin fought to bring

Brackendale's low bridge housing alongside but below the bridge of the old freighter. The two vessels were moving at ten knots no more than a hundred-feet apart. The water squeezing between hulls thrashed and boiled its way astern and Thorburn felt the need to issue a warning.

'Steady as you go, Pilot, but be prepared to break away without waiting for my order.'

It was to Sub-Lieutenant Martin's credit that he responded with a very firm, 'Aye aye, sir!' and Thorburn turned away to hide a smile. He moved to the starboard wing. There was no obvious signs of life this side of the bridge but he cupped his hands and shouted.

'Hello, *Maria*! I wish to speak with your captain.'

A minute passed without anyone coming out. Thorburn tried again.

'Hello, *Maria*! I wish to speak with your captain.'

This time, after a long pause, a thickset man in a peaked cap came out onto the bridge-wing. He'd brought a loud-hailer and used it to good effect.

'Hallo, you English. I am Capitán Menéndez of the *Castillo de Maria*. What is it you want?'

Thorburn felt relieved by the man's ability to speak English and he took a moment to gather his thoughts. He then called again.

'This is Lieutenant-Commander Thorburn of the Royal Navy. I am ordered to take you to an

English port. If you do as I ask all will be well, if not you will be sunk.'

The loud-hailer blared. 'But we are from Argentina. We are not at war with you. Why must we come?'

'There is a blockade of Nazi occupied ports. You will go no further.'

The man scratched his jaw before replying. 'Wait. I must speak with my crew.' And before Thorburn could refuse he had gone back inside.

Armstrong stepped closer. 'Do you really intend to sink her, sir?'

'Only if I'm left with no option. My orders were clear at the outset and I won't hesitate if that's what it takes.' He chuckled. 'I suspect there'll be a bit of an argument going on. Follow my instructions and head for England or become prisoners in the next few minutes.'

A geyser of water shot up between the vessels and *Brackendale* lifted to a wave, twisting.

'Watch her head, Pilot.'

'Steady, Cox'n,' Martin said loudly.

Thorburn heard the reminder and let it be, but relying on whoever was on the wheel in the freighter had become a little nerve wracking. The door to *Maria's* bridge-wing reopened and Menéndez raised his loud-hailer.

'I have spoken with my men. They are not happy but they have listened and agree to what you ask.'

Thorburn snatched a glance round at Martin.

'Give me a course for home.'

'Three-three-oh, for now, sir.'

Thorburn cupped his hands. 'Change course to three-three-oh degrees. Maintain speed. Do you understand?'

Menéndez waved a hand and without using the loud-hailer shouted back.

'I understand. You had better stand clear.'

Thorburn recognised the necessity to break away; he'd just ordered the *Maria* to turn in *Brackendale's* direction.

'Mister Martin, take us out to port and then drop back. I want to hold station within visual distance.'

'Aye aye, sir,' Martin said, leaned to the wheelhouse pipe and began issuing orders.

'Port ten,' he said and *Brackendale* veered out from the freighter's bulk. The small destroyer began to drift gently astern.

Thorburn noted the guns traversing slowly as Carling kept them aligned with the freighter's bridge. Arriving on station a thousand-yards off the freighter's stern rail, Martin ordered an increase to ten knots. The sleet drove in from the port beam but visibility remained fair.

'What are we steering, Pilot?'

'Three-three-oh degrees, sir.'

Thorburn reached for the back of his chair and stared at the rusting freighter's curved stern. Vaguely seen across the wide, bulbous transom the words *Castillo de Maria* had been painted in large gold lettering. Faded and worn with the passing years they gave weight to every sailor's common description of a 'tramp steamer'.

He straightened and blinked sleet from his eyelids. Martin's alteration of course had turned the freighter almost north-northwest, thirty degrees west of her previous bearing. That should be enough to throw the chasing pack off the scent, but one could never be sure. And if he had to turn *Brackendale* to fight off a German hunter, who knew whether or not *Maria's* captain would make a break to the east? Thorburn felt he'd been extremely fortunate thus far in twice finding her whereabouts, he might not be so lucky a third time. What, he wondered, could he do to prevent such a happening. If anything?

He narrowed his eyes against the sleet and found himself looking at the Bowchaser. And slowly, little by little, Richard Thorburn came up with an answer to his conundrum. A piece of history from the time of Nelson's navy had come to the fore. He grinned into the night and looked round.

'Number One.'

'Sir,' Armstrong said from the back of the bridge, and lowered his binoculars.

Thorburn guessed he'd been watching astern for any sign of the Germans.

'Anything?' he asked.

'No, sir, just the occasional glimpse of

something on fire.'

Thorburn motioned for him to step forward. 'Join me.'

Armstrong moved warily across the decking and came to stand at Thorburn's shoulder. 'Sir?'

'I've had an idea, Number One.' In the muted glow of the lamp he saw Armstrong give him a wary glance.

'You have, sir?'

'I have, yes. I want you to assemble a boarding party.'

Armstrong nearly choked. 'A boarding party, sir?'

'Yes, Number One, exactly that. You've hit the nail on the head.'

'But, sir . . . ?'

Thorburn chuckled at Armstrong's obvious consternation. He'd probably only ever heard those words spoken as a theoretical exercise.

'Seven men, all armed. That includes the Cox'n but leave him to me. Two Stokers, a Signaller, a helmsman, and a couple of Special Sea duty men. And perhaps you'd ask Sub-Lieutenant Labatt to join me?'

Armstrong raised an eyebrow, shook his head in disbelief and moved away with a subdued, 'Aye, sir.'

The sleet thinned, becoming more like rain, and in turn it became a fine drizzle, still dense enough to act as a visible barrier at two-thousand yards.

Thorburn bent to the wheelhouse pipe.

'Cox'n!'

'Sir?'

'Come up.'

'Aye aye, sir.'

In less than a minute Falconer came to attention and gave Thorburn a quick salute. 'Sir?'

Thorburn beckoned him over to the port wing. 'Give us some room, Jones.'

The lookout straightened from the screen and moved away to the back of the bridge. Thorburn tucked himself into the corner and Falconer took a pace nearer.

Quietly, Thorburn explained. 'I'm putting a boarding party on that ship, eight of you altogether. The First-Lieutenant is assembling them now. I volunteered you as 2i/c.'

Falconer's teeth gleamed as he grinned in the darkness. 'Thank you, sir. Very kind.'

'I thought you'd like that,' Thorburn said, and leaned closer. 'You'll be taking her to England. Sub-Lieutenant Labatt will be in command and I expect you to give him every assistance. Particularly,' he added, 'when our young man is unaware he needs it.' Around the ship they could hear shouted orders and the thumping of sea-boots on ladders.

'Leave it with me, sir. I'm sure the young officer will be more than capable.'

Thorburn pursed his lips, satisfied that Falconer would act in a timely manner if needed.

'Good. I trust you'll not let him come to any real mischief?'

'Not if I've got anything to do with it, sir.'

'Right, carry on, Cox'n, and I believe the armoury's open, you'd better draw a weapon.'

'Very good, sir,' Falconer said, snapped up a salute and made for the starboard ladder. As his footsteps faded, near at hand someone came clambering up the port ladder. The smiling face of Sub-Lieutenant George Labatt appeared above the plating.

'You wanted me, sir?'

Thorburn nodded and gestured for him to come closer. 'Indeed I do, Sub. I've lined up a job for you.'

'Yes, sir?' Labatt said, curiosity piqued.

Thorburn pointed to the freighter's half visible stern. 'How would you fancy taking command of the *Castillo de Maria* and sailing her home?'

Labatt's eyes widened in surprise, his mouth slightly open, and even in the poor, half light on the bridge, a look of total bewilderment registered on his face. It slowly dawned on him that his Captain was serious.

'You want *me* to take her back to England, sir?'

Thorburn couldn't keep the smile off his face. 'That would be the general idea. But not, of course, if you don't think you could manage?'

Labatt straightened to his full height. 'I believe I could get her back to England, sir. Certain of it.'

Thorburn put a hand on his shoulder. 'Good, well said. I'm giving you seven men to form a boarding party. The Cox'n will be your second-in-command. When you get aboard make sure the ship's crew are placed under lock and key with someone to guard them. The rest I leave to you.'

Labatt was already beginning to think ahead. 'What if they put up a fight, sir?'

'Deal with it as you see fit.'

Armstrong stepped on the back of the bridge and came forward.

'Well, Number One?'

'One boarding party assembled, sir. Volunteers to a man. I could have had three times the number so the Bosun drew names from a hat. The Cox'n has just joined them on the boat deck. Some of the other volunteers will be the boat's crew.'

'Weapons?' Thorburn asked.

'Rifles and pistols, and more than enough ammunition.'

Thorburn nodded and turned again to Labatt. 'You'd better go and draw yourself a side arm. Might come in handy.'

Armstrong intervened and held out a revolver with belt and holster. 'Thought of that,' he said, 'so I grabbed one of these. And a box of ammo.'

Labatt took it and buckled it round his waist. 'Thank you,' he said simply.

Armstrong grinned. 'I'll have the boat's crew

stand by,' he said and made for the ladder.

Thorburn turned to look over the bows. 'Right, Mister Labatt. Time I got the old *Maria* to stop.' He glanced at Martin. 'Pilot, bring us up on her starboard side. Fifty-yards or so.'

'Starboard side, fifty-yards, sir,' Martin acknowledged and within a minute *Brackendale* increased speed and veered to starboard, presenting her port side to the freighter. It wasn't long before Thorburn raised his own loud-hailer and called across the water for *Maria's* captain.

The door to the bridge-wing opened and Menéndez lifted his hailer.

'What now, English?'

'I intend to board you. Heave to.'

'But this is not correct. We do not cause you any trouble. You say steer three-three-oh and we do it. Is that not so?'

Thorburn suppressed a grin. Everything he said was true but he wasn't to know the real reason behind the instruction.

'Yes, captain, you are right, and you have done all I ask. But now you must stop to be boarded.' Choosing his next words carefully he said, 'I do not wish to harm the *Castillo de Maria* but if you do not stop I *will* open fire.'

Menéndez let the loud-hailer hang by his side and Thorburn could see the disconsolate shake of his head.

'All right, English, I will order my engine room

to stop *de Maria*. I have only a rope ladder. It will be this side.'

Thorburn raised a hand to acknowledge the man's difficulty in agreeing. 'Thank you, Captain. I have a boat ready as soon as you are stopped.'

Menéndez turned away and stepped inside out of sight and shortly thereafter the *Castillo de Maria* began to slow. Thorburn laid his loud-hailer on the chair and looked up. 'Pilot, plot a course for home and transfer it onto a fresh chart. Mister Labatt will need it. Quick as you can.'

'Aye aye, sir,' Martin said, and disappeared down the ladder for the chart house. After what seemed an inordinate amount of time the old freighter finally heaved to and sat wallowing in the waves.

Thorburn moved to the back of the bridge where he could see down over the port ladder to the boat deck and the waiting boarding party. The 'whaler' had already been lowered to the waves, the crew with raised oars, waiting. With both vessels stopped *Brackendale* had drifted out to almost two-hundred yards, still an easy row for the boat's crew. He turned to face young Labatt.

'Now listen, Sub. If you have any concerns about what to do next, speak to the Cox'n. The Chief has a lot of sea going years under his belt. He'll more than likely have an answer. Understood?'

Labatt settled the belt round his waist and nodded, the normally smiling face severe in the extreme.

'Yes, sir,' he said sharply.

'Very well, then,' Thorburn said and reached out to shake his hand. 'Good luck, 'Captain' Labatt, and I'll see you in England.'

That brought the broad grin back to Labatt's face. He released the hand shake and gave Thorburn a smart salute.

'Thank you, sir,' he said and stepped onto the ladder. He dropped out of sight and reappeared moving swiftly to Armstrong's side.

Martin came out with a folded chart and passed it over. 'Good luck, George.'

Labatt thanked him, tucked the chart inside his jacket and where the guard rail had been parted lowered himself onto the Jacob's ladder and down into the whaler.

Chief Petty Officer Barry Falconer gave the order to "shove off" and two of the oarsmen pushed with their blades against the hull. The boat cleared the immediate vicinity of the ship's side, oars were dipped, and the crew began to row.

Thorburn, still watching through the drizzle, found himself smiling at Sub-Lieutenant George Labatt. He was sat bolt upright in the stern-sheets next to the Cox'n and looking every inch the Captain-in-Waiting. He certainly looked ready to take up his new appointment.

Thorburn let the smile fade and returned to the bridge-screen. From there he watched the boat reach the foot of the freighter's rope ladder.

The first man grabbed hold and began to climb. At the top he swung a leg over the gunwale and clambered inboard. He slipped his rifle from his shoulder, leaned over the side and called for the next man to join him.

The Cox'n moved to the boat's waist and began to climb. Thorburn turned to the wheelhouse pipe. 'Stand by,' he said, and looked up. It wouldn't be long now.

CHAPTER TWENTY-FIVE ..
FIRST COMMAND

Sub-Lieutenant George Labatt stood swaying with the boat's movement and stepped forward to where the Leading-Hand steadied the bottom of the rope ladder. He would be last man up, all eyes on him, with the icy rain set to make the climb more precarious than it might otherwise be. The boat rose and twisted as a wave slapped the ship's side and he gave himself more time, steeling himself for a controlled lunge.

The moment came. A foot on the gunwale, reaching with both hands, and the other foot finding a wooden rung. His hands gripped onto coarse rope side-rails made greasy by the rain, and thankful he'd not made a fool of himself, he began the climb. Careful not to slip off the wet rungs, he made it to the top and gratefully swung a leg over the side. Glancing back down the side he saw that the boat's crew were already pulling strongly for *Brackendale*, so he turned inboard to assess his position. Two of the boarding party had waited for him to step on deck.

Able-Seaman Joe Branaghan motioned with his rifle. 'The Cox'n's up on the bridge, sir. It's through there.'

Labatt peered into the gloom of the bridge

superstructure and found an open door creaking with the ship's motion. With a sudden feeling of insecurity he pulled the revolver from its holster and eyed the two seamen.

'Right then,' he said, 'let's find out what they're up to.' He strode across the iron deck to the door, entered and halted at the foot of a stairway. If it was dark out on the main deck it was pitch black inside and he took a moment to let his eyesight acclimatise. A wooden handrail led up the left bulkhead and as his vision partially returned he mounted the steps. A half-landing gave way to a right angle turn, and after climbing the remaining stairs he found himself on a square platform with a glazed door at the far end. The faintest of orange lights glimmered feebly from the space beyond.

He pushed through to be greeted by a rifle pointed at his chest.

'Sorry, sir,' said the seaman lowering it to one side.

The Cox'n spoke up. 'Heard you coming, sir. Can't be too careful, don't know how many crew there are.'

Labatt looked round the enclosed area. In comparison to *Brackendale's* bridge this old freighter had been built to a luxurious standard. She had a fully glazed wide bridge-screen, a well worn but comfortable looking leather captain's chair, and the ship's wooden wheel glistened with its ornate spokes and brass fittings The space was lit by a masked lamp that offered a small amount of light through a narrow slit. Hanging from an articulated arm from one end of the chart table it was obviously the original lamp modified to suit the current situation. After the pitch black of the stairway it seemed to offer more than enough light. And then over by the shaded starboard side of the bridge three men stood leaning against the glass windscreen. One of the boarding party stood guard with his rifle at the ready.

Labatt felt the weight of his pistol and decided it was an unnecessarily theatrical addition to his authority. He tucked it back inside the flap of his holster.

'Who've we got here then, Cox'n?'

Before Falconer could answer the taller of the three men took a pace forward. The seaman with the rifle stopped him, prodding his chest with the muzzle.

'All right, Jameson, let him be,' Falconer said, and Jameson stepped back, rifle still held chest high.

Having moved into the light the man straightened his cap and drew himself up to his full height. Labatt caught the dull gleam of gold braid on the peak.

'I am Capitán Carlos Menéndez and the *Castillo de Maria* is under my command.'

Labatt, having been schooled in the traditions of Royal Navy protocol, was not blind to the importance of diplomacy. He came smartly to attention and snapped up a salute worthy of any parade ground Petty Officer.

'Sir,' he began, according the man all the respect due to his rank. 'I am Lieutenant George Labatt of His Majesty's Royal Navy, and I have orders to take this ship to England. I would be grateful if you would instruct your men not to interfere.'

Menéndez slowly returned the salute and Labatt felt the man's frustrated annoyance at having to accept the situation. Especially when having to obey such a young whippersnapper's orders.

'If that is what you wish, Lieutenant.'

'It is, Capitán, and I intend to continue on course three-three-oh.'

'I must call the engine room and have my helmsman on the wheel,' Menéndez said, pointing to one of the other men standing in the darkness.

'No need,' Labatt countered. 'We'll manage.'

The Cox'n moved towards the last man. 'And who's this?'

The man answered for himself in broken English. 'I am Sailing Master, Ricardo Francella. For many years.'

Labatt called Falconer to one side and gave his first command. 'Have our two Stokers escort the man down to the engine room. I want this ship up and running in fifteen minutes. Think they can manage?'

Stoker Jameson, with four years service aboard coastal freighters before joining the Royal Navy, had overheard. 'Begging your pardon, sir, but I could sort these engines in my sleep.'

The Cox'n was about to admonish him for interrupting but Labatt held him back, a hand on his arm. 'You certain?'

Jameson grinned. 'Me and Oldridge, sir, we know coal boilers like the back of our 'ands.'

Begrudgingly, the Cox'n nodded.

Labatt eyed Jameson for a moment, remembering he was a willing volunteer. 'Very well, but take this Francella person with you anyway, he might be useful. When you're sure you've got the hang of everything down there I want one of you to escort all the engine room crew back up here. Clear?'

'Clear as a bell, sir.'

The Cox'n looked about the bridge. 'Oldridge! You're with Jameson. And take this so called Sailing Master with you.'

The pair moved toward the door, Jameson with his rifle levelled at Francella's back. 'Move,' he urged, and all three filed out.

Chief Petty Officer Barry Falconer crossed to the wheel and studied the compass housing. It followed the usual layout, no surprises.

'Lockwood,' he said to the volunteer helmsman. 'See what you think.'

The man took the wheel, turned it from port to

starboard and back, and nodded. 'All right in 'ere, 'innit Cox'n. Nice and cosy.'

'Don't look so happy, sunshine. You'll be glad of that by the time you finish your watch.'

The smile disappeared as Lockwood realised there was just the two of them to share the load.

At the table, Labatt unfolded Martin's chart and spread it out. The plot showed clearly enough. Three-three-oh degrees at ten knots for one-hundred and twenty-miles until the given point of intersection, then change course onto a bearing of oh-four-oh for another hundred and sixty-miles to Devonport. The trouble was, he thought, daylight would come hours before they reached the intersection. If the weather cleared by dawn the Luftwaffe would be up searching at the first opportunity.

He straightened from the table and walked to the forebridge. Leaning on the polished wooden handrail he peered out through the glass and picked out the dark shape of the big hatch cover protecting the midships cargo hold. He must try and inspect the cargo before too long; not many people managed to examine a stash of gold bullion.

In the meantime there was command of the ship to exercise and if possible, enjoy. After all he was now 'Captain' of the *Castillo de Maria*, and although she might be an old rusting freighter, it was something every sea going officer aspired to. He must not be found wanting.

Beneath his feet he felt the first tremor of the propeller turning. Jameson and Oldridge had obviously mastered the engine and he turned to find Falconer.

'On our way, Cox'n. Next stop England.'

Falconer smiled at Labatt's youthful enthusiasm. A lot might happen between now and then. Fingers crossed for a trouble free passage.

The man called Emil Lorenz had looked on with growing alarm as the boarding party took control of the ship. Melting into the shadows he retreated to his store room where the sub-machine gun was hidden. Through many days of growing familiarity as dark as it was he quickly unearthed the gun along with spare magazines and slung it over his shoulder. The canvas hammock that served as his bed he took down, rolled up and placed on a shelf with other stores. Knife, fork, spoon and plate he tucked into an engineering spares cupboard and slid his tin cup inside his jacket. A final check by feeling around the store room convinced him he'd done all he could to hide his presence. Now it would be a case of avoiding a search party. After that he knew exactly where to hide himself.

In no way was Emil Lorenz ever going to voluntarily give himself up to the British.

The *Puma* was flinging up sheets of spray from her raked bows as Korvettenkapitän Wolfgang

Herzog increased speed and used the sudden deluge to break away from the engagement. Once again he found himself chasing after the old freighter. But he felt the weather had intervened at exactly the right moment. The Royal Navy fleet destroyer had begun to get the better of things, but as visibility began to decline Herzog saw the destroyer turn away. Her captain had clearly decided not to take chances in such poor conditions.

'Leitner,' he called to his First Officer, 'alter course to three-five-five degrees. We will hold that for five minutes and then steer zero-zero-five degrees for a further five minutes. Alternate between those two bearings until I order otherwise. I think the *Maria* will maintain her heading for Cherbourg and this gives us the best chance of finding her.'

Oberleutnant Rolf Leitner clicked his heels. 'Jawohl, Herr Kapitän. And she is very slow, will not be far away. We will soon find her I am sure.'

'I am reassured by your confidence, Leitner. Let us hope you are right. The Führer will not be happy if we fail.'

Leitner passed the order to the wheel and the *Puma* leaned into the turn. On the gun decks the clatter of shell cases being cleared away echoed up to the bridge, and minor damage to the superstructure was receiving improvised repairs.

So far, Herzog thought, things had gone better

than he might have expected. A Royal Navy cruiser had been severely damaged, if not sunk. His flotilla had beaten off two attacks by the British although he had lost one destroyer sunk and had two others badly damaged. Given what might have been the outcome with the cruiser running wild he felt he still maintained the upper hand. The British would be licking their wounds and going to the aid of the cruiser.

And then came a call from a lookout reporting the sighting of one of the flotilla joining.

It gave Herzog every reason to believe he would soon re-engage with the *Maria* and end the night successfully. He returned to his chair and sat. He was determined to escort the *Castillo de Maria* into Cherbourg harbour. Nothing would stand in the way of Korvettenkapitän Wolfgang Herzog.

CHAPTER TWENTY-SIX ..
GUNNERS AND SHIPMATES

Thorburn caught the moment the old freighter began to move and had to assume that the bridge and engine room were now in the hands of a scratch Royal Navy crew. So far so good.

'Pilot!' he said loudly.

'Sir?'

'We'll drop back astern of the *Maria*. Five-hundred yards should do it.'

'Five-hundred yards, aye aye, sir.'

Armstrong clattered up the ladder and onto the back of the bridge.

'Number One,' Thorburn called.

He stepped forward to stand at Thorburn's side.

'Any hiccups?'

Armstrong shook his head. 'Not from my point of view, sir. The boat crew said they all got aboard without a hitch.'

'Good, at least that bit went well. The next problem is implementing a useful defence in case of discovery. So I've decided to maintain a 'tail-end-charlie' approach and zigzag port to starboard around *Maria's* mean course.'

'What will you do when the weather clears?'

Thorburn couldn't help but grin. 'Don't ask

awkward questions. I think we'll just play that one by ear.'

'*Cheriton* and *Kingfisher*, sir?'

'I'll leave them out of it for now. If *Vibrant's* still afloat she'll need all the help she can get. And I don't want to give away our position. You never know what Jerry might have in the way of eavesdropping. I've heard recent talk of 'triangulation' to get a fix on where signals came from.'

'*Maria* signalling, sir.'

Thorburn looked across the bridge-wing, the gap between *Maria* and *Brackendale* growing larger by the minute. He caught 'flags' being waved.

'Tell me.'

'Reads, "Captain and crew secured. Following Pilot's plot." End of message, sir.'

'Very well, acknowledge,' Thorburn said, and turned up his collar against the wind. He looked at Armstrong.

'I'm going to take a turn round the ship. The bridge is yours.'

Armstrong straightened from the screen, a question on his face but unwilling to give Thorburn the satisfaction of hearing him ask. 'Very well, sir,' he said simply. 'I have the bridge.'

Thorburn turned for the starboard ladder and lowered himself nimbly to the flag deck and then down onto the fo'c'sle. He walked forward beneath the Oerlikon mount, past the door leading to the wardroom and cabins, and stepped up to the forward 4-inch gun mounting. The gun crew were stood to, flash capes protecting their head and shoulders, steel helmets strapped under their chins. The gun-captain saw him arrive, straightened to attention and whipped up a salute.

Thorburn returned it. 'Relax,' he said, peering at the individuals under the darkness of the splinter shield. 'Everything alright?'

'Aye, sir,' one of them volunteered, and another, 'Fine, sir.'

'Good,' he said easily. 'Just wanted to put you in the picture. Our boarding party has taken over the freighter and Sub-Lieutenant Labatt is charged with getting her to England. I suggested any port would do, thought it best not to tax his skills as a navigator.'

A few chuckles told him they appreciated their Captain's feeble effort of a joke. A voice added, 'Better than the Cox'n having a go.'

It was his turn to smile and he nodded. 'I can't argue with that.' He paused to pass an eye across each one. 'You're doing well, keep it up.' And with that he turned on his heel and headed for the quarterdeck.

Behind him the gunners grinned at one another, praising the Skipper's thoughtfulness in coming to see them. It showed they were not forgotten, valued, strengthening their resolve. Exactly what Thorburn had intended.

He dropped down the ladder to the main deck, dodged the motor boat, skirted the 21-inch searchlight housing and paused as he came alongside the galley. The quadruple Pompom was mounted above it and he called up to the gun crew.

'All right up there?'

Petty Officer Harry Garwood leaned out and looked down. He'd been the automatic choice to take over in Labatt's absence. 'Yes, sir!' he snapped. 'All's well.' The wind tore at the words.

'Good, got everything you need?'

Garwood's teeth gleamed in the darkness. 'We could do with something to shoot at, sir.'

Thorburn laughed. 'You frightened 'em off. Wait your turn.' He heard laughter come from within screen. 'Stay sharp,' he reminded them. 'The Germans aren't done yet.'

Garwood touched his steel helmet. 'Aye aye, sir,' he said. 'We're ready.'

Thorburn acknowledged by touching the peak of his cap and moved to the quarterdeck main armament, the gunners fully warned of his presence. The gun-captain saluted into the rain and gave a crisp, 'Sir!'

Thorburn nodded and touched his peak. 'Just wanted you to know we're not done with Jerry yet. We'll be acting as rearguard while the freighter pushes on for home. And if they don't find us in the dark, target practice will be resumed at dawn.'

'We'll 'ave 'em, sir! We're proper gunners.'

A cheer went up from the others and Thorburn couldn't help but grin; it was contagious.

'Right,' he said, 'in that case it sounds like I can rely on *Brackendale's* 4-inch gunners.' Again he touched his cap. 'Bloody marvellous. Carry on.'

He left them open mouthed and smiling, and then he arrived at the depth-charge rails. This part of the quarterdeck was fully exposed to the elements and Thorburn felt it. The wind and rain lashed in from off the port side and with the quarterdeck riding low in the water the sea foamed and splashed across the deck. It was a tough environment and called for a great deal of resilience to withstand the pounding.

Petty Officer Mathew Gregson saluted. 'Steady, sir, it's a bit rough at the moment.'

Thorburn reached for a depth-charge rail as extra support, feeling the water tugging at his boots. The cold rain soaked his face, ran down the inside of his collar, and he shook his head to clear it.

'Sorry about this, Gregson. I think you should grab what shelter you can in the lee of the galley. And tell Cook I want hot drinks all round. If you are needed, which I doubt at the moment, I'll make sure you're given ample warning.'

Gregson peered at him and grimaced. 'Thank you, sir. Hot drink won't go amiss.'

'Right then,' Thorburn said, 'I'll get out of your

hair. Don't forget now, hot drinks.' He turned away for the port side, and careful not to stray far from some form of handhold made his way back along the main deck to the bridge. Climbing the ladder he remembered the two Oerlikon gunners and once on top he made a point of leaning over each wing and making sure they were alert to the situation.

It was only then, having reassured himself he'd done all that he could to personally bolster the morale of his gunners, that he returned to his chair and jammed a boot against the bracket. All he could do now was wait.

And in the darkness south of *Brackendale*, a pair of German destroyers powered after the old freighter. Korvettenkapitän Wolfgang Herzog was determined to break the British blockade.

H.M.S. *Vibrant* lay dead in the water. *Cheriton* had arrived along her starboard side, within touching distance if need be. Rutherford was certain *Vibrant's* crew would have to be taken off. The cruiser was too low in the water and at least one torpedo had detonated level with her boiler rooms. Fitzpatrick must have flooded the compartments either side of the ship to maintain her current equilibrium, the water lapping close to the height of the main deck.

Then out of the thick weather to the east, *Kingfisher* hove into view, circled west and came up along the cruiser's port side. Rutherford stepped over to the port-wing and watched some of *Vibrant's* sailors hauling a hose along the deck towards the fo'c'sle. He looked across at *Kingfisher* and pursed his lips, thinking. The cruiser was in the best possible position for her crew to be rescued. Sandwiched in between the two destroyers, whatever remained of her crew would easily be catered for. Her entire Ship's Company couldn't have numbered much more then five-hundred. Split them between the two destroyers and they'd be home in no time.

'Hallo, *Cheriton*!' An officer was calling from the flag deck.

'We hear you,' he called back.

'Captain Fitzpatrick has a broken back and will be taken aboard *Kingfisher*. In the meantime he wants both of you to commence taking off survivors. Bulkheads are holding for now, not sure how much longer. I will remain aboard to check everyone is off, including the dead. Captain Horwood has agreed to finish *Vibrant* with a torpedo. Is that clear?'

Rutherford gave him a thumbs up. 'Yes, understood.'

'Good. I'll have your lines tethered as soon as you're ready.'

Rutherford waved and called out to the quarterdeck party. 'Get your heaving lines across and prepare to help them aboard. Injured to the Sick Bay.'

'Aye aye, sir,' a Petty Officer acknowledged, and

the Leading-Hands went to work.

Rutherford stepped back and took a long, deep breath. Stopped in the water alongside the stricken cruiser sent shivers up his spine. Having just taken on one U-boat that had only resulted in an unconfirmed kill, who was to say others were not lining up *Cheriton* through their periscopes? He gritted his teeth, sucked in more air, and keeping the negative thoughts to himself, again moved to the back of the bridge.

The lines went across, heavier ones followed and the gangway was positioned, angled down from *Brackendale* to *Vibrant's* almost submerged boat deck.

And so began the painstaking business of assisting the wounded aboard, limping and hobbling up the gangway, some supported by shipmates, the walking wounded guided below decks. Stretcher bearers carried the more severe cases, and even in the darkness white bandages showed dark patches where blood had seeped through. By the time the last body had been brought up and carefully laid aside, Rutherford's First-Lieutenant reported one-hundred and fifty-nine of *Vibrant's* crew accounted for as unharmed, thirty-one wounded, and nine bodies on the quarterdeck.

Rutherford gave him the standard reply, the singular, unemotional response that seemed to cover each and every situation a Captain might be confronted with during the course of his duties.

'Very well, carry on,' he said.

And then returned his gaze to the cruiser's upperworks, waiting for the lone officer to reappear and confirm there was no-one else left aboard.

Minutes passed without him showing and Rutherford frowned. This couldn't go on. Where in hell had he got to?

Vibrant lurched unexpectedly and tilted alarmingly towards *Cheriton*, her deck taking on a steep incline. Where moments before all had seemed stable, in seconds the illusion was gone.

He shouted to the quarterdeck. 'Release those lines and stand by.'

Two crewmen scurried down the gangway and released the tethers, then stood feet braced against the cruiser's gunwales in an attempt to prevent *Cheriton* from breaking away.

A movement caught Rutherford's eye and from a doorway at the foot of the bridge superstructure the officer struggled into view half carrying a wounded sailor.

'Get help over there!' he shouted, and two or three men lunged down the precariously balanced gangway to run awkwardly up and across the sloping deck. They quickly relieved the officer of the wounded man, lifted him off his feet and carried him down to the gangway. Willing hands hauled him on deck and a sick berth attendant took over.

'That's it!' the officer called and half skated, half slithered down the incline before clambering onto *Cheriton's* quarterdeck.

Rutherford took that as his cue and called for the two men to release the lines and get back aboard. The gangway came last and the First-Lieutenant waved a hand.

Rutherford bent to the wheelhouse pipe. 'Stop starboard, slow ahead port. Wheel amidships.'

Cheriton eased away from the cruiser's side and once she gained enough clear water to manoeuvre without undue risk he took her out to stand off a half mile ahead. *Vibrant* lay listing almost twenty-five degrees to starboard but had again settled, wallowing gracelessly in the rain swept seas.

Kingfisher could be seen pushing out from her port side until she lay parallel with the cruiser at something like fifteen-hundred yards. Rutherford saw the port side torpedo tubes deploy over the side and raised his binoculars. A single torpedo ejected from its tube, splashed into the waves and was lost in the water. He switched to watch the cruiser and seconds later the torpedo exploded level with her engine room. A torrent of water shot skywards, an orange-red flame streaking the dark, followed almost immediately by the dull thunder of the detonation reaching their ears. The warship shuddered and the upheaval subsided. Then, slowly, very slowly, the five-thousand ton Royal

Navy cruiser lost her fight to stay afloat. The stern slid under, bows lifting, and she twisted to the vertical, the fo'c'sle remaining stubbornly exposed. But the unwieldy mass hanging beneath the surface overcame the resistance of trapped air beyond the bulkheads and with a final screaming hiss of venting pressurised air, H.M.S. *Vibrant* succumbed to the inevitable and sank from view. The violently disturbed surface of the sea slowly subsided until, other than a few scattered remnants of debris, all the evidence of *Vibrant's* passing ceased to exist.

Rutherford lowered his glasses and shook his head. It was sad. He hoped the loss of a cruiser was worth it.

To the pipe he ordered, 'Half ahead together. Make revolutions for twenty knots. Steer three-five-oh degrees.'

He heard the quartermaster answer and turned to face the wind. It was vital now to get home. Whatever had happened to the *Castillo de Maria* was out of his hands. You didn't voluntarily look for trouble with a deck full of survivors. An uninterrupted passage would be more than welcome.

CHAPTER TWENTY-SEVEN . . BROADSIDE

Brackendale performed a beautifully choreographed slow corkscrew across a large roller and then thumped the flank of the next. Richard Thorburn ducked as spray drenched the bridge, but was too late to avoid it. He swore and wiped the worst of it from his face.

It crossed his mind that just for once he would prefer to be anywhere rather than in the bloody Bay of Biscay. Without doubt the sea and weather could be a right bastard, and he had to admit that right now it was all was proving to be somewhat trying. He grimaced and moved across to the port-wing. The ship was on a westerly leg of her latest zigzag and with his back to the rain he raised his glasses and took a long look to the south. After a full minute he lowered them to his chest. If the Germans were coming they were taking their own good time about it. At the moment there was still no sign. He swung round to face forward and again raised the binoculars. Through the driving rain he caught a glimpse of the freighter ploughing on to the north. So far so good he thought.

Abruptly, the rain vanished. Finally. And the moon's pale light revealed the oncoming seas, the wind-whipped waves breaking into tumbling crests. Clearly visible in the grey light, the *Castillo de Maria* pushed solidly ahead, her heavy bulk maintaining the reliable ten knot momentum.

'Ship! Bearing Red one-hundred, range six-thousand!' The call came from a lookout at the back of the bridge.

Thorburn stepped back across to the port-wing and trained his binoculars a few degrees astern of ninety. He had to be sure of what they'd spotted, it might well be *Kingfisher* or *Cheriton* on the hunt. It took him all of twenty seconds, but when the ship swam into his lens there was no mistaking that it was an enemy destroyer.

'Guns - Bridge!'

He answered the pipe. 'Bridge'

'Two enemy destroyers. One at Red one-hundred and one fine on the port quarter. Range, six to seven-thousand.'

Thorburn lifted his glasses. 'Stand by,' he said from the corner of his mouth. He relocated the first destroyer and traversed left towards *Brackendale's* stern. Exactly as Guns had reported, a second destroyer came into view. He dropped the glasses to his chest and swung round to the bridge-screen, eyes narrowed, thinking. His first instinct was to attack, charge the enemy, anything to throw them off course. His priority was to give *Maria* more time to put as much distance as possible between her and the Germans.

And then the leading German destroyer opened fire and he grinned. Decision made.

'Hard a-port. Speed twenty-five knots.'

The wheelhouse confirmed. 'Hard a-port. Revolutions for twenty-five knots. Aye aye, sir.'

The small destroyer heeled hard over, the starboard main deck swamped, the quarterdeck bearing the brunt of foaming seas. Twin columns of water erupted in *Brackendale's* wake.

'Midships! Steady.' The ship lurched upright, came out of the turn.

He bent to a pipe. 'Open fire!'

The fo'c'sle guns roared, a pair of shells whipping across the sea. Smoke ballooned over the bridge, and the guns crashed again. The leading German turned to the west. Thorburn saw it and clenched his teeth. A broadside or torpedoes and he lifted his glasses. A broadside was the answer and a salvo rippled from its guns. They fell wide off the port quarter.

The second destroyer let loose, muzzle flashes catching the eye. Shells thumped the sea, water lifting into towering fountains.

'Starboard twenty!' he called down the pipe. The ship swayed into the turn and he let it run, twenty . . , thirty . . , forty seconds.

'Port twenty!' *Brackendale* wriggled back to the left, thumping splashes rising in her wake. This time he waited until the turn had described a ninety degree arc. 'Midships . . . , steady.'

It gave Carling the chance to fire his own

broadside. And he took every advantage.

All four guns of the main armament bellowed in unison, hurling their high explosive shells at the leading German. An orange-red glow flamed on the German's boat deck, the fire illuminating the midships gun mount.

'Bloody marvellous,' Thorburn snapped, a tight grin spreading across his taut features.

Not that it made any impression on the German's fire power. Another salvo rippled from his guns.

Thorburn took his eyes off the leader and concentrated on the second warship. *Brackendale* was now heading straight for it, bow on against the German's port side. Binoculars up he found the torpedo tubes deployed, and squinted. He couldn't do much more than present the ship as she was, head on. It always gave the best chance of avoiding a torpedo.

Armstrong, binoculars raised in the port wing had obviously come to the same conclusion. 'Torpedo tubes, sir!' he warned.

'I see it, Number One. We'll hold as we are.'

The 4-inch guns cracked off another broadside, the forward muzzles ranged squarely across the starboard side.

'Torpedoes in the water,' Armstrong said calmly.

Thorburn saw the moment, three grey shadows as the torpedoes ejected and splashed into the waves. He sucked air. A great deal of luck would accompany his next moves. They were on a combined closing speed of something like sixty-knots and things happen very quickly at almost seventy-miles an hour. He scoured the water through his binoculars, desperate to pick out the tell tale signs of streaming bubbles.

The 4-inch blasted off another salvo and he flinched. He settled the sockets to his eyes . . . , and found them. Three glistening wakes on a spread pattern. At first glance it looked unavoidable.

Armstrong also found them. 'Torpedoes dead ahead.'

Thorburn grunted an acknowledgement, watching carefully. An enemy shell erupted fine off the starboard bow, shrapnel rattling the side plates. The fountain momentarily disrupted his view until the spray settled. He again acquired the tracks. The middle torpedo was the worry, but the two outside ones also gave cause for concern. It limited his room to manoeuvre. If he dodged the central torpedo he might well run into the trajectory of the others. He hesitated a fraction longer. It looked like the middle one would come in a little to the right. It might be enough.

'Port ten!'

'Port ten, aye, sir.'

Brackendale angled to the left. Now it was all about exercising his judgement on when to straighten up.

He'd seen enough. 'Starboard ten!'

She came out of the turn her bows arrowing down the space between torpedoes. But he must stop the stern swinging too far out.

'Midships!'

'Wheel's amidships, sir.'

'Steady on that.'

'Aye aye, sir.'

Brackendale corkscrewed to a wave, veering a little to port. Too late to counteract. Thorburn held his breath, eyes narrowed, frowning at the tracks.

There wasn't much room to spare but the small destroyer squeezed through, the lethal cylinders powering past and on until they ran out of propulsion.

The guns fired again at the first destroyer but they were closing rapidly on the second, the range shortening all the time.

He bent to the pipe. 'Guns!'

'Guns.'

'Let's direct some fire on our friend up ahead.'

'Aye aye, sir.'

Thorburn followed the fo'c'sle guns as they traversed round to the bows. He heard the breeches slam shut, the muzzles lift to the Control Tower's range finding.

And the guns thundered.

On the bridge, deafened, ears ringing.

Shell cases ejected, rattling to the deck. Reload, acquire target . . 'Shoot!' All in under four seconds. The guns bellowed in unison, shells whipping away at their foe. A lurid flash lit up the German's bridge housing and a seaman shouted.

'A hit! We've hit it.'

Thorburn glued his old Barr and Stroud binoculars to his eyes. He caught a stab of flame from the enemy muzzles. Bridge hit or not, the gunners could still retaliate. Beneath his feet, Thorburn felt the ship heave to a large roller. The bow wave streamed in the wind, foaming water boiling over the fo'c'sle. He braced against the screen and squinted ahead. He judged the range to be no more than four-thousand yards, a little more than two miles. *Brackendale's* fo'c'sle guns cracked off another pair of shells. Both found the target. They struck the Gun Tower abaft the German's bridge. The housing ripped apart, the explosive power killing and maiming. The enemy guns fell silent, and the destroyer veered away to the southeast. Its afterdeck guns resumed firing but the fall of shot was wide of the mark. Local gun control seemed poor in comparison.

Thorburn let the glasses hang. 'Bloody marvellous,' he said between his teeth. *Brackendale* had compelled one to run. Time to return his attention back to the leading destroyer. Not that Guns had ignored it; the quarterdeck mounting had been blasting salvo after salvo at the fast moving ship.

'Guns!' he called to the pipe.

'Sir?' came the shouted reply.

'Well done! But leave it now. Let's have another crack at the leader. I'll turn across his stern if I can. Give you time for a few broadsides.'

'Aye aye, sir!' Carling answered, enthusiasm colouring his brief acknowledgement.

To the wheelhouse pipe Thorburn gave the order. 'Starboard thirty, steer two-one-five degrees.'

Confirmation echoed up the pipe. 'Thirty of the starboard wheel on. Two-one-five degrees, aye aye, sir.'

Thorburn braced, knee bent, as once again *Brackendale* tore into the turn, heeling over in the opposite direction. He waited, watching. As she steadied out of the turn glistening lines of lazy tracer arced towards *Brackendale*. Lazy turned into a flashing hiss as the incendiary rounds whipped overhead, the stream of dancing lights being dragged down in a wavy line and the 20-mm rounds finding *Brackendale's* upperworks. Glass shattered and ricochets bounced alarmingly. The starboard Oerlikon joined the action, tracer criss-crossing that of the enemy, and the multi-barrelled Pompom thumped into action, its staccato beat cracking off shell after shell.

Thorburn gripped the rail, involuntarily hunched against the incessant secondary gunfire. He glanced left and caught Armstrong with a mad grin on his face. Their eyes met momentarily and he grinned back, caught up in the savage ferocity of the moment. He thumped a fist on the rail. If he could just get *Brackendale* well enough positioned for Guns to give the German a couple of well aimed broadsides. It wouldn't be easy, the destroyer was already countering his move, turning sharply.

Wolfgang Herzog used the back of his hand to wipe his mouth and cursed. This Englander was no amateur. It was the same 'Hunt' class that he'd previously tangled with, but then the weather had intervened. He gave a mirthless smile. By the look of it, the weather maybe not so much this time, and he was determined to make his extra power count. The *Puma* could run rings around this Englander.

'Hard right!' he shouted, and grabbed for a bridge-phone. 'Gun Tower? Hold fire until we straighten. Then give the British destroyer three broadsides. And maybe we repeat. Understand me?'

'Jawohl, Herr Kapitän. Straighten from the turn, all guns for three times, and again,' the officer said, and the barrels in the turrets lifted.

With his ship swinging wide to circle round on to the small destroyer, Herzog let his anti-aircraft gunners loose. The ship was well armed. A pair of 20-mm canon below the bridge, three single mounts stationed round the rear funnel, and two more twins either side of N0-3 gun on the quarterdeck. And all his gunners with a line of sight took full advantage. Tracer streamed across the intervening space, dazzling in its brilliance, a multi-coloured rainbow that belied the lethal quality of its purpose.

It took just short of two minutes to complete the turn.

And Herzog's primary weapons thundered again. He raised his glasses, wanting an accurate salvo. But only a single column of water lifted close astern, and he assumed the other shells must have gone over. He could see no evidence of a strike. The guns bellowed again as he watched. A twisted smile contorted his mouth. A hit! Near the stern rail, difficult to tell, wreathed in smoke. And a third salvo blasted from the guns, smoke and flame erupting from the muzzles.

He swore. Gun control had over compensated, the shells falling in a neat row metres ahead of the small destroyer, three rising columns announcing the miss. But then a sudden thought came to him, a way of circumventing this Britisher and resuming the search for *Maria*. If he closed at maximum speed, all the *Puma's* guns engaged, he could probably disengage heading north and leave the enemy floundering in his wake.

'Hard right!' he demanded and the *Puma* responded, leaning left, the bows biting round in a tight curve. The frantic array of tracer continued to lash out at the British warship. In a minute or so, he thought, his gunners would blast the enemy again, only closer.

He smiled thinly, hard. Deception was a major part of any battle and right now he was about to achieve one of the greatest.

Sub-Lieutenant George Labatt stood outside on the *Maria's* port bridge-wing and raised a pair of the ship's binoculars. Looking across the transom rail he studied the flashes of gunfire. They were faint, and his attempt to observe what ships or how many were involved proved impossible. Vague lines of coloured tracer strengthened and faded and the sound of heavy artillery echoed in from astern. He lowered the glasses mulling over whether to change course? The assumption had to be that at least one German ship had encountered *Brackendale*. That meant even though the *Maria* was well west of her previous bearing it had not been enough to throw them off the scent. He went back inside and crossed to where Falconer stood staring out of the screen.

'You hear that, Cox'n?' he asked.

Falconer gave a thoughtful nod. 'Sounds like the old girl's in a fight.'

'Do you think we should ignore the chart and head further west?'

The man from the heart of Newcastle's dockland, rubbed his nose and then licked his lips.

Labatt waited for the answer, respectful, knowing better than to try and rush him.

'What could you see?' was the eventual response.

'Gun flashes, not much else.'

Falconer turned and in the dim light of the table lamp he gently smiled. 'I think, sir, it's time to ignore the chart and go due west. Hold that course for two hours and then head directly for Falmouth.'

Labatt worried his lower lip, wanting to believe the advice was sound.

'Two hours?'

'That's right, enough to put us over the horizon by dawn. Then we can make for Falmouth.'

The distant rumble of gunfire reached their ears and Labatt allowed himself to be convinced.

'Right Cox'n, due west it is.'

Falconer stuck out his chin and nodded. 'Aye aye, sir,' he said and strode over to Lockwood on the steering.

'Change of course. Port ten. Steer two-seven-oh degrees.'

Lockwood nodded, peering down at the ornate compass rose. 'Port ten, two-seven-oh, aye aye, Cox'n.'

He eased the spokes through his fingers and then held them, eyes fixed to the dial. The freighter lumbered into the turn, her single rudder and large thumping propeller never designed for sharp alterations of course. After more minutes passed than either man had expected the *Maria's* prolonged turn approached the fresh bearing and Lockwood let the wheel return to centre.

'Steering two-seven-oh, Cox'n.'

Falconer looked over at Labatt.

'Due west, sir.'

Labatt turned to face the bridge-screen and clasped his hands behind his back. 'Very well,' he said using the time honoured response. 'Two hours.'

It began to drizzle.

CHAPTER TWENTY-EIGHT ..
HOODWINKED

Thorburn had seen enough, he was being out-manoeuvred and it was not something he was prepared to put up with. *Brackendale* had just avoided the worst of two broadsides, although she'd been hit on the quarterdeck somewhere. He was still waiting on the damage report. Other than that, power and steering didn't seem to have been affected.

He flinched as a fresh stream of tracer hammered the bridge, sparks flying, steel shards buzzing dangerously. A lookout yelped and grabbed the back of his neck, swore loudly, but went back behind the sockets of his binoculars.

Drizzle swept in, an icy squall lashing the bridge. Thorburn turned his face away, and found himself peering directly at the German destroyer. It was attempting to get on *Brackendale's* stern, mid turn, heeling hard to port.

'Bastard,' Thorburn mouthed, and in that instant made a decision. 'Hard-a-port!' he snapped to the wheelhouse.

'Hard-a-port, aye aye, sir!'

As the ship heeled into the turn Thorburn moved to the back of the bridge, port side, and waited for the enemy to appear astern. He was well aware of the risk he was taking in leaving *Brackendale* open to a torpedo strike, but turning out on the port side to double back gave Guns the ability to strike with a broadside of his own. It was the only way he could think of to outfox the German, and with gritted teeth he waited. The rain increased, visibility the poorer, but still acceptable. And the enemy came into view, still turning to starboard, the ship's portside guard rails almost submerged.

Thorburn gave a thin smile. Now to take advantage. He lunged for the wheelhouse pipe.

'Midships!' he ordered, and *Brackendale* shimmied upright, the mast swaying back beyond perpendicular and then settling.

'Steady!' He looked over the port bow. The German was reacting, straightening from the turn but the guns had not yet come round.

From the wheelhouse, 'Midships, steering one-nine-five.'

'Very well,' he acknowledged, and changed pipes. 'All yours Guns!'

In the Range Finder Director, 'Guns' Carling, for the first time in the engagement, found himself presented with a positive, unhindered view of the enemy. His own Trainer and Layer settled their sights squarely on the enemy forward gun.

'Broadside,' he warned the gun mounts. 'With semi-piercing . . . . Load.'

Behind the shields the gun crews followed the

director's output, traversing and lifting onto the target.

Carling allowed *Brackendale* a few vital extra seconds.

'Shoot!'

The guns crashed in unison, and four 38 pound shells, accelerating at 2,660 feet per second, whipped across the sea. Three found the target, exploding on the fo'c'sle, flame and smoke flaring towards the bridge. Carling waited moments for the smoke to clear . . . , nodding at the result. The gun had been torn from its mounting, shattered and pointing aimlessly skywards. There was no sign of the gunners and the flames grew rapidly. He changed target, to the German's quarterdeck guns. Sights on, he snapped the order.

'Shoot!'

But both destroyers had passed each other, at high speed, the gap widening rapidly. *Brackendale's* shells missed well short. The German effort to return fire went wide.

Thorburn called Armstrong. 'The quarterdeck, Number One. See what's happened.'

Armstrong gave a quick, 'Aye aye, sir,' and ran for the ladder.

The quarterdeck guns blasted another pair of shells at the German's stern with no discernible result.

And then Thorburn felt a moment of utter desperation. He'd made an unforgivable error of judgement. His entire reasoning in placing *Brackendale* between the *Castillo de Maria* and the Germans was to fend off any hostile action. As he watched the German disappearing he glanced at the compass. *Brackendale* was headed south-ish and the enemy looked to be fading into the north-west. He turned from the compass and lifted his face to the sheeting rain. The ice cold precipitation stung his skin, battered his closed eyelids, and he took a deep breath through clenched teeth. All he could do now was try and make amends while hoping the *Maria* had steamed far enough away to be out of sight. Firstly change course and get after them.

'Starboard thirty,' he said to the wheelhouse.

'Starboard thirty, aye, sir.'

Armstrong came up the ladder to report. 'Two wounded, they're in sick bay. Port depth-charge rail and hoist damaged. The Chief has it in hand, says it's repairable.'

'Good, thank you,' Thorburn said, and shook his head. 'But we're in a deal of trouble.'

Armstrong looked perplexed. 'We are, sir?'

'I've been hoodwinked, Number One. Well and truly bloody hoodwinked!'

'Sorry, sir, I'm not with you.'

Brackendale was coming round to the north-west, listing sharply under full helm, and he needed to counter the turn. 'Midships,' he said . . . . Steady . . . . Steer three-two-five.' The acknowledgement came.

He pointed after the enemy. 'He came at us like it was some kind of duel, broadside to broadside, all guns blazing. But look at him now, and don't for a minute think he's fleeing the field of battle. He's not, he's after the *Maria*.' He shook his head. 'Hoodwinked, the bugger hoodwinked me.' The rain turned to hail, heavy, a white wall instantly building a layer in hidden recesses. Sea boots slithered and men cursed.

Brackendale powered on, blind and alone. Thorburn gripped the bridge rail and wondered if he should signal *Kingfisher*? This might be the time. He'd done all that he could with what he had at his disposal, but the speed of a Hunt was never going to match the German. Whereas *Kingfisher* . . . ? well that was a different kettle of fish. She had both the speed and weaponry.

'Number One.'

'Sir?'

'I need to send a signal.'

'Sir,' Armstrong said, and called the bridge messenger to warn the W/T office.

A minute later a Telegraphist stood waiting with a message pad.

Thorburn thought for a moment and then said, 'Take this down . . . . "Admiralty, repeated to *Kingfisher*. *Castillo de Maria* on course 330, speed ten knots. Royal Navy skeleton crew aboard. *Brackendale* engaged two enemy destroyers, one damaged, one in pursuit of *Maria*." Get our position from Pilot and add it.'

The Telegraphist nodded, finished scribbling and looked up for anything more to add.

'That's all,' Thorburn said. 'Get it coded up and sent off soonest.'

'Aye aye, sir,' the man said and turned for the ladder.

The hail eased, turning to sleet, the darkness less dense. Thorburn wiped his face and moved to the bridge-screen. Armstrong joined him.

'Be lucky to find them again in this,' he ventured.

Thorburn reluctantly nodded his agreement. 'True. But they'll have heard the commotion. I just hope young Labatt's used his initiative. That's a big expanse of water out there.'

'The Cox'n knows that, sir. He'll have given his tuppence worth.'

'And what would you do, Number One? Put yourself in their shoes.'

Armstrong dropped his chin and Thorburn gave him time, let him think. *Brackendale* rode a trough, spray lashing the screen. She twisted and lifted clear.

'I think I'd want to change course, get clear of the land. Daybreak's coming and if the *Maria's* not been caught tonight the Germans are bound to begin an aerial search.'

Thorburn pursed his lips, tilting his head. His First Lieutenant had a point and there was no guarantee that the weather wouldn't clear. 'So what are you saying, head west?' he asked.

Armstrong blew out his cheeks. 'All I can think of.'

Thorburn was inclined to agree. 'Fair enough,' and he grimaced, 'let's just hope Jerry doesn't think the same.'

The Telegraphist returned. '*Kingfisher* and Admiralty acknowledged, sir.'

'Very well, carry on.'

Brackendale pushed on through the murk, he and Armstrong lapsed into silence.

Korvettenkapitän Wolfgang Herzog congratulated himself on achieving such a clean break from the encounter. It had all taken place exactly as planned and with little battle damage to show for such an ambitious manoeuvre. More than that, the weather had closed in at exactly the right moment, the Englander quickly fading from sight.

He moved to the chart table and made a few calculations of his own. He plotted a line for the *Castillo de Maria* and re-established the *Puma's* course and speed. In less than thirty minutes the freighter would again be under his orders. Then he would make directly for Cherbourg. No deviation.

Wolfgang Herzog was convinced the Gods were on his side.

High on the *Castillo de Maria's* exposed lifeboat station, Emil Lorenz squeezed out from beneath the starboard boat's heavy tarpaulin and dropped lightly to the deck. His chosen refuge had served him well, now it was time to make himself useful.

A ladder took him down from the after deck-house to the main deck, and crouching low he skirted the rear hatch covers to No-4 and 5 hold, before clambering up the stern ladder to the quarterdeck. A pair of steel stowage compartments straddled the central walkway and he squatted between the port side container and the taffrail. Completely hidden from anyone looking aft from the bridge, Lorenz produced a torch from inside his leather jacket and resting the tube on his left forearm began to deliberately send two flashes at random intervals. After about quarter of an hour he paused for a while before starting again.

He couldn't be sure that a German warship would ever re-establish contact, but the least he could do was to try and help them find the *Maria.* Cold though it was, but protected from the worst of the weather by the bulk of the stowage bins, Emil Lorenz continued to send the narrow beams of light flickering out across the dark waters. As he did so he was well aware that the light could be intercepted by the Royal Navy. Either way he was determined not to sit idly by while the Englanders in charge of the *Maria* escaped to the British Isles.

It was a fifty-fifty chance, and one he was

willing to take.

Brackendale slammed into a breaking wave and Thorburn cursed. Attempting to focus his binoculars wasn't helped by the ship's behaviour. The wind had changed, coming round to blow hard from the west, but it had cleared the clouds and for that he was thankful. What he wasn't so keen on was that first infinitesimally faint lifting of the horizon to the east. He let the glasses hang and rubbed his eyes. He was tired, a lot more than he cared to admit, but so were the crew. Long hours in thick weather, cold and wet, did nothing for a man's well being.

'Guns - Bridge?'

Thorburn turned to the bank of pipes.

'Captain.'

'Sir, there's a small light blinking on and off at Red four-five. Irregular, and I don't think it's Morse.'

Thorburn tried his binoculars again, braced against the ship's movement. The western seas were as yet still in total darkness and he scoured the water for any sign of the light. Nothing. He bent to the pipe.

'Can you still see it?'

'Not this minute, no, sir.'

'Keep looking. I'm going to alter course. We'll investigate.'

'Aye aye, sir,' Carling said, and Thorburn moved to the compass. He checked *Brackendale's* heading and leaned to the pipe for the wheelhouse.

'Port twenty.'

'Port twenty, aye aye, sir.'

And the small destroyer clawed into the turn, fighting her way round to the west.

Thorburn judged the moment by eye. 'Midships!'

'Wheel amidships, aye, sir.'

'Steady.'

There was a brief pause before the answer came. 'Steering two-eight-oh, sir.'

For Thorburn that was near enough. 'Very well.'

'Guns - Bridge. I can see it again. Fine off the port bow.'

Thorburn raised his binoculars and scanned the bearing. And this time he found a faint suggestion, a shimmer of light twinkling from far away. And as Guns had said there seemed to be no regular pattern, a couple of flashes, a pause, then a couple more, then nothing. He leaned to a pipe.

'I have it, Guns. A bit odd. We'll stand to, see what we find.'

'Aye aye, sir. Standing to.'

Sub-Lieutenant George Labatt welcomed that first hint of daylight on the far horizon. He'd been woken from a fitful sleep by Falconer, the two of them sharing the watches. And although the Cox'n would be perfectly entitled to get his head down for a couple of hours, he'd chosen to rouse the freighter's cook and get some breakfast on the go.

In the meantime, with the help of that greying dawn, Labatt had decided to take a turn round the ship and find out how the engine room was coping. Content in the knowledge that all of *Brackendale's* scratch crew were armed and alert to the possibility of an attempt by the *Maria's* crew to take back control, he moved through the door to the staircase. Instead of retracing his steps by descending to the main deck he turned and followed the staircase upwards to the flying bridge. A minute later he opened a door and took a pace out into the cold air. The flying bridge was not a place to linger at this time of year and having satisfied himself that all was well he went back to the stairwell and headed down for the engine room.

From the main deck, iron steps took him below to the warmth of the boiler room where Stoker Oldridge watched over two of *Maria's* crew shovelling coal. In the engine room Leading-Stoker Jameson assured Labatt that everything was under control.

Relieved to find all was in order he mounted the steps back to the main deck and emerged into the pre dawn grey brightening from the east. Moving aft past two hatch covers he came to the port side ladder that would give him access to the quarterdeck. With one foot on the bottom rung he hesitated. A pale glimmer of light had reflected off the wall of a housing above him and he paused, watching to see if he was mistaken. But no, there it was again.

The old freighter swayed to a long roller and he took a firmer hold of the side rails. Determined to find out more he climbed quietly to the top and carefully stepped onto the quarterdeck. To his left he found a passage between two stowage cases and about to move through he thought better of it and stopped to take out the revolver. This time the weight of the weapon seemed a lot more appropriate, comforting. Slowly, with great care, Labatt shuffled forward, the revolver outstretched in front.

Crucially for the *Puma* and Wolfgang Herzog, a sharp eyed lookout at the back of the bridge caught a brief glimpse of wavering light. In the normal course of his duty, the lookout had again traversed his binoculars from square off the portside beam and aft until fine off the port quarter, and it was there, at the extremity of his arc, that he'd spotted the flash of light. Uncertain as to exactly what he was seeing he lowered the glasses for a moment, blinked, and then levelled them to focus on the same patch of sea. When the flash came again he was ready, locked in on the spot, and a second flash convinced him to report it.

'A light, Herr Kapitän!' He checked the bearing. 'Portside off the stern.'

Herzog turned and raised his binoculars to encompass the stern quarter and scoured the sea. To the west it was still dark and there was no sign of a light. He searched again. Nothing.

'A light you say,' he snorted. 'I see only the waves. No lights, only the sea.'

The lookout was not to be intimidated by his irritable commander and held his ground. 'I am sure certain I saw a light, Herr Kapitän, three flashes. The first isolated, then two more together. I have seen no more.'

Herzog let the glasses rest on his chest and pondered his lookout's words. He was adamant there had been a light, was not to be dissuaded by his senior officer's doubts. And there had been no sign of the *Castillo de Maria* moving north. He felt he had nothing to lose by turning about to investigate.

'Come hard left!' he snapped at the helmsman, and the *Puma* heeled over, the bows thumping waves as the turn increased. As the ship swung towards the west he ordered the helmsman to centre the steering and hold that bearing.

Whatever was out there, he thought all would soon be revealed.

George Labatt froze. Whether it was sixth sense or a simple need for self preservation, something warned him of extreme danger and his breath caught in his throat.

And against the soft grey of the eastern dawn the shadow of an armed man filled the space between containers. In the split second before he fired the revolver, Labatt recognised the silhouette of a sub-machine gun being levelled at him. The gun jumped in his hand, and the bullet slammed into the man's chest, knocking him backwards. The sub-machinegun rattled into life, bullets spraying high and wide.

Labatt fired again, before the man hit the deck, and the sub-machinegun dropped, steel clattering on steel. For a few seconds Labatt stood stunned, the noise and flash of the guns at close quarters an unexpected shock. He could see no movement from the inert figure sprawled on his back and took a step closer. The man's face was turned to one side, eyes open, staring, but already very dead. Labatt leaned down to study his features but couldn't recognise him. He certainly hadn't been on the bridge when they'd boarded. And then the cylindrical shape of a torch rolled a short distance across the deck, the evidence of the man's intentions all too obvious. The ship twisted and the torch rolled back. Labatt picked up the sub-machinegun, flicked the catch to 'safe' and slung it over his shoulder. Knowing now that the man had been trying to attract attention made Labatt squint over the stern rail at the eastern horizon. By the naked eye it was empty. He sighed and moved to the ladder. Before he could turn to descend he heard the Cox'n calling.

'You all right, sir?'

'I am, yes,' he called in reply, and then spotted Falconer coming past the hatches. He had his revolver in hand.

'We heard the shooting.'

Labatt made it down the ladder and moved to join the Cox'n. 'There was a chap on the quarterdeck using a torch for signalling. He's dead now. I left him where he fell.'

Falconer nodded and gave Labatt a smile of encouragement. 'You did well, sir. Let me have the machine-gun.' He took it, saw the 'safety' was on and cradled it across an elbow. Together they headed for the bridge, both wondering if the enemy had taken note of a small beam of light.

But Sub-Lieutenant George Labatt had only checked the seas immediately astern of the *Castillo de Maria*, the most obvious place to look if you thought you were being followed. In reality, two warships were closing on the old freighter. From the north came the Kriegsmarine's *Puma* under the command of the determined Korvettenkapitän Wolfgang Herzog. From south-east came the small but battle hardened *Brackendale*, her White Ensign flying proudly from the masthead and her entire Ship's Company stood waiting at Action Stations. Two opposing warships heading west at speed were on route for a fight.

Capitán Carlos Menéndez was summarily escorted to the bridge where Labatt demanded to know who amongst the ship's crew was prepared to betray their whereabouts to the Germans?

'Without you showing me a body I cannot be sure,' Menéndez said. 'But at a guess I would say you killed a man called Emil Lorenz. He was a Nazi sent from the Embassy in Buenos Aries to oversee our progress.'

Labatt frowned and gave Menéndez a scathing look. 'And how many more of these men will go against your word? You promised cooperation Capitán. Is this your way of showing it?'

'My word is my honour, Lieutenant, but I speak for myself, for me. You understand? I cannot guarantee for all.' He gave an expressive shrug of his shoulders.

Labatt felt angry, upset, and he knew the real reason was because it was he who'd had to shoot the man. He fully accepted he'd killed other men since becoming an officer in *Brackendale*, but that had been at a distance and from behind large calibre weapons, not personal and close up.

He glanced at the reliably solid figure of Chief Petty Officer Barry Falconer and slowly common sense came to the fore and he reluctantly dismissed Menéndez.

The Cox'n then pointedly looked at his watch. 'Dawn, sir. Time to alter course for Devonport.'

Labatt nodded staring out of the bridge-screen. The grey light of day had well and truly arrived, but luckily the clouds were low, threatening, scudding along with the westerly wind. He turned to the helmsman and nodded again.

'Starboard twenty.'

'Starboard twenty, aye sir.'

'What course, Cox'n?'

'Three-four-oh, sir.'

The helmsman acknowledged. 'Three-four-oh, aye aye, sir.'

Beneath their feet the lumbering old steamer came out of the turn and steadied on the given bearing.

'Steering three-four-oh, sir.'

'Very well,' Labatt said, turned to the screen and clasped his hands behind his back. After all, a lowly Sub-Lieutenant he might be, but he *was* still Captain of the *Castillo de Maria*.

!CHAPTER TWENTY-NINE . . SHOOT

It was Jones in *Brackendale's* port wing that gave the first warning.

'Ship! Red twenty!'

A bridge full of binoculars focussed on a patch of sea fine off the port bow. Richard Thorburn also raised his pair of Barr and Stroud to study the waves. Lieutenant Carling in the Range Finder Director heard the shout and brought the tower round from where it had been searching to the north-east. At a range of six miles he found the outline of a 'Carnivore' class German destroyer.

'Guns - Bridge! Enemy in sight, bearing three-five-five. Range six miles.'

Thorburn found the stern of the destroyer at the exact same moment Carling made his report. With Armstrong stood next to him at the bridge-screen, Thorburn shook his head.

'It's a pity, Number One, but the bugger's out of range.'

Armstrong continued to watch through his glasses and from the corner of his mouth made an observation. 'I don't think he's anywhere near top speed. Maybe we could get in range before he's aware.'

Thorburn studied the destroyer again, careful to take note of the bow wave, or at least the little they could see of it.

'You could be right. No harm in trying.' He called to Martin. 'Full ahead, Pilot. I want to see if we can close the gap.' Then he leaned to Carling's pipe.

'Guns?'

'Sir?'

'I'm trying to close in. If you get the range, open fire.'

'Aye aye, sir.'

With daylight strengthening Thorburn felt certain it was only a matter of minutes before the German would detect *Brackendale's* approach. And if he chose not to engage but increase speed . . . ?

'Ship! Red four-five! The *Maria*, sir.'

Thorburn heard the call, fully aware it was from Jones . . . , again. The keenest pair of eyes on the ship. Binoculars up, Thorburn grinned. It was the *Castillo de Maria* all right, presenting her starboard quarter to the chasers while ploughing on for home. The downside, unfortunately, was that bloody German destroyer, a lot closer to the merchantman than *Brackendale*.

He nudged Armstrong. 'D'you think Jerry knows the ship's in our hands?'

'Doubtful. How could they know? I'm sure the *Maria's* wireless room will be under our control.'

'So when they join up the Jerry destroyer will just become another close escort. Only this time they'll be defending a Royal Navy transport.' He chuckled. 'How strange are the ways of war.'

The wind whipped salt laden spray over the side and men hid their faces. Momentarily. Then it was teeth clamped, eyes squinting, and back on the job. Overhead, abaft the bridge, the White Ensign flapped vigorously, the halyards whining to the gusts. And Thorburn noted the waves had quickly become angry, curling and breaking into ragged spindrift. He glanced to the west expecting to see a rain front moving in but the daylight revealed only low white-grey clouds, no ominous darkening as a prelude to a squall.

He looked up beyond the bows, the waves slapping hard against the port side, fully aware of the helmsman's fight to keep *Brackendale* on course. Sheets of spray enveloped the Bowchaser, a heavy mist streaming away to starboard. Already the bows thumped hard as waves chased from left to right.

'Enemy slowing, sir!' Armstrong pointed.

Thorburn looked over the screen, stretching taller, exposed to the cross wind. And what he saw immediately gave him pause for thought. The German destroyer was suffering under the combined onslaught of wind and waves. The bows were more submerged than afloat, huge fountains of spray being thrown at the bridge, the forward gun hidden by the deluge.

He worried his bottom lip. Somewhere in the back of his mind he remembered hearing a snippet of information regarding the sea worthiness of the 'Carnivore' class destroyers. In heavy weather they suffered from being 'wet' ships, the poorly designed 'flare' of the bows contributing to severe issues with handling. It was a design flaw that resulted in poor "weather helm", an inability to hold course against a driving wind on either beam. *Brackendale* on the other hand, although rocking and rolling, easily lifted her bows to the waves, the foaming seas sweeping back along the gunwales and guard rails to be quickly dispersed over the side.

With that differential in mind, Thorburn wondered how he might take advantage of the German's predicament. Manoeuvrability was a key component of the Hunt class destroyer. Small, and with a quick turn of speed, the ability to turn on a sixpence was *Brackendale's* true asset. She might not win many marks for top speed but for agility she was first rate.

'It's the weather, Number One. He's struggling with the weather. Not so capable in high seas.'

'Certainly looks like it.'

Thorburn made a decision. Close the gap, get on his tail and use *Brackendale's* dexterity to stay out of trouble. He stepped up onto the compass platform and checked the bearing. A glance at the enemy and he bent to the pipe.

'Starboard ten,' he ordered.

'Starboard ten, aye, sir.'

Brackendale veered right, pulling across into the German's wake.

'Port ten.'

'Port ten, aye aye, sir.' The small destroyer eased left and Thorburn brought her into line astern of the German.

'Midships.'

The helmsman centred the wheel. 'Midships, aye sir. Steering three-four-five.'

'Very well,' Thorburn acknowledged and leaned to the Control Tower pipe. 'What's the range, Guns?'

'Seventeen-five, sir.'

Thorburn hesitated. That was under ten miles, within range, but Carling had held back.

'Problem?'

'No, sir. It's just that the sea's a bit too lumpy for accurate grouping. If we could close in by another thousand, sir?'

Thorburn grinned into his mouthpiece. 'For you, Mister Carling, I'll get Mister Dawkins to hurry it up.' He heard Carling chuckle.

'That would do nicely, sir.'

The bellow of German gunfire brought the light hearted exchange to a sudden close, and a pair of shells exploded fifty yards off the port bow.

'Port ten!' Thorburn ordered to the pipe, deliberately altering course towards that fall of shot. The German gunnery officer would be correcting to his left. *Brackendale* would no longer be on that trajectory.

'Starboard ten . . . , midships.'

And came the flash of gunfire from ahead. Thorburn smiled grimly. Two columns of foaming water erupted off the starboard quarter. He glared at the enemy over the screen. A minute since Guns had requested he close the gap, almost nine-hundred yards gained, excluding whatever the German destroyer was making. Another minute of taking it before *Brackendale* retaliated.

'Starboard five!' he snapped, and the ship jinked a little to the right, enough hopefully, to upset the enemy calculations.

'Midships!'

The small destroyer came out of the turn angling out to starboard across the German's stern. All of *Brackendale's* main 4-inch armament traversed a little to port, muzzles lifting.

'Guns - Bridge!'

'Captain.'

'Ready!'

Lieutenant-Commander Richard Thorburn lifted his eyes to the enemy. 'Open fire!'

The guns thundered, spitting flame, and four high-explosive shells whipped across the void. Empty brass cases clanged to the deck, breeches reloaded, closed.

'Shoot!' from Carling.

Thorburn had his binoculars levelled at the enemy quarterdeck and saw the first salvo bracket the destroyer, all four shells erupting close. The destroyer made a turn to starboard and he smiled. He couldn't have wished for a better response. *Brackendale's* second salvo missed to port but Thorburn didn't mind in the slightest. The *Castillo de Maria* had gained ground, the enemy destroyer fully distracted by Thorburn's tactics.

'Port ten!' he called down the pipe and watched the bows come left. To position *Brackendale* between the *Maria* and the enemy would now be the ideal. Preventing the enemy from closing in on the merchantman had to be the main purpose. Time was the critical factor and with low cloud cover reducing the risk of aerial reconnaissance, the longer Labatt could push on for Plymouth the less chance of Thorburn having to obey Fitzpatrick's order to sink the old steamer.

Brackendale's guns swung from left to right as the Control Tower corrected to follow the warship. More enemy shells shrieked overhead, winging into the distance.

Thorburn put the ship into a series of zigzags, deliberately sacrificing Carling's accuracy to ensure the German was kept guessing. Sooner rather then later, he felt sure the enemy would throw caution to the wind. It was all a matter of timing ... Theirs.

Wolfgang Herzog snarled at the Englander's persistence.

'Verdammt!' he spat. Always that small ship

interfered. And now the weather had also turned against him. Gusting winds with a marked increase in the height of the waves did the *Puma* no favours. A decrease in speed was the only way to overcome the erratic handling and to give his guns a more stable platform. And all the while this accursed Englander would not give up.

A pair of shells exploded astern, seething foam rising into fountains. He swivelled round to look for his First Officer.

'Oberleutnant Leitner!' he barked.

'Jawohl, Herr Kapitän.' The young officer strode forward.

'I intend to increase speed. You will go round the ship and make certain the crew is aware and that all is tightly secured. You understand me, Leitner?'

'I think so, Herr Kapitän. But for why? Must we leave the freighter?'

'Never!' Herzog growled, angered by such a suggestion. 'Never.' He wiped his mouth convinced that the Fuhrer would follow every last twist and turn of his exploits.

'The *Puma* may be the last of our flotilla but I have only to defeat this Englander and the prize is ours.' A tight smile returned to his face. 'And remember, Leitner, we have two torpedoes not yet used.' He gestured vaguely towards the bows. 'Now I will show this Englander how we Germans can fight at sea. I will take us ahead of the *Maria* and then make a turn back down her far side. Then we will see how brave this Englander is. Will he shoot with the freighter in the way? No my young friend, he will not dare.' He turned to the wheel. 'Ahead full! Steer north.'

'All engines ahead full. The bearing is north, Herr Kapitän.' The engines increased in tempo, the bows plunging with the waves. In a very short space of time the *Puma* had reached two-thirds of her power.

But then a full salvo of *Brackendale's* main armament plunged down to bracket the *Puma*. Only one of those high explosive rounds hit the target but it struck the main deck above No-2 boiler and detonated in a lurid ball of fire. The blast fractured an ancillary pipe carrying superheated steam through to a turbine, and though not critical to the *Puma's* momentum, the warship's starboard propeller instantly lost half its power.

On the bridge, Herzog grimaced at the glow of dancing flame.

'Shwinehund!' he shouted, almost in disbelief. All that he'd gone through and then one lucky strike. He looked ahead over the port bow and shook his head in frustration. The *Castillo de Maria* sailed serenely on, not a care in the world. The orange glow from the explosion subsided, the fire crew winning the against the flames.

A telephone buzzed on the panel.

'Ja?'

'Engine room, Kapitän. We have lost power.'

Herzog squeezed his eyes shut and took a deep breath. 'Tell me,' he demanded.

'We have only two-thirds remaining, Herr Kapitän.'

Herzog opened his eyes. A loss of power was not something he'd envisioned. 'You can repair it?'

'Not quickly. I need time.'

'So be it,' Herzog snapped, and slammed the receiver back on its cradle.

A lookout called in alarm. 'Herr Kapitän! The enemy.' He pointed frantically.

Herzog leaned to peer astern and found the enemy considerably closer, much too close for comfort. His quarterdeck guns fired and he raised his glasses for the outcome. Missed wide. The Englander was throwing his ship about as if she were a power boat and not a thousand ton warship. Hitting such an elusive target owed more to fortune than dedicated experience. As he watched he saw her forward guns belch smoke and he tensed.

'Come right!' he ordered in a belated reaction. *Puma* leaned to the turn and columns of water reared up close by the port side. Shrapnel rattled the hull.

'Make our bearing northeast.'

'Northeast, Jawohl, Herr Kapitän.'

Herzog leaned on the back of his chair and dropped his head. With the alteration of course the wind now blew from the port quarter and the ship felt much more manageable. And even though down on power there was enough of a differential for the *Puma* to make significant headway. His original idea to swing round to the far side of *Maria* could still be executed. Who knows he wondered, he might be able to launch the torpedoes by a fast manoeuvre out from behind the freighter. In the meantime he must keep this dog of an Englander at bay. He moved to the screen and planted his feet firmly apart.

In a flurry of leaping spray the *Puma* powered on.

CHAPTER THIRTY .. HOME RUN

Richard Thorburn saw for himself the fiery explosion as Guns dropped one on the German's main deck. He also took note of the rapid change in direction.

'Jerry's on the run, sir,' Armstrong said at the same time.

'Yes, and I'm inclined to let him go. Our first duty is to the *Maria*. I should think Mister Labatt is getting somewhat concerned.'

Armstrong laughed. 'That's putting it mildly. I should think he's having kittens.'

Thorburn grinned at the thought. He fixed the old freighter with his binoculars, studied her for a moment, and then swung the glasses round to focus on the German. Its direction of travel was now firmly established, north-east towards Cherbourg. Was it quitting the field of battle? Joining reinforcements? Had Guns possibly inflicted more damage than was apparent? Whatever the case *Brackendale* was better off as nursemaid to the freighter. With daylight firmly established beneath the low cloud cover at least they'd have plenty of warning if the enemy reappeared.

'Pilot,' he said, lowering the glasses. 'Be so good as to station *Brackendale* off the *Castillo de Maria's* starboard beam.'

Martin looked over with a grin and mimicked the Captain's traditional formality. 'Station *Brackendale* off the *Maria's* starboard beam. Aye aye, sir.' He bent to the pipe. 'Port five. Make revolutions for fifteen knots.'

Faintly, Thorburn heard the helmsman's repeat, and the ship eased serenely to port. Martin steadied her at the appropriate moment and for the first time in long hours the crew took the opportunity to relax at their posts.

Thorburn moved to his chair and delved in a pocket for his cigarettes. He extracted one and lit it behind cupped hands. As he blew smoke he glanced at Armstrong. 'Let them smoke if they've got them, but they're to stay alert.'

The word was passed and it went quickly through the decks. Pouches of rolling tobacco made an appearance and pipe tobacco was deftly tamped into bowls.

Armstrong lit his own cigarette and leaning on the screen casually remarked that there was more smoke now than when the guns had been fired.

Thorburn glanced round and agreed. 'Looks like Whitby's kipper smokehouse,' he said. 'Couldn't see a hand in front of your face up there.' He smiled at the memory.

'Twelve knots,' Martin ordered.

Brackendale slowed, to gently close a cable's length off *Maria's* starboard quarter. Gradually the small destroyer overhauled the freighter until finally, at ten knots, and with both bridges aligned, a young Sub-Lieutenant walked out onto *Maria's* wing and gave *Brackendale's* navigating platform a salute.

Thorburn stepped up and returned the salute. 'Well, Mister Labatt,' he shouted, 'how're things?'

'All's well, sir.'

'Any problems?'

There was a slight hesitation before the answer. 'Nothing of importance, sir.'

Thorburn accepted the report at face value, without challenging. He wasn't really in any position to argue.

'Good,' he said. 'Navigation? You're not really where we expected to find you.'

'Diverted west before heading for Plymouth. Seemed like a good idea at the time, sir. But any advice from Mister Martin would be more than welcome.'

The wind strengthened, gusting hard over the freighter's bulk. *Brackendale* reacted to the pressure, drifting away before the helm was corrected. Thorburn raised his voice. 'If you hold this course and speed we estimate Plymouth in five hours.'

'The Cox'n reckoned more like four,' Labatt called with a grin.

From *Brackendale's* flag deck a sarcastic voice piped up. 'Couldn't read a bleedin' map let alone navigate a chart.'

Laughter rippled round the upperworks.

Armstrong frowned as expected of a First Lieutenant but didn't press it.

Optimistic went through Thorburn's mind. 'Right,' he said, 'anything you need?'

'No, sir, we can manage.'

'Very well, Mister Labatt, I'll get a berth arranged. I expect a tour of your command when I come aboard.'

Labatt's boyish grin lifted the gloom. 'Aye aye, sir,' he said and gave a smart salute.

Thorburn touched the peak of his cap and turned to the compass platform. 'Starboard ten, Pilot. And I want *Brackendale* stationed five-hundred yards off *Maria's* starboard bow.'

'Starboard bow, five-hundred yards, aye aye, sir.

The destroyer peeled away and gathered enough speed to pull ahead and take station as Thorburn wanted. He checked his wristwatch. 07.45 hours, and he smiled. They were on the home run, might even be back for a late lunch.

He moved back to his chair and jammed a booted foot onto the pipe bracket. It was beginning to look as if the *Castillo de Maria* might well have escaped the attentions of the Kriegsmarine. Maybe. Fingers crossed. He looked up at the scudding clouds, the wind still gusting at least Force 7. The Luftwaffe wouldn't be making an appearance either.

Doc Waverly sat in his cabin and pored over

the last three signals that had been intercepted. The first two had no bearing on *Brackendale's* deployment. He decoded the messages and entered them into the log book. The third was addressed to *Brackendale* directly and he set about unravelling its mysteries. Encrypted signals were received in four letter groups and the Doctor decoded them using the specified code books. The first characters of any message indicated which book and what page to use for decoding the remainder of the message. When not in use, the code books were placed into special canvas bags equipped with lead weights. There were standing orders to throw them overboard in the event that the books might fall into enemy hands.

But as always, his note pad and pencil were being put to good use as he sought to decode the third message. The Telegraphist had jotted down in a hurry and legibility was proving difficult. But letter by letter, group by group, the signal was deciphered until he had the words written out on a message slip in plain language. And it didn't make for good reading. This one, he thought, he would deliver to the Captain personally.

He reached for his cap and hurried to the bridge.

Thorburn stood with Martin and studied his navigator's latest plot, dividers and parallel rule much in evidence.

'So that's your best estimate?' he asked.

'Yes, sir. I managed only the one sighting last night. It's been all guess work since. And with this wind . . . , well I really don't know how far off course we might be.'

'Captain, sir.'

Thorburn turned at the seldom heard voice of Doc Waverly.

'Doc?' he queried in surprise.

Waverly's eyes were serious as he offered a message slip. 'From the Admiralty, sir. Came in about twenty minutes ago.'

Thorburn opened the folded paper. Written in the Doctor's neatly applied long-hand he saw the message was indeed addressed to H.M.S. *Brackendale*. It read,

"Enemy destroyer reported north-east of your last known position. Four E-boats departed Lyme Regis area at 07.00 hours heading south. Three Motor Gun Boats in pursuit. Air cover will be despatched when weather clears." It was signed by the Chief of Operations at the Admiralty War Room.

Thorburn thoughtfully refolded the paper and handed it back to Waverly. 'Thanks, Doc,' he said, and gave a meaningful sideways glance to Armstrong who not long since had tried to convince his Captain to get Waverly out of the decoding business. 'I think things are about to get busy.' Armstrong averted his eyes and managed to look extremely preoccupied by examining his binoculars.

The Doctor went back to his cabin, Sub-Lieutenant Martin studied his chart, and the lookouts dutifully watched over their sectors.

Lieutenant-Commander Richard Thorburn went back to his chair and jammed his boot on the bracket. That old tramp steamer, he thought, with one of His Majesty's destroyers acting as close escort, was fast becoming the centre of attention. The trouble was it sounded as if at any moment all their endeavours might suddenly amount to nought.

Brackendale rolled, her narrow hull wallowing obscenely at the enforced reduction in speed. At a subdued ten knots she and her valuable consort ploughed on towards England's southern coast.

Wolfgang Herzog stood braced at the *Puma's* bridge-screen. He'd brought the ship round until the bows were pointing straight into the westerly wind. It was a way of overcoming the bad behaviour and even with the reduction in top speed the hull rode the waves well. A check on the time had him smiling and he turned to the helmsman.

'Come left ten degrees.'

'Ten degrees left, Jawohl Herr Kapitän.'

Herzog watched the compass, the bows swinging round to the south and he immediately felt the power of the wind against the starboard beam.

'Rudders central!' he ordered, and the helmsman middled the wheel. Another glance at the compass showed he had the *Puma* now heading a little east of south, exactly as he'd planned when he broke contact with the enemy. If his calculations were correct the *Castillo de Maria* should appear any time soon.

'Achtung! Gun Boats, Herr Kapitän.' It was the starboard lookout pointing across the beam.

Herzog stepped over to the side and raised his glasses. He found them easily enough, three boats leaping the waves at high speed on a parallel course to *Puma*. Four kilometres range at a guess and showing no interest in a German destroyer. Their very presence raised more questions than answers but Herzog found himself unable to draw any conclusions.

He cursed. They would be reporting the *Puma's* location; too late to prevent it. For the first time since he'd departed Cherbourg harbour, Herzog began to have doubts. It might be that he must use the torpedoes to sink the *Maria*. It had been mentioned only once in all the planning, and she was only to be sunk if there were no other possibility. He raised his chin and stuck out his chest, he was not done yet.

CHAPTER THIRTY-ONE ..
FIGHT OR DIE

Lieutenant-Commander Richard Thorburn sprang to his feet and looked round for Armstrong. He found him watching the freighter through his binoculars.

'Number One,' he said, urgency in his tone.

'Sir?'

'That signal . . . , the first part about the destroyer. It was a warning.'

'Yes, sir,' his First Officer agreed as if that was stating the obvious.

'No, I mean a warning aimed at the *Maria*. If she holds course she's a sitting duck. I've got to send her west, due west, out of harm's way.'

'But if we stay on this bearing help will arrive shortly. It must do.'

'I can't take the chance, it might not. Or the skies might clear and the Luftwaffe finds her first. No telling what might happen.'

Armstrong gripped the rail and stared out to sea, thinking it over, and Thorburn gave him the space. It was a stark choice. Stay the shortest course and pray help arrived before the enemy, or turn west for the Lizard and aim for Falmouth. From Thorburn's point of view, sitting on his backside and waiting to have the prize package whipped from under his nose was not an option.

Armstrong rubbed his jaw and looked round at his Captain. 'Due west it is. George won't like it, but you're right. It's for the best.'

Thorburn patted him on the shoulder. 'Good man, I knew you'd see reason. As for Mister Labatt, he'll obey my order.' He raised an eyebrow. 'Will he not?'

'Of course, sir. Better let him know.'

'Very well. No time like the present.' And Thorburn passed instructions to slow *Brackendale* before once more taking station off *Maria's* starboard side. Bridge to bridge, Labatt came out onto the wing.

Thorburn cupped his hands. 'I have fresh orders for you, Mister Labatt.'

'Yes, sir?' came the shouted response.

'You are required to set a course for Falmouth.'

There was a prolonged silence before an obviously crestfallen young officer called, 'Might I ask why, sir?'

Thorburn thought that was a fair question and deserved an answer. 'A signal from the Admiralty. Enemy forces ahead.'

Labatt looked down at his feet and shook his head, visibly disappointed. But only for a moment. When he looked up it was with his usual bright determination. 'Falmouth,' he yelled. 'Aye aye, sir.'

'I'll inform the Admiralty,' Thorburn elaborated. 'They'll have someone meet you.'

'Thank you, sir.'

Thorburn hesitated, loath to send them off unescorted. But he was determined *Brackendale* must act as decoy and draw the Germans into battle and away from the scent of titanium and gold. There was little else to say except a simple farewell.

'Good luck, Mister Labatt . . . , and God speed.'

They exchanged salutes across the intervening void and turned away, duty calling.

Thorburn held *Brackendale's* course and speed a little longer, just long enough to catch the *Castillo de Maria* commence her turn away to the west. And then he moved to the forebridge, rubbing his hands in anticipation.

'Pilot,' he said, deliberately raising his voice. 'There's an enemy destroyer to the north. Course and speed to intercept, if you will.'

'Three-five-eight degrees at twenty-five knots, aye aye, sir.'

'Very well,' Thorburn said. The hint of a smile lifted his face. It would soon be time for battle.

'Three Gun Boats off the starboard bow!'

Thorburn reached for his glasses and focussed on the leader. They were pouring on the power, bows raised to skim the waves, plumes of foaming seas in their wake. Then the leader began flashing a signal from the flying bridge.

'What's she saying, Yeoman?'

'Enemy destroyer bearing oh-one-five, range fourteen-miles, speed thirty knots, heading one-eight-oh.'

It was a concise report, accurately detailed.

'Acknowledge,' Thorburn said. He stepped across to the starboard wing and as the boats powered by towards the stern he raised his cap in thanks. An arm waved from the leader and was then lost in spray.

Richard Thorburn moved back to the screen, mind churning over the situation. His quarry was well ahead at approximately Green two-oh and on a heading that would take it in the opposite direction down *Brackendale's* starboard flank. With a closing speed of nigh on sixty miles an hour the two destroyers would be within sight of one another in mere minutes. And of course, Thorburn's reasoning for sending the *Maria* off to the west was for *Brackendale* to act as decoy. Right now, he thought, the best way to achieve that would be to alter course east across the path of the German. It would be a major gamble and definitely not subtle, but surely a move the enemy couldn't resist.

'Number One.'

'Sir?'

'You heard that?'

'Yes,' Armstrong said, replacing the bulkhead handset, ' and Guns reports, "Enemy in sight", sir.'

'I'm going to swing across that bastard's nose, provoke a response. If I've learnt anything about that commander, it'll be too much for him to resist. If nothing else we'll engage, see if we can't sort the bugger out.'

Armstrong grinned. 'Not being reckless are we, sir?'

Thorburn raised a wicked eyebrow. 'Who me? Never.' He glanced around the bridge and found a number of half hidden smiles. Most men aboard were aware of the Admiralty's earlier criticisms of their Captain's behaviour.

He stepped up to the compass platform and grasped the binnacle.

'I have the bridge,' he announced. 'Action Stations, Number One.'

Armstrong hit the button and the alarm resounded throughout the ship, and those of the crew not already at their stations scrambled for their posts.

Korvettenkapitän Wolfgang Herzog fumed at the ship's lack of handling. The helmsman, try as he might, was simply unable to hold the *Puma* on course. Even with the helm theoretically turning the bows hard right, the power of the westerly wind was too much. Given the reality, it was up to the ship's commander to implement a course and speed that was appropriate to the conditions. For Herzog it seemed like an admission of failure, not something he willingly accepted. But with a prolonged sigh he ordered a further reduction in speed to help alleviate the amount of lift from the bows. Less lift from out of the troughs should reduce the amount of pressure against the exposed hull. But before he was able to judge the improvement the bulkhead telephone buzzed.

He snatched the receiver from the cradle. 'Ja?'

'Range Finder, Herr Kapitän.'

'What is it?'

'British destroyer ahead. Range sixteen-kilometres, coming north.'

'Type?' Herzog queried.

'Hunt class. I think it was with the *Maria*, Herr Kapitän.'

'So . . . , our paths cross again. That is good, very good. Prepare to open fire but wait on my word.'

'Jawohl, Herr Kapitän, but I also have a sighting of top masts to the west. It could be the *Castillo de Maria* on the horizon.'

'First the destroyer,' Herzog insisted, returned the receiver to the cradle and raised his binoculars. Spray whipped across the bows blocking his view and the *Puma* corkscrewed right to left. The spray cleared and a moment later he had the enemy in view. And the one thing in Herzog's favour was the *Puma* now behaving less erratically.

'Leitner,' he rasped.

'Kapitän?' His First Officer came to attention.

'The Englander approaches. This time we do not play games, Leitner, you hear me? There will be no fancy tricks, no pretence at leading him on. No, Leitner, this time we meet head to head and we will see how brave is this captain of the Royal Navy.' Herzog grimaced. ' Look and learn, Leitner, and I will teach you how to wage war. This Englander is about to swallow the bitter taste of defeat.'

'And the *Castillo de Maria*, Herr Kapitän?'

'Do not worry your head over the freighter, there will be ample time to deal with the *Maria* when this Englander is finished.'

The young First Officer had already dared to query his commanding officer, he was not about to make any further argument.

'Of course, Herr Kapitän, as you say.'

'Exactly, it is always as I say.'

Oberleutnant Rolf Leitner clicked his heels and gave a formal nod. 'Jawohl, Herr Kapitän. I will see to the men.'

Herzog dismissed him with a wave of his hand and turned back to the screen. The Englander was noticeably nearer and he stuck out his chin. A battle was about to commence.

Thorburn had the German fixed firmly in his lens and an underlying impulse stirred his senses. He knew that it was really the thrill of the chase, the proximity to danger, an excitement admitted to no-one. But that feeling could manifest itself in many ways and in this case he called over his shoulder.

'Raise the Battle Ensign!'

In less than a minute the large flag broke free at the masthead, followed almost instantly by the crisp sharp flapping of a wind blown Ensign rattling the halyard.

He leaned to the Control Tower's pipe. 'Guns!'

'Guns, sir.'

'Prepare to engage.'

Carling acknowledged. 'Prepare to engage. Aye aye, sir.' Below the bridge the twin barrels of the fo'c'sle turret traversed a fraction to starboard, lifting to encompass the range. Behind the shield the gun crew stood tense in helmets and anti-flash capes, all concentrating on serving the guns that were *Brackendale's* primary weapons.

'Number One, I'm going in close before we turn. I want all secondary armament to engage.'

'Pompom and Oerlikons, aye aye, sir.'

'Guns - Bridge?'

'Captain.'

'In range now, sir.'

Thorburn lifted the binoculars and focussed on the enemy ship.

'Open fire!'

'Shoot!'

The pair of 4-inch guns bellowed, shells ripping across the sea. A rapid reload followed. 'Shoot!' and another salvo winged away. The acrid sting of cordite blew across the bridge and Thorburn coughed, eyes watering. *Brackendale* thumped the flank of a wave and heaved out, twisting over the crest.

An enemy shell exploded off the port bow, shrapnel rattling the hull. Thorburn lowered the glasses, better able to judge the moment to turn across the German's nose. A shell hissed by the starboard wing and exploded far astern. And now, with the range decreasing to below four miles he spotted Kennedy and his loader hurrying up the fo'c'sle for the Bowchaser.

The German veered to port, enough for his quarterdeck guns to join the fight, shells from both destroyers bracketing one another, but as yet without success. The gunfire increased in tempo, range down to five-thousand yards.

Armstrong shouted for the Bowchaser to open fire and the gun's thumping bark resounded back to the bridge. The Oerlikons joined the fight, tracer streaking across the waves, pretty to watch, lethal on arrival.

Thorburn waited no longer. 'Hard-a-starboard!' he shouted above the din.

'Hard-a-starboard, aye aye, sir,' echoed up the pipe, and the ship reacted. As the German's 20-mm anti-aircraft guns burst into life, Thorburn braced to *Brackendale's* turn. Her main armament fell silent as she heeled hard to port, thumping the waves, the mast leaning far out over the sea. Men leaned into every corner, fingers searching for hand holds. Sea boots slipped on steel decks, the guard rail swamped, green seas rushing aft. She clawed her way east, dipping and winding to the waves, carving through the sea in a welter of flying foam.

'Midships!' Thorburn snapped and *Brackendale* rolled upright, to beyond the perpendicular before rocking back to right herself.

'Steady . . . , steer oh-eight-five.'

'Steer oh-eight-five. Aye aye, sir.'

Thorburn looked up across the port wing just as Carling ordered, 'Shoot!' and *Brackendale* reeled to a full broadside. Smoke and flame ripped from the muzzles and four high explosive shells chased away at the target. The rattle of machine-guns accompanied the roar of main armament and the Oerlikons and Pompoms added to the noise. A fury of tracer lashed out at the enemy, the first hits sparkling with ricochets.

Richard Thorburn bared his teeth and waited. The German must surely take the bait.

Wolfgang Herzog couldn't believe his eyes. Amidst all the gunfire and tracer he watched in amazement as the Englander turned across his bows. There was a brief respite as the enemy destroyer's port side rails were engulfed in water but as soon as she straightened her guns blasted again.

'Verdammt!' he mouthed, realising at the same moment that the Britisher was fleeing to the east. And that was not part of Herzog's plan. Not at all.

Tracer latched on to the bridge, bouncing and fizzing in the confined space. The Spandau gunner gasped as a spent phosphorous round hit his neck scorching the skin, burning.

Herzog scowled at the turn of events. This time it was the Englander who made the running but the difference now was that the *Puma* chased, and even with a damaged power train the *Puma* would still outrun the Royal Navy.

'Come left full rudder,' he spat. 'Hard over!'

The helmsman span the wheel and the ship heeled, propellers churning, rudders fully angled. The *Puma's* bows clawed round, straining to close the quarter turn.

Herzog ducked from glowing tracer, and a pair of shells exploded off the port beam. 2-pounder Pompom shells raked the Gun Control station.

'Rudders central!' he ordered, and *Puma* lurched out of the turn. The forward gun roared again, and the 20-mm hammered into action. The tracer swept across to the Englander's quarterdeck, plucking at the Pompom platform, smashing the steel screen.

'Do you see, Leitner?' he called above the noise. 'I told you I would teach you how to wage war, did I not? See how he runs. Look and learn, young man. Look and learn.'

Leitner only managed to nod, mesmerised as he was by the enemy destroyer's agility. And he wasn't so sure the Englander was running. It seemed to Leitner the turn east was a deliberate ploy, not done in panic. Glowing red tracer arced out from the enemy bridge wing, curving in at the *Puma*. He saw it coming, a weaving line growing faster the nearer it came. The bridge screen shattered into flying fragments, shells humming.

A jagged steel splinter hurtled through the air and sliced into Leitner's right arm. Muscle and sinew were torn in two, blood pumping, the arm hanging limp. Leitner screamed his agony and crashed to the deck, overwhelmed by the surging wave of pain. The severed artery gushed dark red, the blood pooling.

More tracer scoured the bridge space and the helmsman fell, a bullet to the chest and another to his thigh. He lay half slumped against an electrical switchbox his body contorted with pain, losing blood, unable to lift himself. Another sailor grabbed the spokes, dragged the ship back on course.

The *Puma's* bridge-wing anti-aircraft guns took up the battle, green luminescent tracer reaching out for the British gunners. Hits could be seen walking along the port waist, rising to the boat deck.

It was then that the young Oberleutnant Rolf Leitner lost his fight to live. Too much blood had pumped from his body, draining his vital organs. Grey faced and short of breath, and with an incoherent cry for his mother, Leitner finally slipped away, eyes wide, lifeless.

Herzog had his binoculars focussed on the back of the Englander's port bridge-wing. An

Oerlikon was locked in on the *Puma*, tracer spraying a constant curtain of shells. One thing was clear, the *Puma* was gaining ground and the two remaining torpedoes might yet come into their own.

'Leitner!' he shouted. There was no answer and he called again. 'Leitner!'

'The First Officer is dead, Herr Kapitän.'

He lowered his binoculars for a brief moment, accepted the news, and raised them again. Men died, this was war.

'Get me the Torpedo Officer. Schnell!'

Watching the Englander he began plotting how he might surprise him with a late deployment of the tubes.

A British shell hit the Range Finder and exploded, an orange ball of flame surging aft to envelope the forward funnel. Three men died including the Gunnery Officer. Another cartwheeled into the sea, and one was blasted onto the deck below, horribly burned from the flames. The main armament continued to fire, but with no-one in overall charge, the rate and accuracy became erratic at best.

Herzog shut his mind to the chaos, concentrating only on his need to destroy the Englander.

Leutnant Franz Weimar, the *Puma's* Torpedo Officer arrived on the bridge and awaited his Kapitän's orders.

CHAPTER THIRTY-TWO . .
SMOKE AND FLAME

Thorburn stood in the port wing and looked astern beyond the port quarter to where the German warship had turned to follow. He saw the explosion on the Range Finder and watched tracer from *Brackendale's* secondary armament find the German's bridge.

'Bloody marvellous!' he said and narrowed his eyes at the damage. The quarterdeck 4-inch crashed off another pair of shells. One missed short, the second detonated on the German's fo'c'sle deck, forward of the No-1 gun mounting. Shrapnel flew, two gunners died.

Thorburn nodded at *Brackendale's* continued ability to concentrate her firepower on the German destroyer. And more to the point he congratulated himself on being able to draw the enemy away from the freighter. It had been a heart in the mouth gamble which in this particular case had paid off handsomely.

The guns bellowed and this time the fo'c'sle turret joined the salvo, the barrels pointing hard back over the side and just missing the port wing supports. The smoke whipped away and he searched for Armstrong. The First Lieutenant appeared at the top of the starboard ladder.

'Number One,' he called.

'Sir?' and he moved to join his Captain.

'So far so good,' Thorburn said. 'I think . . . .'

Tracer slammed into the bridge, raking the upperworks, punching ragged holes in the superstructure. They both ducked as 20-mm canon shell fizzed and ricocheted round their shoulders. It lasted seconds. When it shifted to a fresh target Thorburn snatched a quick glance round the platform. The starboard lookout stood holding his left arm, blood seeping through his waterproofs.

Armstrong reacted. 'Get that man to the sick bay.' The bridge messenger stepped over to give support and guide him towards the ladder.

Thorburn licked his lips. 'As I was saying, I think we've succeeded in our main aim.'

'Can't argue with that, sir.'

Thorburn fixed his First Officer with a determined gaze. 'But I want to finish it now, take him on, no quarter given.'

Armstrong turned to look at the German destroyer. 'Me too. Need to teach that bugger a lesson he won't forget.'

Thorburn grinned and clapped him on the shoulder. 'Well said, Number One, let's get to it.' He strode to the raised platform and bent to the wheelhouse pipe.

'Hard-a-port!'

The wheel went over and *Brackendale* answered, swinging left in a tight turn. She heeled to starboard, heaving across the waves, powering toward the enemy. And now the small destroyer met the westerly wind, the rolling seas breaking on the sharp stem.

'Midships! Thorburn called, eyes fixed firmly on the enemy. *Brackendale* straightened and the helmsman answered.

'Steering two-six-five, sir!'

'Very well!' Thorburn acknowledged. The turn came to its natural conclusion with the ship travelling in exactly the opposite direction, which meant both ships would pass starboard to starboard. He stepped forward off the platform and leaned up against the damaged screen, just as Lieutenant Carling resumed the fight. The forward pair of guns blasted a fresh salvo at the enemy.

Smoke and flame mushroomed from the base of the German bridge-housing and for Leutnant Franz Weimar, hurrying to his torpedo station, the war ended. The explosion lifted him bodily into the air and flung him into the sea. He was dead before he hit the water.

Thorburn gave a grim smile. *Brackendale* trembled to the power of the guns. Whether it was enough to make any difference, he could only hope. And now the two warships were rapidly coming together, opposing courses. Would the enemy shy away, think better of it? Thorburn steeled himself against the violence to come. This was not for the faint hearted. He braced to call the German's bluff.

Seaman-Gunner Les Pope, who manned the starboard bridge-wing Oerlikon, swivelled the gun to target the German's bridge. A young man just turned twenty but already with two ME-109 'kills' to his credit, he knew what he was about. Ordinary-Seaman 'Ted' Skinner stood at his shoulder as 'loader', a canister of sixty 20-mm shells waiting to be slapped in place.

The 4-inch guns crashed off another salvo, smoke billowing over the bridge-wing. But although the main armament let rip, Les Pope waited to reassure himself that the target had closed to within four-thousand yards.

Ted Skinner asked the question.

'What you aiming for, Les?'

'The bridge, take out the officers.'

'Right,' Skinner said. 'Any minute now.'

Seconds later they heard the First Lieutenant's shout of 'Open Fire!' and with the enemy destroyer's bridge filling his sights, Pope hit the trigger. The judder of the gun rocked his shoulders, the curved rests transmitting the recoil. Tracer whipped away at the enemy, missing right. He corrected, still 'leading' the target by a few feet, but watching the shells beginning to make inroads, hammering the steel upperworks.

Shrapnel flayed the *Puma's* bridge, lethal shards of steel humming in all directions. A shell deflected off an angled stanchion and found soft flesh. Wolfgang Herzog screamed at the pain, the 20-mm round gouging a burning furrow in his right thigh. He screwed up his eyes and grabbed for the wound, his fingers finding a deep bloodied groove. A second piece of shrapnel struck his chest, buried itself deep. He writhed in the agony of intense pain. The muscles of his thigh went into spasm and his leg gave way. He crumpled, squealing like a pig and lay sobbing.

Then, German tracer flashed from a pair of mountings between the funnels, curving in a lazy arc before hurtling down on *Brackendale*. 20-mm cannon shells slammed into her bridge housing, ricocheting wildly snd punching holes in steel panels.

Pope's Oerlikon clanged to a stop. Skinner whipped off the empty mag and slapped on the fresh one, tapped Pope on the helmet. The gun chattered into action.

Les Pope gritted his teeth and changed targets, attempting to silence the guns. He stuck with it, concentrating on the base of the flashes, and the guns hammered on.

On the Bowchaser Kennedy traversed with the moving target and settled on the enemy bridge. The gun sight found the upper housing and the screen, followed the damaged glazing. The barrel jumped under Kennedy's hands, thumping out the staccato beat, scarlet tracer winging towards the target. Sparks flew and he swung the gun as the two ships began to pass one another. The loader fed in a new 2-lb ammunition belt. Empty shell cases ejected, rattling down the deck and lying in a clattering heap.

Machine-gun tracer hissed by his head and he hunched his shoulders. He took his eye away from the sight and found where the gun was firing from. It came from the boat deck and he gave it a long squirt. The tracer stopped.

All the while the twin turrets of the main armament crashed out salvo after salvo. With the a range coming down to as little as two-thousand yards, Carling and Thorburn began to count the explosions as the weight of *Brackendale's* firepower began to take affect. And the 4-inch guns traversed round as the two ships swept past one another. It was then that Thorburn caught sight of the torpedo tubes arrayed over the side. He raised his glasses for a closer look and saw that only two tubes were loaded. But even then, the moment to fire at *Brackendale* had come and gone. For whatever the reason they remained firmly in their tubes. With the enemy drawing away beyond *Brackendale's* starboard quarter, Thorburn made a snap decision to cross the German's stern.

'Hard-a-starboard!'

Thorburn braced against the tilt, eyes flicking between compass and enemy. A fountain of spray erupted from a near miss and splinters battered the hull. But *Brackendale* clawed her way round, rolling with the heavy seas. He lifted a handset.

'Guns?'

'Sir?'

'I'm crossing his stern. Fire as you bear.'

'Aye aye, sir!' Carling shouted down his handset.

Thorburn barked at the pipe. 'Midships! . . . . Steady.' And *Brackendale* straightened from the turn, leaping upright, her guns swinging ninety-degrees across the beam. The forward pair found the enemy guns and a single 4-inch shell thumped out across the void. As it exploded a second shell erupted from the twin barrel and detonated on the aft housing. Oerlikon, Pompom, and anti-aircraft tracer filled the air, the sound of secondary gunfire rising to a crescendo. Both destroyers received raking 20-mm hits, the inevitable injuries beginning to grow. A German machine-gun targeted Les Pope's Oerlikon and Ted Skinner was struck twice. He was flung bodily against the bulkhead behind, the shells smashing into throat and shoulder. He died in a contorted bloody heap. Pope only realised when he ran out of shells.

On the quarterdeck, both 4-inch guns bellowed simultaneously, stabbing flame at the enemy. Both missed the intended target of the quarterdeck housing but hit the rear funnel instead. The resulting explosion ripped the flimsy structure to shreds and the scream of escaping steam rent the air. Thick black smoke coiled from the base, and for a moment, a red glow indicated something burning.

Thorburn slammed one fist into the palm of the other. 'Bloody marvellous,' he grinned. 'Bloody marvellous.'

An enemy shell exploded close to the starboard quarter, shrapnel lashing the hull and within a minute a bulkhead telephone buzzed.

He picked up the handset. 'Captain.'

It was the warm Welsh brogue of Dawkins. 'Engine room, sir. That last explosion, it damaged the starboard propeller. Something's out of kilter. If I don't reduce speed on that shaft it'll likely shake itself adrift.'

Thorburn rubbed his forehead, pinched the bridge of his nose. Just when he thought they were winning. But it was no good crying over spilt milk. In battle you went with what you had.

'Very well, Chief. What can you give me?'

'On that shaft a hundred revs, no more, sir.'

Brackendale's quarterdeck 4-inch guns thumped a final salvo at the German destroyer, the pair of shells whining across the sea.

Thorburn glanced in the direction of the smoking German, now receding into distant eastern waters at a fair speed. *Brackendale*, having crossed the German's stern, was pushing north, a complete ninety-degrees difference. At least, he thought, the enemy was travelling in the opposite direction to *Maria*. They'd be hard pressed to find her now.

'All right, Chief, give me what you can.'

'Aye aye, sir,' came the reply, and Thorburn replaced the handset. 'Number One.'

'Sir?'

'I hate to say it but that's our lot. We won't catch it now.'

'You think he's given up, sir?'

Thorburn took another look in the German's direction. 'I do. I think we gave it a good hiding. Not totally broken, but with enough damage to force him to disengage.'

'If he goes after the freighter?'

Thorburn glanced at his wristwatch. 'I have a feeling Mister Labatt will be greeting his new escort just about now.'

Armstrong smiled. 'I hope he's made the most of his temporary appointment.'

'I'm sure he has,' Thorburn said. 'Pilot, set course for Weymouth.'

'Weymouth. Aye aye, sir.'

'Number One, casualties and damage report if you please?'

'Sir,' Armstrong nodded and headed for the ladder.

Under Sub-Lieutenant Martin's guidance, *Brackendale* came round to the north and settled down for the trip home.

Thorburn crossed to his chair, jammed a boot onto the bracket and lit a cigarette. Win some, lose some, he thought, and sometimes you settle for an honourable draw.

The *Puma* had caught fire and was burning below decks. The Fire Control division was doing its best to damp it down and had begun to check the spread of flames.

For Wolfgang Herzog, although morphine had dulled the pain he felt the time had come to call a halt to this whole sorry episode. He had a piece of shrapnel embedded in one of his lungs, his breathing shallow, laboured. Blood soaked his chest even though he'd reluctantly allowed the doctor to wrap a bandage round his torso. The heavy bandage round his thigh did little to help give him support. Taking another large mouthful of Napoleon brandy Herzog pushed himself upright in the chair. He went through his reasoning for leaving the field of battle. In his opinion he'd fought a good fight and if it had not been for the atrocious weather he'd have probably succeeded in helping the *Castillo de Maria* to break the embargo.

In normal circumstances, the failure to carry out his duty would have been the end of a promising career, but it had dawned on Herzog that this running battle had produced a victory that could be attributed directly to the *Puma's* leadership. And in particular to the tactical, on the spot, decisions made by Korvettenkapitän Wolfgang Herzog. His order to attack with torpedoes had sunk a British Royal Navy cruiser, a cruiser the recognition books indicated might have been named the *Vibrant*.

With that in mind, when the Englander wrecked the *Puma's* funnel and set fire below decks, and with more than half his firepower unable to carry the fight, he ordered the ship to maintain a heading of due east. It was the opportune moment to slip away from the Englanders clutches.

Cherbourg was not so far and in the meantime he could make certain that all written logs tallied with his version of events. He could brush off any alternative versions by arguing the chaos of battle brought doubt to the sequence of events. With a report that the fire was out he took another swallow of brandy, and coughed hard. The cough wracked his body in convulsions and he spat blood. It cleared and he managed another mouthful. Sinking deeper into his chair, a half smile played on his lips. There would be many women cheering on the quayside.

Forty minutes later all thoughts of great pomp and ceremony faded to nothing. In excruciating pain he was rushed down to the sick bay, but it proved to be too late. Korvettenkapitän Wolfgang Herzog died on the ship's operating table as the surgeon tried desperately to remove the embedded shrapnel from his Kapitän's left lung. A slip of the scalpel as the ship corkscrewed wildly to port and the right lung filled with blood. With one lung deflated and the other full of fluid Wolfgang Herzog lost his fight to survive.

It was late morning when the *Castillo de Maria* entered the outer reaches of the River Tamar and Sub-Lieutenant George Labatt stood aside to allow a Lieutenant-Commander to take over as Pilot and navigate the ship to a safe anchorage. A Fleet destroyer had come to act as an escort for the final leg of their passage before a Sloop took over as very close escort. Labatt made sure her skipper realised there was a scratch crew from the Royal Navy aboard the old freighter. At the same time he received information that *Kingfisher*, *Cheriton* and *Brackendale* had all returned home to Portland.

At the given moment they dropped anchor and with the engine stopped Falconer had the ship's crew brought up and paraded on deck where each man was interrogated by Royal Navy Police from Davenport's shore establishment.

Capitán Carlos Menéndez was the last to be questioned. Having given his inquisitor much freely volunteered information (anything other than the amount he'd been paid) he turned to Labatt and touched the peak of his cap.

'Goodbye, Lieutenant. I hope you enjoyed playing captain of my *Castillo de Maria*.' He reached out to shake hands. 'And I tell you something, young man. Do not lose any sleep over the shooting. Emil Lorenz was a German Nazi and a very evil man. You rid the world of a rat who would spy on others, and kill without mercy. And because of you my familia are safe. One day, and I don't know how long, my wife and my children, we will be reunited.' He relaxed the shake of hands and straightened his cap.

Labatt gave him a crisp salute, his face lit up with gratitude.

'Thank you, Capitán. I am grateful that you kept your promise. I wish you well for the future.' He stepped back to show their conversation was over and a Master-at-Arms came forward to usher Capitán Carlos Menéndez into captivity.

The Sloop, still hanging about in close proximity, edged closer along the port side. Her skipper made an appearance and shouted across.

'Sub-Lieutenant Labatt?'

'At your service, sir.'

'I have orders for you and your crew to report ashore and catch a train up to Weymouth where you'll rejoin ship. The harbour launch will be with you shortly.'

'Very well, thank you,' Labatt replied, and the Sloop veered away to take station a couple of cable lengths astern. Devonport's senior officers were obviously taking no chances with *Maria's* cargo.

A short while later the launch arrived at the bottom of the Jacob's Ladder and Falconer led them over the side. There was a formal farewell between the 'Pilot' Lieutenant-Commander, and Labatt, after which he made short work of the

Ladder and settled in the cockpit.

As the boat pulled away for the quayside, Labatt turned to take a last look at his first ever command. It had been short and sweet, not even a day, and yet he would not soon forget the *S.S. Castillo de Maria*. Streaked with rust and with her red paint flaked and peeling, the battered old three-thousand ton tramp steamer had served him well. He grinned, wouldn't be long before he was once again back to being a junior officer and reporting for duty aboard the small Hunt class destroyer, H.M.S. *Brackendale*.

It was nearing 10.00 hours the following morning when Thorburn entered Portland's Naval Headquarters adjoining the old Clock Tower. In a large office on the first floor he found himself ushered to a seat next to Paul Wingham. To his right sat Lieutenant Kendal, and Charles Rutherford of *Cheriton* sat behind. Near a window overlooking the harbour, *Kingfisher's* Captain T. Horwood lounged with one foot on a chair to his front.

At the stroke of ten Vice-Admiral Sir John Tennant, R.N., K.C.B., C.B.E., entered, took his place behind the desk and dropped his cap on the highly polished surface.

'Gentlemen,' Tennant began, 'Let me start by congratulating you all on what turned out to be a very successful mission. I appreciate that with the loss of *Vibrant* you might not be so quick to agree, but I can assure you that the capture of S.S. *Castillo de Maria* intact has been widely seen as a major victory.' He paused to come out from behind the desk and then jammed his hands in his jacket pockets.

'It's a sad fact that from the beginning of Operation Buttercup to the present time we've suffered a fair amount of casualties. But what you've all achieved has saved the lives of more men than you'll ever fully understand.' He looked at the floor before continuing.

'It is the nature of war, gentlemen, especially the war at sea, that more often than not we don't have all the information to hand. In time of battle no one guarantees the outcome. We who must make tactical decisions are often deceived by the inevitable fog of war.' He ran a hand through his greying hair and smiled gently. 'Unfortunately, we've already had the newspapers sniffing around and we've put out a release to say a blockade runner was apprehended and ship and crew have now been interned for the duration. Needless to say no mention has been made of her cargo. The Admiralty will deal with *Vibrant's* sinking and there will of course be a Board of Inquiry looking into her sinking but I'm sure that under the circumstances no blame can be apportioned.' He glanced round the room and his gaze settled on Charles Rutherford.

'You're *Cheriton*, I believe?'

'Yes, sir.'

'In the short term, we've been unable to verify your U-boat but I don't doubt that with the passage of time the evidence will show you did indeed sink that boat. Congratulations.'

'Thank you, sir.'

'So, there we have it, overall a successful conclusion to a tricky operation. Any questions?'

Horton leaned forward. 'If I may, what is the condition of Captain Fitzpatrick?'

The Admiral grinned. 'Not as bad as first thought. He has one partially collapsed vertebrae and he's quick to remind anyone within ear shot that it's causing him some considerable pain. According to the surgeon it's likely pinching a nerve. A couple of months rest should see him up and about.' He held their gaze. 'Any more?'

Richard Thorburn raised a finger. 'Yes, sir, I have a question.'

'Go on.'

'The *Castillo de Maria*, sir . . . , a young officer under my command wanted to know what prize money he might be able to count on?'

'As I'm sure you're aware, Commander, the Royal Navy no longer subscribes to that practice.' He smiled. 'But you may tell your young officer there was no harm in trying.'

Laughter rippled round the assembly and Thorburn nodded. 'Thank you, sir. I'll make sure he receives your advice.'

The Admiral took a last look at the seated

officers and smiled. 'Well, gentlemen, I've said my piece and I hope by the time you leave here you'll each take away a better understanding of how things unfolded.'

And with that, Vice-Admiral Sir John Tennant retrieved his cap from the desk and hurried out to the lobby.

The discussion that followed slowly revealed the true extent of what happened during the entire operation. From the minute Kendal off loaded Wingham's Raiders on Telegraph Bay, to the fighting withdrawal and subsequent unexpected revelations let slip by the German Officer.

Captain Horton had gathered a fair amount of detail with regards to the battle itself. He also clarified the decision to vacate the battle and get the two destroyers full of rescued survivors out of harm's way.

For his part Thorburn explained the running fight *Brackendale* had with the *Puma*, and his own decision to disobey Fitzpatrick's order to sink the *Maria*. There was general agreement over the vagaries of the weather and how luck had intervened at opportune moments.

Shortly after, Horton announced it was time for him to leave and the meeting came to a natural conclusion. As he shook hands and prepared to depart a rare smile crossed his sombre features.

'I wish you all the best,' he said. 'As for *Kingfisher*, me and her, we're off to sunnier climes. Gibraltar for us.' And with an exaggerated bow he chuckled and left them with, 'I bid you farewell,' as he slipped out of the door.

Thorburn turned to Wingham and Kendal. 'I have orders to ship you and the Raiders back to Chatham. Apparently General Bainbridge wants a word.'

Charles Rutherford stood and offered his hand. 'I'm going nowhere,' he said. 'This is *Cheriton's* new station, something about convoy escort.'

Thorburn smiled his understanding and shook the hand. 'The quiet life, Charles, I know.'

And so they went their separate ways, battles fought and with new horizons waiting.

H.M.S *Brackendale* eased gently to the quayside of Chatham's Royal Dockyard and her Special Sea Dutymen began the familiar ritual of tying up to the bollards. Lieutenant Robert Armstrong stood on the fo'c'sle overseeing his hands, and on the quarterdeck, Sub-Lieutenant George Labatt made certain the wires were well secured. A wave from bows and stern, and Thorburn bent to the wheelhouse pipe.

'Finished with main engines.'

As Kendal and Wingham's Raiders finally took their leave, Thorburn spared a glance in the direction of Captain Pendleton's office windows.

He felt certain he caught a brief glimpse of Jennifer watching the quayside and a thought struck him.

'Pilot,' he said to Martin. 'What day is it?'

'Mmm . . . , Saturday, I think. Why, sir?'

'Oh never mind, just a thought.' And he hid a smile. If the lovely Jennifer Farbrace had acted on her suggestion there might well be a table for two waiting somewhere close by. He stretched and yawned.

A hot bath wouldn't go amiss.

Printed in Great Britain
by Amazon